International Conference on e-Health 2017

Held at the Multi-Conference on Computer Science and Information Systems (MCCSIS 2017)

Lisbon, Portugal
20 – 23 July 2017

Editors:

Mario Macedo
Piet Kommers
Pedro Isaias
Luís Rodrigues

ISBN: 978-1-5108-6529-7

Printed from e-media with permission by:

Curran Associates, Inc.
57 Morehouse Lane
Red Hook, NY 12571

Some format issues inherent in the e-media version may also appear in this print version.

Printed by Curran Associates, Inc. (2018)

For permission requests, please contact International Association for Development of the Information Society (IADIS) at the address below.

International Association for Development of the Information Society (IADIS)
Rua Sao Sebastiao Da Pedreira
No. 100, 30, 1050-209
Lisbon, Portugal

Phone: 351 21 3151373
Fax: 351 21 3151244

secretariat@iadis.org

Additional copies of this publication are available from:

Curran Associates, Inc.
57 Morehouse Lane
Red Hook, NY 12571 USA
Phone: 845-758-0400
Fax: 845-758-2633
Email: curran@proceedings.com
Web: www.proceedings.com

INTERNATIONAL CONFERENCE

E-HEALTH 2017

part of the

MULTI CONFERENCE ON COMPUTER SCIENCE AND

INFORMATION SYSTEMS 2017

PROCEEDINGS OF THE INTERNATIONAL CONFERENCE

E-HEALTH 2017

Lisbon, Portugal
JULY 20 - 22, 2017

Organised by
IADIS
International Association for Development of the Information Society

Volume Editor:
Mário Macedo

Computer Science and Information Systems Series Editors:
Piet Kommers and Pedro Isaías

Associate Editor: Luís Rodrigues

TABLE OF CONTENTS

SHORT PAPERS

REFLECTION PAPERS

POSTERS

FOREWORD

These proceedings contain the papers of the International Conference on e-Health 2017, which was organised by the International Association for Development of the Information Society, 20 - 22 July, 2017. This conference is part of the Multi Conference on Computer Science and Information Systems 2017, 20 - 23 July, which had a total of 652 submissions.

The use of ICTs (Information and Communication Technologies) in Healthcare Services is the main mechanism to improve efficiency and effectiveness. The e-Health (EH) 2017 conference aims to draw together information systems, practitioners and management experts from all quadrants involved in developing computer technology to improve healthcare quality.

Submissions were accepted under the following 3 main areas in the field of e-health within specific topics:

-Research Issues
-Management Issues
-Applications

The e-Health 2017 conference received 84 submissions from more than 25 countries. Each submission has been anonymously reviewed by an average of five independent reviewers, to ensure that accepted submissions were of a high standard. Consequently only 15 full papers were approved which means an acceptance rate of 18%. A few more papers were accepted as short papers, reflection papers and posters. An extended version of the best papers will be published in the IADIS International Journal on WWW/Internet (ISSN: 1645-7641) and also in other selected journals, including journals from Inderscience.

Besides the presentation of full papers, short papers, reflection papers and posters, the conference also included a keynote presentations from an internationally distinguished researcher. We would therefore like to express our gratitude to Dr. Alexandre Valentim Lourenço, President of the South Regional Council of the Medical Doctors Order, Portugal, for accepting our invitation to be the keynote speaker.

This volume has taken shape as a result of the contributions from a number of individuals. We are grateful to all authors who have submitted their papers to enrich the conference proceedings. We wish to thank all members of the organizing committee, delegates, invitees and guests whose contribution and involvement are crucial for the success of the conference.

Last but not the least, we hope that everybody will have a good time in Lisbon, and we invite all participants for the next edition of this conference.

Mário Macedo, Universidade Atlântica, Portugal
e-Health 2017 Program Chair

Piet Kommers, University of Twente, The Netherlands
Pedro Isaías, The University of Queensland, Australia
MCCSIS 2017 General Conference Co-Chairs

Lisbon, Portugal
July 2017

PROGRAM COMMITTEE

E-HEALTH CONFERENCE PROGRAM CHAIR

Mário Macedo, Universidade Atlântica, Portugal

MCCSIS GENERAL CONFERENCE CO-CHAIRS

Piet Kommers, University of Twente, The Netherlands
Pedro Isaías, The University of Queensland, Australia

E-HEALTH CONFERENCE COMMITTEE MEMBERS

Abdel-Badeeh M.Salem, Ain Shams University, Egypt
Adel Taweel, Kings College/Birzeit University, United Kingdom/Palestine
Alain Pruski, LCOMS Université de Lorraine, France
Alexander Hoerbst, UMIT - University for Health Sciences, Medical Informatics and Technology, Austria
Amir Hajjam el Hassani, University of Technology of Belfort Montbeliard, France
Andreas Schrader, University of Lübeck, Germany
Anna Bianchi, Politecnico di Milano, Italy
Antonio Lanatà, University of Pisa, Italy
Asa Smedberg, Stockholm University, Sweden
Ayse Bener, Mechanical and Industrial Engineering - Ryerson University, Canada
Bert-Jan van Beijnum, University of Twente, Netherlands
Bobak Jack Mortazavi, Yale School of Medicine, USA
Bridget Kane, Karlstad University, Sweden
Carlos Fernández Llatas, Universitat Politècnica de València, Spain
Cesar Caceres Taladriz, Rey Juan Carlos University, Spain
David Hansen, Australian e-Health Research Centre, Australia
David Isern, University Rovira I Virgili, Spain
Edward Kacki, EFMI, Poland
Elena Villalba, Universidad Politécnica de Madrid, Spain
Elizabeth Krupinski, Emory University, USA
Elske Ammenwerth, UMIT - University for Health Sciences, Medical Informatics and Technology, Austria
Emmanuel Andres, Université de Strasbourg , France
Enzo Pasquale Scilingo, University of Pisa, Italy
Eric Campo, LAAS-CNRS, France
Farid Naït-Abdesselam, Paris Descartes University, France
Georg Duftschmid, Medical University of Vienna, Austria
George Okeyo, Jomo Kenyatta University of Agriculture and Technology, Kenya
Guillaume Lopez, Aoyama Gakuin University, Japan
Jan Aidemark, Linnéuniversitet, Sweden
Jan Vejvalka, Charles University, Czech Republic
Jaspaljeet Singh, Universiti Tenaga Nasional, Malaysia
Jesuk Ko, Gwangju University, South Korea
Jose Luis Sanchez , Laboratorio de Computadoras y Control, Spain

Full Papers

A QUALITATIVE STUDY OF THE IMPLEMENTATION AND USE OF A NATIONAL INFORMATION SYSTEM

Line Lundvoll Warth and Kari Dyb
Norwegian Centre for E-health Research, P.O. Box 35, N-9038 Tromsø, Norway

ABSTRACT

In Norway, a national digital tool for critical information sharing (CIS) was implemented in the period 2013–2017 for sharing critical patient information among and between primary and specialist healthcare professionals. The health authorities considered access to patient information across levels and institutions of care so important that it warranted an amendment. In September 2017, qualitative interviews were conducted with 12 project leaders (PL) responsible for the implementation of CIS and 25 doctors with access to CIS. The interviews were semi-structured, and they lasted 20–80 min each. They were recorded, then transcribed, and analyzed according to their content. The PL considered that they had succeeded with their implementation work, but practitioners seldom used the new technology for the purpose of providing critical information. CIS also gives access to prescribed medicaments, which is the most useful tool for them. As CIS is a national initiative, practitioners are implementing more long-term strategies. While PL consider their work to be finished after technology implementing and training, practitioners predict that CIS is one of several small steps toward a national journal for sharing even more patient information.

KEYWORDS

National information system, implementation, interviews, general practitioners, project leaders

1. INTRODUCTION AND BACKGROUND

In Norway, CIS (in Norwegian; Kjernejournal) is the first national, digital system for information sharing between professional at different levels and institutions in health care (The Norwegian Directorate of eHealth, 2017). A CIS provide the same information whether the health professional work as a General Practitioner (GP), in emergency units in primary care (EUs) or in emergency rooms (ERs) in hospitals /specialist care. The national tool was implemented in the period 2013–2017 for sharing patient information between and across primary and specialist healthcare professionals. CIS gives healthcare professionals access to selected and important information regardless of where in Norway a patient receives treatment. This is the first national solution in Norway for sharing information across levels of care (The Norwegian Directorate of eHealth, 2017), and it meets a defined national demand for giving healthcare professionals and patients quick access to a limited set of information across organizations and levels of care (Ministry of Health and Care Services, 2011) . This practice of sharing information is new. The Norwegian health authorities considered access to patient information across levels and institutions of care so important that it warranted an amendment (Ministry of Health and Care Services, 2011 and 2013), in Norwegian (Helse og Omsorgsdepartementet, 2011, Helse og Omsorgsdepartementet, 2013).

The contents of an Electronic Patient health Record are divided into three types: critical information, important information, and other information (Arnesen & Larsen, 2014). CIS contains the same subjects, however the objective is to provide "critical information" (The Norwegian Ministry of Health and Care Services, 2012). CIS contains information about medications; critical information such as allergies, implants, and relevant chronical conditions registered by the GP; automatically synchronized history of hospital visits; and information registered by the patient him-/herself.

Prior to CIS, patients' health information were stored locally where the patient has received health care. Health personnel spend valuable time on gathering information from the different places where the patient has been treated. In emergencies, this might have fatal consequences. Lack of vital information about the patient can cause unintended events, in worst case patient injury or death (The Norwegian Directorate of eHealth, 2017). CIS was established because the need for a national tool to share selected information across levels of healthcare was deemed essential.

When the government started implementing CIS in 2013, CIS was aimed at providing selected patient information that would be crucial if health care providers lacked information about the patients and patient was unable to give an account of him-/herself, typically if a citizen became ill when travelling and there were no local health record of the patient accessible. This selected information would be crucial for the choice of treatment and would result in wrong or late treatment if missing. CIS is an e-health system that is aimed to cover the trajectory of emergency medicine. CIS was implemented to enhance patient safety and treatment quality, as patient information is often missing during hospitalization (Arnesen & Larsen, 2014).

All healthcare professionals (GPs and specialists) who are going to use CIS need to undergo an e-learning course and pass an acceptance test. After passing this test, they receive an identity card that allows them to open and use CIS. When opening CIS, the practitioner is identified and the access is logged, hence the patient also knows who has accessed his/hers information stored in CIS.

Norway is divided into four healthcare regions. Each region offers specialist services (e.g., doctors and nurses at hospitals) and primary care (e.g., GPs and accident and emergency units). Before CIS was implemented, the four healthcare regions, including their primary care and specialist services, were not linked together by a common information system. CIS is the first information sharing system across Norway, and it shares selected information between and across primary care and specialist services. This new way of sharing selected information aims to cover the treatment trajectory from medical offices to emergency units (EUs) and emergency rooms (ERs) at hospitals, and it provides information that may be crucial for acute medical treatment. During spring 2017, all Norwegians citizens were given access to their CIS.

This paper aims to contribute to the understanding of the dynamic factors that influence information systems and how such systems are shaped in practice. It also answers the following research question: *How was CIS implemented and how is it used in practice?* Here, we investigate the relation between the work of technology implementers and the practitioners who use the technology.

2. SETTING AND RESEARCH METHOD

Norwegian healthcare is divided into specialist services and primary care. In relation to CIS, primary care consists of GPs who typically treat patient. GPs normally refer patients to specialist services at hospitals. Minor emergencies are handled at emergency units, where GPs work in shifts; EUs are considered a part of primary care. Acute emergencies or accidents are handled at emergency rooms; ERs are considered a part of specialist services. Norway is divided into four healthcare regions.

This is a qualitative study that develops descriptions for the introduction and use of CIS. The sample includes 12 project leaders (PL) who implemented CIS and 25 physicians with access to use CIS. The CIS PLs have a finite term for their position, recruited in each health care region, after an initiative for their position from the national authority. They were selected locally, and 11 out of 12 of them were experienced PLs in the field of healthcare. The PLs represent all regions in Norway, with 2–4 leaders from each region. The participants were interviewed in September 2016. Each interview lasted 45–80 min. One interview was conducted face-to-face as the interviewee and interviewer were occasionally located at the same place. The remaining 11 interviews were conducted by telephone, Lync, or Skype depending on the PL's preference.

To obtain in-depth knowledge about the use of CIS in the trajectory of healthcare, the Trondheim city healthcare region was selected for studying practitioners. CIS was implemented in Trondheim in 2013, and practitioners here have the longest experience with it in Norway. The sample included 10 GPs from 5 medical offices, 5 doctors from EUs, and 10 doctors from ERs at hospitals. Each interview lasted 20–60 min, and it was conducted face-to-face at the workplace in September 2016.

All interviews were semi-structured (Malterud, 1996), with predefined themes and subjects based on the research question. The nature of the interview enabled participants to share their own themes and experiences, regardless of whether these were included in the predefined themes. All interviews were recorded and then transcribed. They were read thoroughly in detail and coded according to the interview content. The findings were discussed among three senior researchers. The utterances are selected and structured according to the main findings. Hence, the stories presented are selected to answer the research question. The data collected are reviewed and concepts are coded. When more data was collected and re-reviewed, the codes were grouped into concepts, and then into categories. The results in this article build on a pattern in the findings related to the introduction and use of CIS, and the analysis is based on grounded theory (Charmaz K, 2014, and Glaser BG, Strauss AL, 2009). Grounded theory, used in social science, is a systematic methodology constructing concepts and theory thorough the analysis of empirical data.

The interviews were handled according to the Regional Committee for Medical and Health Research Ethics (REK) code of ethics. This study does not include project definitions evaluated according to the Health Research law. The study is registered with the data protection supervisor at the University Hospital of North Norway.

3. RESULTS

Here, we present results based on interviews with the PLs who implemented the digital tool and doctors who were in the target group for using CIS.

3.1 Projects Leaders Introduction of the Tool

The implementation of CIS was initialized by the Ministry of Health, led by PLs in each healthcare region, employed by a local or a central hospital for a predefined period. They were responsible for preparing, inform and to implement necessary infrastructure so that professionals who should have access did so. The PLs also encouraged practitioners to complete the e-learning course and to pass the acceptance test needed for using the new tool.

3.1.1 Implementation, a Success?

The PLs were all professional PLs in the field of health care, some were full time involved in implementation of CIS while others held part time positions. After introducing CIS, the PLs moved on to lead the implementation of new tasks or projects. The PLs were asked about the goal and the success criteria of the implementation of CIS. On this question all of them answered that they wanted to offer CIS to practitioners. One PL said the following:

"It is a success, because we have turned it on (...). We have prepared it so that those who want to use it can do so. But, it is up to the clinics themselves to start using it." (PL 3)

Others were more ambitious about the goal his/hers work:

"(...) the goal is to <u>start</u> to use it. It does not say anything about volume, and how often healthcare professionals should use it." (PL 11)

In addition to turn the system on and prepare the professionals to start using it, was the e-learning test mentioned as an indicator of how successful the introduction of CIS was and of whether the training was successful.

"We had a goal for how many took the test, and not for how many logged into the CIS." (PL 10)

This study indicates that the PLs mainly aimed to enable practitioners to pass the acceptance test, to turn CIS on, and to help the practitioners to start using CIS. Volume of use seemed secondary to the PLs. However, as they had access to the traffic data of professionals who had logged into CIS, they could also evaluate its success according to the volume of use. One PL said that she had hoped that all who took the test also would use the new tool.

"The number of CIS users indicates that we did not succeed ... We hoped that all who took the test would use it. We have not succeeded in terms of the number of users ..." (PL 6)

3.1.2 Alternate use of Information Systems?

CIS was aimed at providing critical information about patients to health personnel regardless of time and place. This study show that the number of patient within the scope of CIS are maybe fewer than expected prior to developing CIS. PL 12 noted that only 2%–5% of patients had critical information of relevance for CIS.

> *"We had a focus on critical information in CIS. But, that is not much used ... Only 2%–5% of the Norwegian inhabitants have critical information* (relevant for CIS...). *We should have been more balanced between the critical information and all the other functions that might be ... Important information. Not for saving lives, but more in general. You get this presented as (...) it informs about what needs to be done to save a life in a situation where a patient arrives in an emergency room and cannot give an account of him-/herself. But, it is several other units at the hospital who have a need for the information in CIS. It is important to focus on this in the future." (PL 12)*

CIS was designed to provide critical patient information with a particular focus on acute or emergency situations. The PLs' reports that even if such information might be crucial for some patients, there are in fact few patients in need of healthcare outside their own health region who cannot give an account of themselves, they emphasize that the information in CIS might relevant in other situations and for nonemergency units.

> *"There are several ways of using CIS, not necessary only when the patient is arriving in a coma." (PL 8)*

Furthermore, another PL said the following:

> *"(...) we wish for more functions in CIS, so that it will be used more than it is today." (PL 2)*

Even if the PL consider their own work a success; turning on the system and help professionals pass the e-learning test, they also wanted the system to be used more frequently than today. They therefore searched for new functionalities to increase the use. However, these new functionalities was not related to critical situations. This was expressed clearly:

> *"The use [of CIS] is a challenge when the patient does not have critical information (...) we request use (...) CIS do contain information that might be relevant in several situations, not only critical. You have the medical history, the hospital history, information about relatives ...." (PL 4)*

These quotes indicates that when the PL detect that the use of the new service is low, they seek other ways of using it.

> *"I think we should start an information campaign for CIS, to inform that it is more than critical information." (PL 12)*

Several PLs mention that since information already existing in CIS, the system should not be limited to emergency situations, but also be used for noncritical purposes. "Background information" like; age, residence, phone numbers and relatives are considered useful for health care providers. The two following quotations illustrates how PLs suggest, that professionals, other than doctors, might value the use of CIS:

> *"I think there is still much potential in CIS. The e-learning course is aimed at doctors .... I think that ... nurses have a big need for the information in CIS. History of visits, information about medicines, relatives ..." (PL 7)*

> *"It might a good strategy to approach several ... In the beginning, it focused on emergency rooms and doctors in acute trajectories. But, I think it might be useful to focus on professionals in wards and out-patient clinics as well." (PL 3)*

New ways of using CIS and including professionals other than doctors are closely related. New functionalities in CIS can open up for use among new group of professions:

> *"For doctors, the critical information is most important. But, for those doing all the other work, there might be some other relevant information there. This is an example of exploring CIS. It gets new functionalities, and we are more engaged with other functionalities than when we started. Critical information ... So, what is CIS?" (PL 11)*

The PLs' work mainly aimed to enable practitioners to pass the acceptance test, to turn CIS on, and to help the practitioners to start using CIS, while volume of use were secondary to the PLs work. They still were concerned about the volume of use, reporting low-frequency use. Infrequent use of the system is not surprising as the PLs estimate that just 2%–5% of Norwegian citizen have critical information that is within the scope of CIS. It is interesting to note that instead of regarding CIS a successful system which provide critical information to the target patient group on a national level, some of the PLs were searching for new groups of professionals and new functionalities within CIS. They wanted to expand the functionality in CIS and include new user groups. In the next chapter, we discuss the practice of doctors, who at the time of amendment, development and implementation were the target group of users.

3.2 New Tool in Doctors' Work Practices

The Trondheim healthcare region was the first to implement CIS. CIS was implemented in 2013, and the healthcare region has, in 2017, the highest volume of entries in CIS. In this region, interviews were conducted with doctors at; GPs' offices, EUs, and ERs. The main findings are related to three themes of introducing new tools in everyday work practices: GPs are appointed by the government to produce critical information (content) in the CIS for doctors in emergency care, in everyday work practice CIS are used as a sours of information about patient medicaments, and practitioners predict the expansion of CIS in the future.

3.2.1 Critical Information in Work Practices

In Norway, GPs are often the first to meet the patient. If necessary, they refer patients further to specialist services. GPs are also the "closest" to the patient, and traditionally, they are the ones who have the larger picture of the patient's health, including family and living conditions. GPs are appointed by the government to have a particular responsibility to provide critical information about their patients in the national CIS, so that emergency care practitioners can access relevant information in acute or emergency situations regardless of time and place.

GP's in primary care feed information into the CIS while the expected effects is at another level of care. One GP said the following:

> *"I thought CIS was a good idea. And I still think it is a good idea ... (...) It is hard for us GPs to see the big value in it." (Doctor 6, GP office)*

The quotation illustrate that while the GP provide information to emergency care practitioners, the GP has little personal use for CIS. While GPs felt responsible for enter critical patient information in CIS, the system had limited utility among GPs. Limited utility of the system was also evident in emergency unites (EU) in primary care. In Norway, at least in the lagers town and cities, patients in emergency situation should arrive at the ERs in hospitals. A doctor working at an EU explained how the use of CIS is supposed to be low in EUs:

> *"I participated in the implementation* (of CIS). *It is a tool for acute and emergency situations, and it's meant to be that. How many patients do we receive here [emergency unit] that are so urgent? It's not supposed to be that at the emergency unit. If it is emergent, they are supposed to arrive at the emergency room." (Doctor 3, EU)*

The two preceding quotes, as well as the next illustrates that at GPs' offices and EUs alike, the use of CIS is described as low, and that it is expected to be low:

> *"I have an impression that both GPs and specialists, to a large extent, don't use the functionality of CIS enough." (Doctor 4, ER)*

At the ER in specialist care, doctors find critical information in CIS of more importance. Nevertheless, these doctors don't distinguish between two of the functionalities in CIS, medicaments and critical information. The doctors working in ERs, refer to medicaments as critical information in emergency situations.

> *"I use several sources, including CIS, to receive information about medicaments." (Doctor 9, ER)*

The study illustrates how doctors at different levels relate to and use CIS. CIS as a tool for accessing critical information is strongly related to GPs' work in providing information about a limited number of patients' condition, while the doctors in ER regard access to patient medicaments as critical in emergency situations. In the next section we will illustrate how CIS was used or not-used in everyday practices.

3.2.2 Use and Non-Use in Everyday Work Practices

All informants, doctors at; GPs' offices; EUs and ERs, referred to information about medicaments as a reason for using CIS:

"When you get new patients, a patient you don't know, it [CIS] is useful to get quick information about allergies, rare diseases and medication, to what kind of medication the patient uses." (Doctor 5, GP office)

While a doctor at the emergency unit said the following:

"Of most importance for me [with CIS] is medicaments. Especially, in the emergency unit, it is very useful to see what kind of medicaments they use (....). And it is very useful to reveal those who should not have more of previously given medicaments, those who want sedative medicaments or pain killers, given from their GPs a few days ago." (Doctor 7, EU)

To have updated information about medicaments is valuable for all patients. The previous and the next quotation illustrates that updated information about medication is viewed particularly valuable in the field of addiction, for those who are treating patients that wish for more medicaments than they have been prescribed. This was described by a doctor in emergency room as follows:

"In relation to the field of addiction, it is of relevance. You do not have to discuss with the patient. It says [CIS] that you got the medicaments three days ago. So, what you say is actually not true. I do not have to argue. It is documented." (Doctor 18, ER)

3.2.3 Expected Increase in Information Sharing

The purpose of CIS is to share information across all levels of care in Norway. The next quote illustrates how sharing information become a threat for GPs, as they get sensitive information given in confidence by the patient. Information that is irrelevant for treatment in emergency situations.

"If [the patient journal] becomes national (...), almost a public document ... I am very reserved on what I write when it comes to sensitive stuff ... Venereal diseases, assault, sexuality, ..." (doctor 6, GP office)

Comparable to how the PLs seek additional functionally in CIS, CIS has also been transformed in clinical practice. Doctors prefer the functionality medicaments to critical information. In clinical practice CIS is used to reveal additions. Furthermore, doctors do expect that the system will expand further, as described:

"W*hen CIS was implemented ... The information I got first. Then, there was a clear expansion on what to register in the CIS from the first to the second meeting. That made med skeptical. Really skeptical. But, as a tool within a defined area, I think it might be very good." (Doctor 12, GP office)*

Another GP defined the shift in intention as follows:

"CIS, in principle, I think it is a very good tool, provided it is used as intended. But, I can see a pattern of one common journal [sharing all information nationally, between levels of care]." (Doctor 12, GP office)

GPs are skeptical of a fully shared patient journal, and they predict that CIS is the first step toward nation sharing:

"This is as if it was step one. We are going to expand, that's my skepticism." (Doctor 10, GP office)

This illustrates how CIS has changes from being about critical information about patients' conditions to patients' medications, and how the solution continues to develop and change. This expected change or development make particular GPs skeptical to CIS. They worry that an expansion of CIS is a threat to the relationship between the GP and the patient; a patient opens up and trusts a practitioner who he/she meets face-to-face.

4. DISCUSSION

PLs consider the work of implementing CIS as a success. They have completed their tasks of preparing CIS, turning it on and having practitioners pass the acceptance test. When discussing the number of users in relation to the number taking the test, they feel that they have not succeeded, even though the implementation was a success. The use of CIS for critical information depends on GPs and the extent to which they enter information into CIS. As the outcome covers the emergency care trajectory, and not their office, they are not motivated to provide critical information.

The PLs communicated the purpose of implementing CIS from the viewpoint of health authorities, with a strong focus on the use of CIS for providing critical information. Health authorities estimate that only 2%–5% of Norwegian citizens have critical information that has to be revealed and registered by the GP. PLs succeeded in providing access to doctors, although the use remained low as the patient base was small.

Traditionally, when introducing new technology, the experience is that it is refused, modified, and/or accepted in practice (May et al 2001, Mort et al 2012, Roberts et al 2012). The results of this study illustrate the untraditional way of searching for other functionalities that will increase the use of the technology. CIS has incorporated other types of functionality, such as information about prescribed medicaments. The practitioners and PLs try to resolve their main concerns about CIS by changing the meaning of the tool. The change in the use of CIS and the move away from its central use is also changing who CIS is made for. New functionalities will include new groups of professionals, such as nurses. As the results show, both practitioners and PLs are searching for new ways of using CIS to make it more relevant in work practice. Inspired by grounded theory (Charmaz K, 2014, and Glaser BG, Strauss AL, 2009) the results form a new category, not refusing, modifying and/ or accepting the tool, but changing the meaning of the tool.

Both in primary and specialist care, physicians' purpose for use is information on medicaments in general. None of them had used CIS for critical information in an acute situation. Factors encouraging the use of CIS include updated information on prescriptions made only a few days ago, so that physicians, whether they meet patients at their office, at EUs or ERs, do not prescribe the same medicaments twice within just a couple of days. This updated information about prescriptions prevents repeatedly prescribing medicaments to those having addictions, and it also serves as written documentation on what has been prescribed previously. This is an additional feature that goes beyond the use for "critical information".

Both physicians' and PLs predict that the definition of critical information will change over time. CIS remains a useful tool for providing critical information. However, it is becoming more than that. These results illustrate a change in the purpose of the use of CIS, from critical information provided by GPs to automatically synchronized lists of medicaments. The PLs have facilitated information sharing, so that patient information is accessible. GPs are skeptical about this sharing culture, and even though practitioners use an identity card when accessing CIS, they would not like to share sensitive patient information that is irrelevant for acute care. Both PLs and GPs see a change in the purpose of the use of CIS since the implementation started in 2013.

CIS is considered a step toward a common national patient journal, in which information that was previously shared only between the patient and his/her GP might be exposed to all practitioners in a common journal. This way of using a technological tool might be of special relevance because this is a nationally initiated implementation. Smaller projects are often brought into use, modified, or refused without such thorough consideration from practitioners. Larger, nationally initiated actions facilitate more long-term strategies from the users. As the PLs consider their work finished, the practitioners predict that CIS is one of several small steps toward a national journal for sharing even more patient information. The continuing change in CIS's use might be stepwise adjustment to a new work practice where information is shared between organizational levels in health care.

5. CONCLUSION

By studying the relation between the work of those who implement the technology and the practitioners who it is developed for, the results show how the PLs define their success in relation to the project period and how they set goals with a focus on the implementation of the technology. Local work practices influence how the technology is used, and even though the PLs consider the technology a success, its use is not as expected.

Smaller development and implementation projects and standalones are often ended when the project period is over irrespective of whether they have succeeded or not. Implementing a national project over time makes it possible to modify the purpose of use during and even after the implementation period. When the PLs have finished their work, authorities can keep the work going and change the direction and the purpose of the technology and thereby enable new work practices.

Inspired by grounded theory (Charmaz K, 2014, and Glaser BG, Strauss AL, 2009) the results form a new category for handling practice. The CIS are not refused, modified and/ or accepted as a traditional way of responding to smaller implementations initiatives. The practitioners and the PLs are changing the meaning of the tool. Both practitioners and PLs are searching for new ways of using CIS to make it more relevant in work practice. It is a change in the use of CIS, a move away from its initial and central use, and there for a change in who CIS is made for. New functionalities will include new groups of professionals, such as nurses.

As CIS has been implemented over the years in Norway, we were able to explore the implementation and use of CIS across all health regions that had implemented it between 2013 and September 2016. The study was limited by the fact that the informants had used CIS for unequal periods of time. Some had finished the project period a long while ago, whereas others had just started. This might influence the results. In the future, it might be interesting to explore work practices that are closer to the work done by the authorities.

ACKNOWLEDGEMENTS

The authors would like to thank the Norwegian Directorate of eHealth for funding this research project and to all the study participants. The authors would like to specially thank Nils Kolstrup, PhD, MD.

REFERENCES

Arnesen E.N, Larsen B.N, 2014: Kritisk informasjon i kjernejournal. *Tidsskrift for den norske legeforening*. 20 (134) pp. 1927-1928.

Charmaz K., 2014: *Constructing grounded theory*. Sage.

Glaser B.G, Strauss A.L., 2009: *The discovery of grounded theory: Strategies for qualitative research*. Transaction publishers.

Helse og omsorgsdepartementet (The Norwegian Ministry of Health and Care Services) 2011, *Prop.89L(2011-2012): Endring i helseregisterloven (opprettelsen av nasjonal kjernejournal*). Oslo.

Helse og omsorgsdepartementet (The Norwegian Ministry of Health and Care Services) 2013. *Forskrift om kjernejournal (kjernejournalforskriften).* Oslo.

Malterud, K. 1996: *Kvalitative metoder i medisinsk forskning. En innføring,* Aurskog, Tano Aschehoug.

May C, Gask L, Atkinson T, Ellis N, Mair F, Esmail A. 2001: *Resisting and promoting new technologies in clinical practice: the case of telepsychiatry,* Social Science and Medicine, 52: pp. 1889-1901.

Mort M, Roberts C, Callen B. 2013: *Ageing with telecare. Care or coercion in austerity?* Sociology of health and illness. 35(6), July 2013: pp. 799-812.

Roberts C, Mort M, Milligan, 2012, *Calling for Care, "Disembodied Work, Teleoperatiors and Older People Living at Home*; Sociology, 46 (3); Sage, pp 490-560

The Norwegian Directorate of eHealth, 2017 (https://ehelse.no/english) [accessed, 03.04.2017]

The Norwegian Ministry of Health and Care Services, 2017 (https://www.regjeringen.no) [accessed 03.04.2017]

ENVIRONMENT- AND USER-FRIENDLY POWER-SUPPLY CONCEPT FOR RF-COUPLED HEALTH AND SPORT SENSORS

Hans Weghorn
BW Cooperative State University Stuttgart, Kronenstrasse 53A, 70174 Stuttgart, Germany

ABSTRACT

Nowadays during sports and in health activities, various electronic monitoring tools are in use quite commonly. Patients or sports persons often are embedded into a personal body sensor network, which traces different facets of their physiological activity. Widespread are heart rate sensors, but all kinds of meters, e.g., for counting foot steps and pedal turning are often also used in parallel. As technical construction, it has commonly established that these sensor devices are autonomously operated as very tiny computer systems from built-in lithium battery cells. Exchanging such sensor batteries from time to time is expensive, the mechanical handling of this process is not very easy due to the small sensor housings, and it has to be reminded that use of throwaway batteries represents a waste of resources. In this work, an alternative power supply for sports sensors is investigated, which bases on the use of so-called supercapacitors. Construction concepts, advantages of the approach related to handling and manufacturing, and the possible application ranges are thoroughly discussed, while the study is complemented with practical experiments from endurance sports.

KEYWORDS

Sport Computers, Health Monitoring, Sport Sensors, Body Network, ANT+, Bluetooth LE

1. INTRODUCTION

Improving health by controlled physical activities plays an important role in our modern and aging societies. Performing personal sports on regular and moderate base from early days represents a valuable key for preserving an extended period with fewer health problems already at middle age (Oguma and Shinoda-Tagawa, 2004) up to higher living ages (Jefferis et al, 2014). Both categories of physiological activities are today usually monitored with the help of electronic devices and tools for achieving optimal response (Arts and Kuipers, 1994). The simplest variants of such monitoring units are pedometers or smartphones with corresponding software tools (Tudor-Locke and Basset, 2004).

A higher professional elaboration level is achieved, when using sports computers with built-in or RF-linked sensors (Malkinson, 2009). One of the most well-known samples of this multi-device monitoring are chest straps with autonomous sensor units for detecting heart rate (HR) from skin surface electrodes. Their measures are sent to other control units for display, evaluation and recording. Figure 1 shows different HR devices, one communicates through the Bluetooth LE standard (Bluetooth SIG, 2017), while the other one (device S) broadcasts its values through ANT+ radio (Dynastream Innov. Inc., 2011). The latter can be received by many sports computer systems and by some smartphones with special RF electronics, while Bluetooth LE is readable by most modern smartphones. It has been reported earlier that the electrical power consumption of the ANT+ system is lower compared to the Bluetooth LE solution (Weghorn, 2015).

Similar sensors exist for different other physiological measures, which are likely to be observed and traced during sports and health exercises. For instance, tread rate in foot stepping, wheel and pedal turning rate in cycling and other information may be of relevance and interest in such applications. Accordingly, many sensor types are available on the market and a training person can be embedded into an extended wireless body network, which consists of one central control unit and several autonomous sensor elements.

Since such sensors are tiny wireless computer modules, they do require also an electrical power supply. For this, commercial devices use lithium battery cells (B in Figure 1), which have to be exchanged and disposed as hazardous waste, when they are emptied. This manual exchange is not easy, because the mechanical components are really small and some systems need considerable force and torque for opening and closing the battery mould covers. Figure 1 shows above each sensor its back case part for the battery cell; for sensor S very small screws have to be handled, which is already inconvenient and complicate for younger people and may render impossible for older people or health patients with reduced sensitivity. Another negative aspect of inconvenience is that these batteries are rather expensive.

In the tiny sensor devices rechargeable batteries are not in use, because such a technology would increase size and price of the systems. Furthermore, wrong maintenance like deep discharge for a longer while damages accumulators and make the entire unit worthless, because the accumulator usually cannot be exchanged. Derived from commercial market like simple time watches, development has concentrated therefore on reducing power consumption of the sensor devices. The energy density of a single-use battery cells allows a continuous operation of the sensors for few days, but in real practical use cases this long operational time is not really required for physical exercises. In medical investigation, in health and sports monitoring, workouts and exercises quite typically last in the order of one hour (USD Labor, 2009).

For long time, possible substitution of batteries with capacitors, which provide much better development opportunities, remained just a very attractive vision for electronic engineers, since the electro-chemical capacitors couldn't reach the required load. Approximately two decades ago, so-called supercapacitors - also named ultracapacitors - could be developed on base of upcoming nanotechnology (Conway, 1999) and since then, capacitor parts caught up to the desirable high storage of one Farad and more. Today after many years of further evolvement, supercapacitor (SC) application is well-known in sports, e.g., as powersupply for boosting temporarily Formula 1 race cars as term of an ultra high power and extreme current cell (Lu, 2013).

Another upcoming field for SCs is the replacement of backup batteries for configuration memory on computer main boards (SC samples are C^x and C^y in Figure 1). This scenario is very similar to what is required for operating sport sensors, since they need also a high capacity value, which is providing very long time a rather small electrical current. Out of the four fundamental SC types, this variant represents a prospective candidate for replacing the throw-away lithium battery cell in autonomous sports and health sensors with a self-sustaining electronic part. Inspired from this existing knowledge and the new technologies, the work here discusses first the general properties of modern supercapacitors with respect to the targeted application frame in sports sensing; next the substitution idea particularly is used for the most common sensor of HR detection in endurance training for a real-world evaluation of the approach. Following this, the derived findings and possible concepts for further applications and improvements are critically reflected in their relevant details.

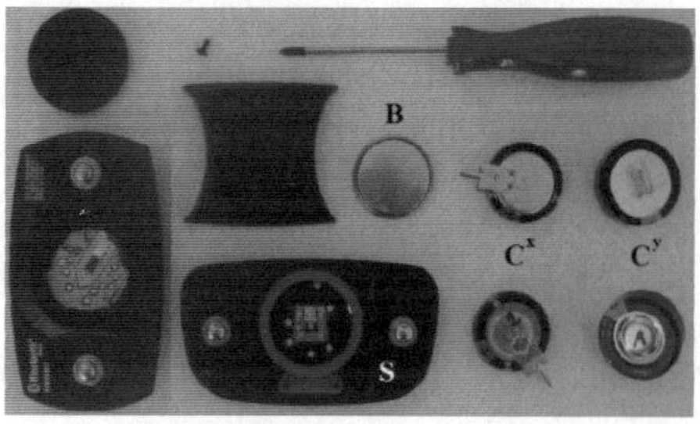

Figure 1. On the left, different heart rate sensors are shown with their covers for the supply battery; the middle cover has to be fixed with 4 tiny screws. On the right, rear and top view of supercapacitors samples are shown, which are possibly feasible for replacing the lithium sensor batteries

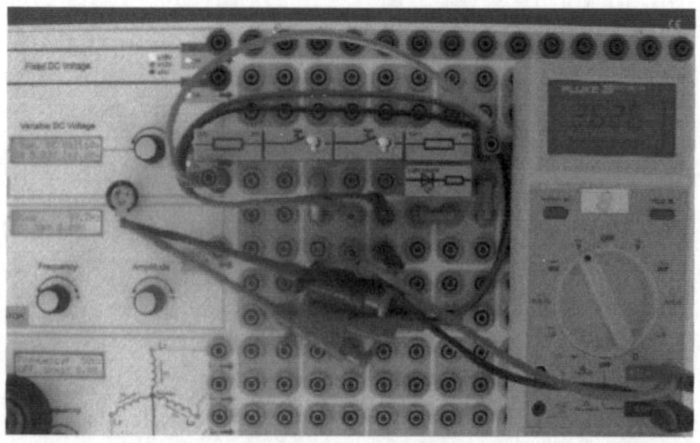

Figure 2. Laboratory board for charging and discharging the supercapacitor probe on the left side. A digital voltmeter measures precisely the probe output

2. PROPERTIES OF FEASIBLE SUPERCAPACITORS

From practical experience through a longer period of on-going investigation about handheld sports tools and sensors, it had been estimated as initial working base, that a SC part in the order of one Farad should provide sufficient energy for at least one or even few hours of sport sensor operation. Practical experience had shown, that a 230 mAh lithium battery can be used approximately one week full week. The error bar of this assumption was rather high, because the advertisement material for the sensors and their technologies promise much longer operational times. Due to low voltages and very small supply currents it is not possible to measure the sensor energy consumption directly with high precision; therefore an indirect methodology was used here in the further investigation for the determination of a sufficient power supply capacity.

2.1 Initial Parts Selection and Laboratory Setup

At first, two different SC types had been selected from a quality manufacturer for passive electronic parts, which are matching the targeted use of low voltage combined with low current. Other important criteria were also, that the parts are available from stock and that the size of the parts is comparable to the size of lithium battery cells. Part C^x is specified as SC with 5.5 Volts maximum and a capacity of 1.5 F, while C^y - despite it has got a bigger housing - comes with the same voltage rating and 1.0 F. For the evaluation of statistical variation in specified ratings, a set of samples was purchased from professional suppliers. The data sheets specify for the storage capacity possible differences from -20% up to +80%, but this wide range is expected to emerge reduced, since the body sensors are used in a narrower temperature band than allowed.

Figure 2 shows the laboratory board setup for conducting the basic experiments. The circuit allows to charge the SC probe through a protection shunt at a defined voltage and to discharge it through a defined load. The load in the test circuit was dimensioned, so that the discharge from 5V down to 3V takes in the order of one hour, since this should be similar like to the minimal estimated working time of a health or sports sensor. This test circuit maps to the following replacement construction for the battery cell: a linear voltage regulator downscales the SC voltage band to the valid sensor supply voltage as yielded by lithium batteries.

Table 1. Discharging time results for the ten SC samples: each probe was charged up to 5.00V, then this load voltage was sustained for a further minute, after which the discharging was initiated. From there, the time delay was measured in seconds for a voltage drop of each probe down to 4.00V and then further down to 3.00V.Below each time measure the corresponding capacity deviation from the parts specification sheet is listed

SC probe	C_1^x	C_2^x	C_3^x	C_4^x	C_5^x	C_A^y	C_B^y	C_C^y	C_D^y	C_E^y
Δt for 5.00V→ 4.00V	534s	555s	490s	491s	478s	456s	422s	457s	422s	394s
deviation from spec.	-27%	-24%	-33%	-33%	-35%	-14%	-21%	-14%	-21%	-26%
Δt for 4.00V→ 3.00V	1155s	1164s	1117s	1123s	1105s	880s	854s	865s	876s	856s
deviation from spec.	-31%	-31%	-33%	-33%	-34%	-13%	-15%	-14%	-13%	-15%

2.2 Determining SC Storage Capacity

Five samples each of the two selected SC parts were tested in a charge/discharge cycle. The goal for this first experimental run was to compare the capacity variation under similar conditions for in a sport sensor. Table 1 shows the corresponding results, and it indicates that the experienced variation of the capacity between different part samples is much lower than specified. The discharging is non-linear, but this doesn't explain completely the high differences among the discharging slope for the two different voltage steps. Super capacitors behave in some aspects considerably different to electrolytic capacitors, since they do stand only low switching frequencies and their internal resistance increases with charging load. As observed in the experiments, it is not sufficient to connect SC for a short while to the desired charging voltage, following the definition of how to measure SC capacity, it would be more required to keep the target charging voltage up for half an hour. Since this is not realistic for the intended application frame here, charging was terminated after an acceptable time. The consequence is, that the discharge rate is over-proportional high in the first phase as seen in the upper row in Table 1.

In the next experimental stage, two reference measurements were conducted for model C^x and C^y for obtaining precise capacity values. The SC probes were charged in the beginning to a higher voltage for an increased waiting time, while afterwards the slope of the discharge curve was measured at a lower voltage frame. Table 2 shows all experimental parameters and the deduced results. The determined reference capacities are much lower than the specified in the data sheets, which claim C^x = 1.5 F and C^y = 1.0 F. The true capacities were used to calibrate the deviation from the nominal capacity. Table 1 lists also these derived differences for the measured capacities, which all arise systematically too low. The difference appears considerably smaller for C^y, for which most measures are even within data sheet specification, but it is still, because the measurement procedure for the nominal capacity bases on a 30 minutes charging time, which is not acceptable for a sports or health sensor that shall be used for just one hour. Instead, 50% oversize in capacity appears as more appropriate approach for the proper SC selection.

Table 2. Experiment of determining absolute capacity values as reference

item/event	mode	C_3^x	C_C^y
$V_{SC}(t_0=0)$	defined & set	5.00V	5.00V
R_L=10k selected	measured resistance	9.93kΩ	9.93kΩ
@$V_{SC}(t_1)$ = 4.50V	measured time t_1	05:16:05	08:44:22
@$V_{SC}(t_2)$ = 4.00V	measured time t_2	05:35:40	09:01:08
t_2 - t_1	calculated	1175s	1006s
C	calculated	1.00 Farad	0.86 Farad

2.3 Self-Discharge Behavior

According to the concept, that the SC should supply a health sensor for the very next use period, which lasts, e.g., around one hour, the sensor would have to be charged each time before. One question for convenience would be, how much delay is allowed directly after charging the SC before using the sensor. Inactive sensors consume only reduced energy; furthermore storage cells in general suffer from self-discharge. Both effects have to be regarded to optimize the entire use cycle starting with any kind of preparation.

Therefore, the self-discharging effect also should be measured for the SC samples. In the corresponding experimental series, C^y was excluded, because its size was so huge, that it wouldn't directly fit into the sensor without major rework of the housing. This part of the fundamental investigation should direct clearly to the final application, therefore the capacitor samples were charged for an extended time to the start voltage of 3.3V, which is what a fresh lithium battery cell would feed to the sensor. Table 3 lists the discharging measures in time; the digital voltmeter was connected always only for a short time when collecting the sample points, so any distortion by the voltage measurement itself was avoided.

Concerning self-discharge, the variation between different SC samples appears high. Another snapshot is seen in Figure 2, which shows the voltage of C_1 three days after starting the experiment in Table 4. From the results it can be derived, that it is advisable to early use the sensor after charging, if a SC is used as power supply cell, since the nominal supply working range for sensors ends at 2.7 Volts. This guides to the design and use recommendation, that either the SC parts are selected with a reliably low self discharge or the user is advised to charge the sensor power just before any workout.

Table 3. Measuring voltage drops from 3.30V (@t_0=0) invoked solely by self-discharge of the SCs

SC probe	C_1^x	C_2^x	C_3^x	C_4^x	C_5^x
t_0 + 1h	3.14V	3.26V	3.30V	3.21V	3.19V
t_0 + 12h	2.87V	3.16V	3.26V	3.01V	2.93V
t_0 + 1d	2.79V	3.11V	3,.23V	2.94V	2.84V
t_0 + 1.5d	2.74V	3.07V	3.20V	2.90V	2.78V

3. PRACTICAL USE OF A SC POWER CELL IN A HR SENSOR

In the next phase of this investigation, the practical application in terms of replacing the lithium battery of a heart rate sensor by a supercapacitor was prepared. Based on the findings, which were collected so far, the following was decided: at first, an ANT+ HR sensor was selected for the rework, because of its low power consumption (unit S in Figure 1); secondly, since SC part model C^x is only barely bigger than the lithium battery (B in Figure 1), it was chosen for limiting the mechanical adoption of the sensor housing. The initial plan was, to charge the SC up to 5 Volts and feed it through a low power linear regulator IC (Figure 4b) to the sensor board. With this construction, a usable voltage range from 2.9 Volts to 5.4 Volts on the SC side can be translated into a stable sensor supply voltage of at least 2.7 Volts.

3.1 Supply Circuit Simplification in First Proof-of-Concept

During the analysis of the battery mould in the sensor cover it turned out, that the selected SC could directly replace the lithium cell battery with few modifications in the sensor housing and at the soldering lugs of the SC (Figure 4a). Hence, the sensor was connected in the next stage directly as supply to the electrical sensor supply inputs. The consequence is that the usable voltage range of the SC had to be limited to a frame between 3.3 Volts down to 2.7 Volts. One further discharge test with these new limits showed that type C^x can provide easily more than 60 minutes sufficient supply voltage at the expected discharge current of the used HR sensor. Therefore, subsequent use tests were performed in this simplified way and the implementation of the regulator circuitry in the sensor was postponed to a later experimental phase.

For the following tests, the SC part of type C^x with the smallest self-discharge rate was selected, so that the power consumption of the sensor in sleep mode could also be qualified. In a first laboratory experiment, the SC was charged to the maximum allowed supply voltage with the board in Figure 2. Then it was installed inside the closed cover of the HR sensor. With a proprietary smartphone App and a sports watch the operation of the sensor was observed, while it was worn for the next hour by an experimenter. During this phase, only lab working activities, but no strain sport actions, were performed (Table 4: first row).

Table 4. First documented test runs of the HR sensor supplied from the SCC

use mode	overall time frame	SC voltage before use	voltage after use
normal work, no physical strain	09:08-10:17	3.29V	2.99V
Slow jogging on a nature trail	10:38-11:43	3.31V	3.03V

3.2 Field Testing

The measured voltage drop of 0.3 Volts in the first practical use of more than an hour suggested that the SC-supplied sensor is directly feasible for a first field test. In this, an endurance training was performed next in terms of a slow jogging for one hour at a controlled speed of 6.5 mph (Figure 3). Two minutes cool down phase by walking was included, the HR sensor was connected to a wearable sports computer, from which the recorded running data could be transferred to a personal computer software, in order to display the results in bigger screen collections and plotting graphs. The whole system worked during the exercise without problems and in a way as known from the normal HR sensor use. In this run, there was some additional preparation time for dressing and moving between laboratory space and the running path outside the building. Again this experiment showed that the simplest concept easily supplies the HR sensor for one full hour while consuming only half of the available capacity. In other words, the ANT+ HR sensor can be operated in this configuration for at least two hours plus several minutes for setup and preparation times.

According to these first positive results, a longer sensor test with a complete use cycle was prepared. Since one of the two chest strap connectors on the sensor housing (Figure 4a) is directly connected to Ground level on the sensor board, only one other electrical access point for the SC positive pole was required. For establishing this, a hole was drilled in the back cover case above the battery mould (Figure 4a right part). After this, the SC could be firmly enclosed into the sensor housing, since charging and voltage measurement was now available through access from outside. Few undocumented experiments with slight overcharging, observation and validation of the SC-supplied HR sensor had been conducted in the following phase.

After all, the participation at a public street run over half-marathon distance was prepared in terms of a complete and quite regular handling cycle by a sports person using and wearing the modified sensor unit. The street run event took place in 50 mi distance from the laboratory environment, therefore typical activities like traveling to the event place, registering for the run and changing clothes was part of this extended field experiment. Table 5 protocols the relevant steps in this experiment.

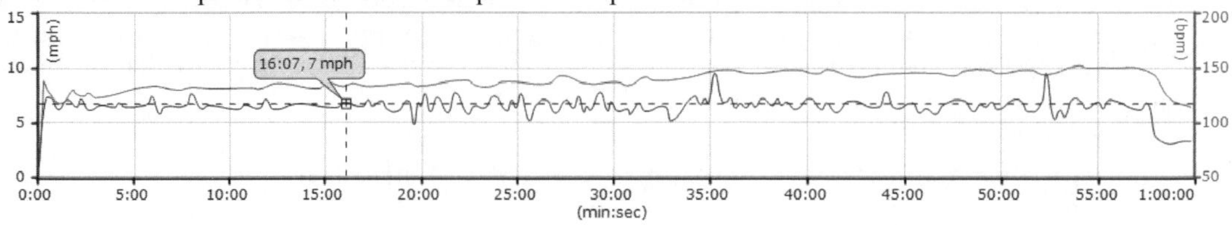

Figure 3. One hour slow jog workout recorded by a Triathlon sports watch linked with the SC supplied heart rate sensor. The plots show the movement speed more or less stable at 6.5 mph and the HR curve with some cardio drift effect

Unfortunately, the correct HR trace failed already 10 minutes after the run was started. After leaving the race arena, an unexpected deep discharge of the SC inside the HR sensor had to be detected. In the following phase of this study, possible reasons were sought for the partially failed experiment. After additional tests and inspections of the sensor, the explanation was found that the measurement distortion is produced by humidity collected inside the sensor. This was validated by several additional field tests on nature trails. At the moment it is left up to the future part of this study to improve insulation of the sensor casing, which was impaired by a slightly too big SC. On the other hand, the entire phase from sensor charging, preparation of the event attendance and first mile of the run showed, that the SC capacity can supply the entire handling cycle when attending such a sports event of two hours duration. The SC discharge contributed by the HR sensor in sleep mode is found being negligible, hence no particular expedition with the sensor in sleep mode is required, even when conducting a two-hour workout with this very simple power cell concept.

The selected capacitors have got a slightly bigger size and a higher weight than a lithium battery cell, while their price is lower. All these differences are not high, but still consequence modifications of the sensor housing. If the complete SC voltage band is exploited and the sensor operation time is specified to the typical value of one hour plus - reasonably - 300% extra reserve, a much smaller and cheaper SC can be used, especially in ANT+ devices. This means, that the sensors could be constructed more slim and lightweight, which would provide a further handling benefit.

Table 5. Protocol for the stages in attending a street running competition with the SC-supplied HR sensor

	9:15am	9:30am	11:30am	11:40am	12:01am	1:42pm	1:50pm
mode/action	charging for 1 min	test after settling time	quiescent discharge test	activation + walk to start	race start	cross finishing line	sensor sleep mode
measure	3.40V	3.37V	3.35V				2.27V

4. DISCUSSION OF RESULTS AND COMPLEMENTING CONCEPTS

The experimental results and the simplified proof-of-concept during the field tests have shown, that the lithium battery cell in sports and health sensors can be replaced by an appropriately selected supercapacitor. Already with a directly connected one Farad SC power cell an operational time of more than two hours can be achieved for the most typical unit of a heart rate sensor. When adding a voltage regulator in the supply path (Figure 4b) as applied during the on-going work in this context, the usable voltage range can be increased from (3.3-2.7)Volts to (5.0-2.8)Volts. This stands for a factor of 3.5 and by that an operational time with one single charge of at least seven hours, which certainly will be enough for most personal applications. Only in extreme cases like attending an Ironman Triathlon this supply capacity wouldn't be sufficient.

It has to be noted that this efficiency applies in such extend to ANT+ sensors, the more universal systems with Bluetooth low Energy would reach due to their higher power consumption only in the order of 2.5 hours total operational time, which is also sufficient for 80% of non-elite sports people (USD Labor, 2009). The electrical power consumption of other sensors is very similar to the HR units, because most energy is required for their RF transmissions. In the experiments here, an additional voltage regulator IC had to be used, because the internal sensor electronics cannot be modified. For a final product on the market, the sensor manufacturers can simply integrate the expanded regulation into the device without additional effort in electronics, since stabilization of supply voltage has to be integrated anyway. When using instead of linear regulation so-called voltage pumps, the supply band could be expanded towards much lower SC output voltages, which would then factorize the working time by another value of approximately 1.5. Hence, with this improved supply electronics, also BT sensors can reach a very reliable operational duration.

Using a SC as power cell of a body sensor provides a series of advantages for construction and manufacturing, for usability and for environment. The SC would be implemented firmly inside the sensor housing, therefore no mechanisms are required for manual exchange by the user. Considering, e.g., sensor S in Figure 1, six mechanical parts could be omitted in the design, which are in detail the four screws, the backside cover and a sealing ring. Furthermore, the sensor housing case could be simplified. This all saves development costs and also in fabrication it saves costs for raw material, production processing stages and production cycle time. The price of the lithium battery cell, which is usually contained in newly sold sensor packages, is even higher than the one for a SC. Hence, either the selling price of the sensor could be reduced, which would represent a customer benefit, or the earnings statement for the vendor could be slightly improved. The cumbersome handling of changing batteries like discussed before could be avoided completely, which represents evidently an important benefit for the customer. Using a self-sustaining power cell is obviously more environment-friendly than any type of throw-away batteries, especially those wasting rare earth metals. Capacitors provide even more advantages compared to accumulators, because the number of charge/discharge-cycles is almost unlimited, and the capacitor cannot be destroyed by deep discharge. This all preserves a much longer use of SC-supplied sensors, also in comparison to the theoretical use of micro accumulators, and therefore again an improvement of environment-friendliness.

One other important aspect hasn't been covered in the discussion up to here: The question how the SC can be charged prior to sensor operation appears also relevant for the degree of handling convenience. For HR sensors, which are equipped with electrodes for their sensor inputs anyway (Figure 4a), the charging could be performed by a DC cable connection through these contact points as well. For other types (Figure 4d), which do not have any electrical connectors to outside, any kind of plug adapter would be required, but for this technical solutions are known and widely in use like, e.g., for charging sports watches (Figure 4c). For such cases, some additional technical effort would be incurred. Use of a charging cable would map perfectly to USB connectors, which are known worldwide as universal system for charging small units and which is partially even enforced by laws. A more modern solution would be inductively charging through an RF field; this would require additional components in the electronic circuitry of the sensor, but may keep the mechanical design for its housing simple. In the end, contact-less charging represents the most convenient method for the user, if the charge loading time is limited to a reasonable time span.

It shall be remarked, that the study here is aiming just for achieving fundamental findings and for demonstrating a proof of concept, or in particular for showing the applicability of a relatively new components technology in electronics to a certain field of use. The development of certified and professional sensor products is left up to companies, who want to implement such ideas into new product generations feasible for mass production and long-term use in health and sports sensing.

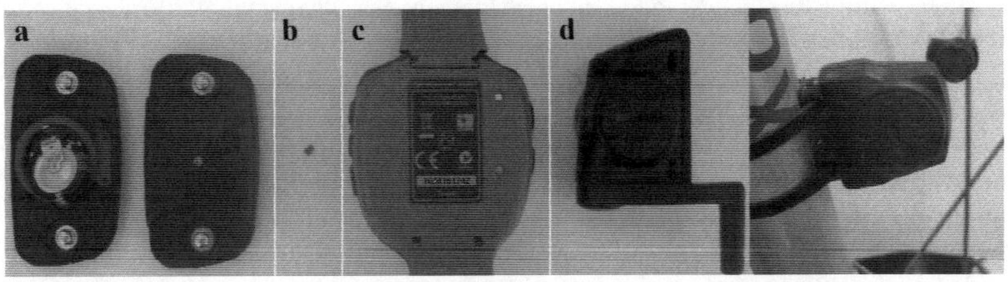

Figure 4. Collection of devices for discussion of charging concepts: a) shows how the SC fits into the backside mould of the open case of sensor S, and how it can be accessed through a pinhole in the closed back cover; b) voltage regulator for experiments; c) commercial solution of contacting device for charging without extra electrodes; d) pedal and wheel turning sensors as samples without regular contacts but battery mould

5. CONCLUSION

As demonstrated and validated in the experiments here, supercapacitors sustain enough electrical power for operating wireless body sensors for a reasonable duration in health and sports workouts. Therefore, supercapacitors can replace the commonly used lithium battery cell in terms of a much more environment-friendly part for most typical sports sensor use. As consequence, the mechanical sensor construction can be simplified, since no exchange of the power cell has to be regarded any more, and cumbersome manual user handling of this can be completely avoided. Hence, the supercapacitor solution arises more comfortable and cheaper than lithium batteries.

Physical workouts are limited for most people to a duration around one hour; during this time frame, the one Farad SC easily delivers enough energy for operating sensors with ANT+ or Bluetooth LE, even if only a limited voltage range like the one of lithium batteries is exploited. Depending on the effort, which is invested in the regulation electronics, a much wider voltage range can be harvested from the SC and the operational time can be factorized considerably, which means that, e.g., an ANT+ HR sensor can be used up to half a day without recharge. SCs can be reloaded in practice infinitely often and they cannot be destroyed by deep discharge; hence SCs provide also clear advantages over the possible, alternative use of micro accumulators. Since feasible SCs have got similar size and weight like the lithium battery cells, there remains no deterioration or restriction during their use as sensor energy supply.

Preparation of the sensor use, on the other hand, represents indeed an aspect of handling convenience, which has not been covered intensely in this study so far. Therefore, the concept work of this investigation will be continued by developing and testing improved discharge and recharge mechanisms like contact-less methods and voltage-pumping. The resulting increased duration for the sensor supply will be validated with further practical experiments especially also for Bluetooth sensors with higher power dissipation, because Bluetooth reaches almost all modern smartphone devices and this may inspire more people for performing also health and sports activities. In addition, the sensor housing shall be improved for overcoming the humidity distortion problems, but up to here, this investigation has shown clearly the potential, that supercapacitors can be used as more comfortable, more cost-efficient and more environment-friendly power supply than the established solution of throwaway lithium cells in sports and health sensors.

REFERENCES

Arts F.J., and Kuipers H., 1994. The relation between power output, oxygen uptake and heart rate in male athletes. *Int. J. of Sports Medicine*, vol. 15(5), pp 228-231.

Bluetooth SIG, https://developer.bluetooth.org/DevelopmentResources/Pages/White-Papers.aspx, last access: April 2017

Conway B.E., 1999. *Electrochemical Supercapacitors, Scientific Fundamentals and Technological Applications*. Springer Science+Business Media, New York, USA.

Dynastream Innovations Inc., 2011. ANT message protocol and usage. http://thisisant.com, Rev. 4.5 (2011).

Jefferis B.J. et al, 2014. Protective Effect of Time Spent Walking on Risk of Stroke in Older Men. *Stroke*, vol. 45, pp 194-199.

Lu M., 2013. *Supercapacitors: Materials, Systems and Applications*. John Wiley and Sons Inc., New Jersey, USA.

Malkinson T., 2009. Current and emerging technologies in endurance athletic training and race monitoring. *Science and Technology for Humanity (TIC-STH)*. Toronto, Canada; pp. 581-586.

Oguma Y., and Shinoda-Tagawa, T., 2004. Physical activity decreases cardiovascular disease risk in women. *American Journal of Preventive Medicine*, vol. 26(5), pp 407-418.

Tudor-Locke C., and Basset D.R., 2004. How many steps/day are enough? Preliminary pedometer indices for public health. *Sports Med.*, vol. 34(1), pp 1-8.

Weghorn, H., 2015. Usability and Engineering Aspects of Competing RF Technologies for Communication with Commercial Sports Sensors in Ubiquitous Applications - Experimental Comparison of Power Consumption and Use Cases for ANT+ and Bluetooth Low Energy Sensor Devices. *Proceedings of the 3rd International Congress on Sports Science and Technology Support icSPORTS 2015*, Scitepress, Lissabon, Portugal, pp 263-270.

USD Labor, 2009. Sports and Exercise. *Spotlight on Statistics*, May 2009, https://www.bls.gov/spotlight/2008/sports/, last access: June 2017.

PROGRESSIVELY DEVELOPING A BUSINESS MODEL TO ASSIST ELDERLY PATIENTS WITH COGNITIVE IMPAIRMENT THROUGH A DIGITAL ECOSYSTEM: A METHODOLOGICAL APPROACH

Paolo Locatelli[1], Federica Cirilli[1], Luca Gastaldi[2], Simona Solvi[2] and Andrea Pistorio[2]
[1]Fondazione Politecnico di Milano· [2]Department of Management Engineering, Politecnico di Milano, Italy

ABSTRACT

Cognitive Impairment (CI) can significantly alter the independent living of people because of its impact on health and wellbeing. This paper illustrates a general Business Model (BM) allowing the delineation of services to ensure independent living for elderly people affected by CI. Furthermore, it describes a methodological approach to fit the general BM into a particular context and applies them in the Italian healthcare setting. The general BM includes a flexible, modular, scalable, and up-to-date organisational model and a digital platform. The first one describes the activities that regulators and service suppliers should accomplish and the second one consists of an easy-to-replicate and innovative information and communication technologies. The methodological approach comprises two steps that allow obtaining the BM Canvas and, then, the Service Model (SM) that includes Country-specific subsets of the elements included within the general BM. Finally, the paper describes the most significant aspects considered to transfer and adapt the developed BM in other contexts.

KEYWORDS

Business models, Service models, Healthcare systems, ICT, Cognitive impairment

1. INTRODUCTION

Prevalence of Cognitive Impairment (CI) in elderly patients is one of the key issues in Western Countries since it involves loss of memory, cognitive slowdown, aphasia, apraxia, sensorial and movement deficit, personality and mood disorders (Alexander et al. 2015; Rizzi et al. 2014). The elderly people with cognitive limits - especially those living in solitude - are significantly exposed to certain risks for their safety: falling, malnutrition or unhealthy nutrition, hygiene issues due to lack of mobility, isolation and depression (Alzheimer's Association 2016). The needs of these patients range from daily aid to dedicated medical assistance (Alzheimer's Association 2016; Miranda-Castillo et al. 2013). Although digital technologies can be one key lever to answer these needs, most of the current solutions are immature for mass implementation (Restifo et al., 2015).

In this context, the double goal of this paper is, on the one hand, to progressively define a Business Model (BM) for supplying assistive services to elderly people affected by CI and, on the other hand, a methodological approach to fit the general BM into a certain context.

2. RESEARCH PROCESS

The overall research process followed to develop the BM and the related methodological approach to fit the BM in the Italian context encompassed three subsequent phases.

The first phase is focused on the general BM design. A literature review has been conducted to discern the most relevant articles dealing with the state of the art, good practices and trends related to the digital solutions used to assist elderly people with CI. The analysis of these articles allowed producing the general

BM to focus the primary variables to be considered to increase the likelihood of providing effective digital services. Web of Science™ and Google Scholar™ have been used to research the articles. The literature has been analysed according to two complementary frameworks. Initially, we relied on the STOF framework (Bouwman et al. 2008), which provides an overall picture of a BM from four broad, interrelated perspectives—service, technology, organisation and finance. Next, we progressively deepened each insight through the Business Model Canvas (BMC) framework (Osterwalder and Pigneur, 2010), which allowed focusing on the main design elements to be considered in service design.

The second phase is focused on the definition of the methodological approach, and related tools, to fit the general BM into a specific context. The methodological approach is based on two steps that allowed achieving a context-specific BM canvas as well as the relative Service Model (SM).

Finally, within the third phase, the BM and the related methodological approach have been applied to a set of real contexts (Italy, Spain, Sweden and Israel). The designed SMs are implemented following a Business Process Reengineering (Hammer, 1990; Champy, 2002) approach, which is characterised by the following activities: (1) design of the care process model, which firstly defines the macro-phases of a general care process for CI patients. (2) analysis of the AS-IS process models; (3) design of the TO-BE process models, underlining the difference between AS-IS and TO-BE process models, also considering digital solutions (Locatelli et al. 2015; Pistorio et al. 2017). In this paper, we report the application in the Italian context.

3. GENERAL BUSINESS MODEL FOR PEOPLE WITH CI

The general BM is characterized by the following 9 building blocks. For each of them we report the main results of the analysis of the literature that has been accomplished.

1. Customer segments are the convenient set of clients with common needs, behaviours or attributes. Following Petersen (2004), the main customer segments to be considered in CI are: (i) patients with dementia; (ii) patients with amnestic Mild CI (a-MCI); (iii) patients with non-amnestic Mild CI (na-MCI).

2. Value proposition is the reason why a customer chooses one product and/or service. In CI domain, a tool adopted to assess the various needs is the Camberwell Assessment of Need for the Elderly (CANE) model (Reynolds et al. 2000). Its application highlights that the patients with dementia have more care needs than MCI patients. Furthermore, there are several solutions for the various actors involved in the care process.

3. Channels are the interfaces used to interact with the customers to deliver a value proposition. Literature shows that the main channels by which care services are provided to elderly people with CI are the following: (i) caregiver; (ii) general physician; (iii) healthcare specialist; (iv) healthcare structure.

4. Customer relationships regard how relating with customer segments. Patients suffering from CI tend to communicate with their caregivers or social workers. These two support patients in adopting and using any digital solution for providing enhanced services. From the viewpoint of the actors involved in the care process, many companies maintain online most of their relationships with caregivers.

5. Revenue streams deal with the cash generated from every customer segment. Following Stroetmann et al. (2003), the main revenues for a digital solution in CI domain are the following: (i) service paid by insurance funds; (ii) service paid by governments; (iii) service paid by the patient or by his relatives/caregivers through out-of-pocket expenses. Three groups of people or organisations pay for the digital solution: (a) Business to Consumer (B2C): the service is sold directly to the patient or his caregiver. (b) Business to Public (B2P): the service is sold to public entities i.e. local authorities, NHSs and housing associations; (c) Business to Business (B2B): the service is sold to private companies and, in some countries, most of them are private medical insurance companies. Furthermore, there could be the following types of transactions between the provider of digital solutions and the healthcare organisation: (1) healthcare organisation purchases the entire system (one-time capital investment); (2) healthcare organisation pays a license fee for each patient connected to the system.

6. Key resources are necessary assets to create and offer the value proposition. From the perspective of the patient suffering from CI, human resources that will be crucial in the establishment of the BM are health professional and caregivers (or the social worker if the patient has not relatives that support her) (Robert et al. 2013). The human resource that is vital for the establishment of the BM is the specialist of digital services

through which assisting people with CI (Kapadia et al. 2015). From the standpoint of physical assets required to provide the service, technologies play a key role both for the patient and for the overall system (Kerssens et al. 2015; Robert et al. 2013; Bharucha et al. 2009). Other key resources are patents, licenses and copyrights.

7. Key activities are actions that should be performed to create and offer a value proposition. From the patient standpoint, the key activities are related to his involvement: (i) engagement of the patient; (ii) maintenance of the relationship with the patient. From the standpoint of the actors involved in the care process, key activities are related to the creation and sustainment of the relationships among these key actors: (a) create the connection between healthcare specialist and caregiver/social worker; (b) maintenance of the relationship between healthcare specialist and caregivers/social workers. Following Ógáin and Mountain (2015), these activities can be supported through the contributions of governmental actors regarding national/regional awareness campaigns, financial incentives to healthcare organisations and healthcare specialist for the adoption of digital solutions to diagnose and treat MCI and dementia. Following Robert et al. (2013), the key activities related to the technology adopted are the production of the equipment and sensors, the selection of the most appropriate technology/sensor, the installation of technologies in patients' home, and the calibration of the sensors.

8. Key partnerships refer to the network of suppliers useful to improve the BM. The literature on CI suggests that some key partnerships could be related to government, research centre/university, local regional community (Kapadia et al. 2015), private organisations (König et al. 2015), and networks between the providers of digital solutions and healthcare organisations.

9. Cost structure deals with relevant costs characterising a feasible BM. Literature suggests that the main costs for a digital solution in the CI domain are the following (Kapadia et al. 2015): (i) training costs; (ii) personnel costs; (iii) installation and maintenance costs; (iv) purchasing and manufacturing costs; (v) customer service costs.

4. FITTING OF THE BM IN A SPECIFIC CONTEXT

The methodological approach to fit the general BM in a specific context is based on two steps that allowed to obtain, starting from the general BM, the BM_{Canvas} and, then, the Service Model (Figure 1). BM_{Canvas} represent the Country-specific subsets of the elements included within the general BM. SM contain configurations mainly focused on value propositions.

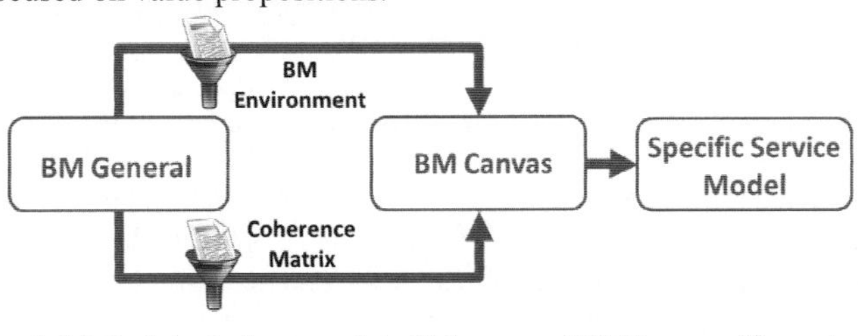

Figure 1. Methodological approach to fit the general BM in a specific context

The first step is made through two tools: (i) the Business Model Environment (BME) (Osterwalder & Pigneur 2010); (ii) a Coherence Matrix (CM). These tools have been used to reduce the multitude of elements proposed in the general BM.

The BME organises and describes the key contextual variables useful to synthetically characterise each context involved in the research, according to the four macro-areas: (i) key trends; (ii) macroeconomic forces; (iii) industry forces; (iv) market forces.

The CM has been developed by the research group and is characterised by the following five dimensions: (i) country; (ii) customer segment; (iii) functionalities; (iv) actions to address the needs of the patient and of the overall system; (v) relevance of the specific need. The CM describes the underlying interrelations among these dimensions and allows discerning between: (a) coherent and incoherent pairs functionality-action to address the need (i.e. need of the patient or of the overall system); (b) relevant and not relevant pairs functionality-action to address the need; (c) Country-specific and common among Country pairs functionality-action.

In addition to BME, the implementation of the CM returns different combinations of coherent, relevant and context-specific technological functionalities and actions to address patients' needs.

The synthesis of the findings related to the application of BME and CM allows defining the $BM_{Canvases}$. The latter, though grounded on already established frameworks (e.g. Business Model Canvas, BME), take advantage of the flexibility of the tools adopted to build them, thus making them adaptable to the various possible contexts (i.e. specificities of the various countries) or other patients' clusters different from those adopted in this research. The second step reduces the complexity of the vast number of elements present in the BM canvas focusing on the key building blocks of value proposition and customer segments.

5. APPLICATION IN A REAL CONTEXT

In this paragraph, we describe the application of the BM and the methodological approach in the Italian context.

5.1 Design of the Italian Service Model

The needs marked by clinicians as extremely relevant have been highlighted and clustered as follow:

N_1. Diagnosis and assessment: (i) overall medical condition; (ii) behavior and mood; (iii) assess the risk of malnutrition; (iv) Activities of Daily Living (ADL); (v) risk for falls; (vi) immobility detection for elderly monitoring at home (indoor) for patient physical needs; (vii) fall detection for elderly monitoring at home (indoor) for patient physical needs.

N_2. Patient psychological needs: (i) cognitive stimulation; (ii) online cognitive training.

N_3. Clinical team needs: (i) coordination of care; (ii) clinical team information sharing; (iii) improve diagnosis method; (iv) advising on deciding course of action; (v) better access to and relevance of non-pharmacological therapies; (vi) standardised care pathway.

N_4. Follow-up: (i) monitoring overall condition; (ii) measurement of adherence and compliance of patients to treatment; (iii) assess timely changes evolving needs for social care support.

Given Italian specific needs, further specific elements of the Italian SM are available: (iii) trend analyses performed on data gathered from various patients' monitoring activities for diagnosis and assessment & for caregivers needs; (iv) registering of pre-scheduled activities performed by the patient (patient is formally required to provide a yes/no answer) for patient environmental needs & for patient physical needs; (v) automatic reminder to patients for the performing of a scheduled activity for patient environmental needs & for patient physical needs; (vi) availability of personalized and adaptable remote-based training programs automatically tailored to individual patient's characteristics for patient physical needs; (vii) drug management for patient physical needs.

Starting from these clusters, it is possible to cluster also the technological functionalities that allow meeting these needs, and which are common to all Countries. Regarding the patient layer, the following 5 clusters have been identified (technological functionality in brackets):

TFP_1. Patient's status (monitoring): (i) automatic remote-based measurement of patient's blood pressure; (ii) automatic remote-based measurement of patient's O_2 saturation; (iii) automatic provision and submitting of questionnaires (of various nature, including patient's health status and to support change detection) to care-involved subjects; (iv) gathering on non-structured information on patient's health status from informal caregivers or social caretakers; (v) evaluation and monitoring of cognitive skills and monitoring of decay curves and other trends; (vi) Immobility detection for elderly monitoring at home (indoor); (vii) Fall detection for elderly monitoring at home (indoor);

TFP_2. Patient's status (alert): automatic provision of feedbacks and alerts on patients' progress or deterioration.

TFP_3. Patient's status (communication-cognitive stimulation): (i) cognitive games/exercises to stimulate patients to preserve cognitive/ executive functions; (ii) tele-consultation (tele-presence) functionalities allowing patients and professionals to communicate to each other visually.

TFP_4. Patient's Activities (alert): (i) automatic provision of remote real-time feedback on patients' activities, including non-pre-scheduled activities; (ii) automatic provision of remote real-time patient-tailored motivational messages based on patients' activities, including non-pre-scheduled activities; (iii) automatic

provision of remote feedback on patients' activities, building on long-time data analysis on patients' status; (iv) provision of automatic reminder to patients for the performing of a scheduled activity; (v) availability of personalized and adaptable remote-based training programs automatically tailored to individual patient's characteristics;

TFP_5. Patient's Activities (monitoring): (i) activity monitoring through accelerometer for elderly monitoring (also outdoor, with batch data download once reconnected to base station): stand / sit / walk / steps + intensity of activity; (ii) GPS-based patient monitoring and structured health-based data gathering for outdoor step counting or activity monitoring (including detection of falls); (iii) registering of pre-scheduled activities performed by the patient (who is monitored real-time by sensors when performing the activity); (iv) trend analyses performed on data gathered from various patients' monitoring activities; (v) registering of pre-scheduled activities performed by the patient (patient is formally required to provide a yes/no answer);

TFP_6. Patient's status (storage and sharing information): (i) activity monitoring through accelerometer for elderly monitoring (also outdoor, with batch data download once reconnected to base station): stand / sit / walk / steps + intensity of activity; (ii) GPS-based patient monitoring and structured health-based data gathering for outdoor step counting or activity monitoring (including detection of falls); (iii) registering of pre-scheduled activities performed by the patient (patient is monitored real-time by sensors when performing the activity).

Regarding the actors involved in the care process, the following 4 clusters have been identified:

TFS_1. Care providers (communication): informal communication (messaging) among various actors (e.g.: family members and doctors);

TFS_2. Care providers (teamwork): enablement of multidisciplinary teamwork across care providers, doctors and informal caregivers (or some of these);

TFS_3. Care pathway/treatment plan (monitoring): coherence check between clinical guidelines/protocols and data gathered as part of care activities, drug management.

TFS_4. Care pathway/treatment plan (sharing information): sharing of a treatment plan among caregivers, doctors and family members (or some of these).

5.2 Application of the Italian Service Model

The analysis highlighted four common phases to every care process for people with CI: (i) noticing symptoms and first detection; (ii) assessment and diagnosis; (iii) treatment and care service definition; (iv) service delivery and maintenance.

We will describe in detail the Italian As-Is process model, in Palazzolo Institute of Fondazione Don Carlo Gnocchi Onlus in Milano, following the four macro-phases.

A. Noticing symptoms and first detection: the process starts with the first meeting between patients and physicians, like a check-up visit, or after an acute episode in a long-term care facility. The visit can be owned by the GPs or specialised physicians (both within Palazzolo Institute as well as external). Once patients with certain kind of characteristics have been identified during a physician's visit, their path continues in the care process.

B. Assessment and diagnosis: in case there are symptoms of CI, a basic assessment can be performed. Note that usually the GP points out the patient to specialists (at Palazzolo Institute or externally). This initial assessment consists of a basic examination of the patient with suspected CI, aimed at understanding more regarding patients' health conditions and social situation. In case the basic assessment strengthens the initial suspicion of CI, a comprehensive assessment follows. At Palazzolo Institute, for a comprehensive assessment, patients can be referred to a specialised geriatrics unit, which starts the assessment protocol aimed at reaching the diagnosis.

C. Treatment and care service definition: in Italy, it is common that patients' relatives or caregivers take the responsibility for organising the care pathway of the patient. The care pathway can be managed through the activation of home-based and facility-based services, whose activation is discussed together with the family.

D. Service delivery and maintenance: Palazzolo Institute delivers an integrated socio-healthcare service to patients affected by CI. During the service delivery, the patient is continuously monitored by the professionals of the Institute.

As regards the TO-BE process models, we will describe in detail the differences between the Italian AS-IS and the TO-BE process model. The fundamental differences from AS-IS and the TO-BE process models are linked to some new technologies, which ensure the sharing of information among the various actors enabling independent living.

A. Noticing symptoms and first detection: during the visit, physicians visualise the patient's medical records on the DECI platform connected with the databases of local hospitals and GP.

B. Assessment and diagnosis: data collected by the specialised geriatrics unit are entered in a tablet and immediately shared (through a cloud service) with the other stakeholders of the care network.

C. Treatment and care service definition: A first needs analysis can be performed by the patient/caregiver filling an on-line questionnaire on the DECI platform. Then a visit could confirm the results of the questionnaire.

D. Service delivery and maintenance: A wearable sensor could be used to detect abnormalities in the level of activity and send alert messages to family members or assistance operator. The GP and specialists can share the information collected through the DECI platform and plan together a revision of the medication and treatment plan, and schedule visits. The program can alternate sessions in physical presence of the physiotherapist with tele-rehabilitation sessions. Some cognitive stimulation and rehabilitation exercises could also be done at home through the online platform. The platform can also be used by the case manager to communicate with the patient or the caregiver.

6. TRANSFERABILITY INSTANCES

In this paragraph, we describe the main instances that we can consider to evaluate the transferability of the Business Model (BM) in different Countries of the EU, validated within the DECI project.

Firstly, we must consider the level of integration of services to support elderly patients affected by Cognitive Impairment. As described by Leutz (1999), there are three levels of integration: linkage, coordination and full integration. "Linkage" allows people with mild to moderate or new disabilities to be cared for properly in systems that serve the entire population without having to rely on outside systems for special relationships. At this level, there is no case management and the information is provided when asked and asked when needed. At the second level, "coordination", explicit structures and individual managers are in place to coordinate benefits and care across acute and other systems. Coordination is a more structured form of integration than linkage, but it still operates largely through the separate structures of current systems. At this level, there are case managers and linkage staff; the information reports/items are defined and provided routinely in both directions. The third level, "full integration", creates new programs or units where resources from multiple systems are pooled. At this level, teams or "super" case managers control all care and, to share information, they adopt a common record as part of daily practice and management.

In our view, to be applied the Business Model, the Country can have in place all the three integration models – linkage, coordination or full integration - as we have applied it from linkage models (e.g. Spain) to full integration models (e.g. Israel).

Then, we must also consider the population Information Technologies (IT) readiness, measured as the percentage of the population that access to the internet and use it at home every day (Lupianez *et al.*, 2013). Indeed, if patients, or at least their caregivers, and socio-healthcare providers have not a minimum level of digital literacy it is not possible to successfully apply the DECI Business Model. As reported in the research of the Internet World Stats, the four Countries involved in the DECI project 62% of the population at minimum uses the internet: in Sweden, the internet users percentage is 94.6%, in Spain is 76.9%, in Israel is 72.7% and in Italy is 62%. For these reasons, we can say that, to be applied the DECI Business Model, the EU Country must have a minimum of 62% of internet users. As reported in the Internet World Stats research, there are very few EU countries with a percentage of internet users minor than 62 % (Bulgaria 56.7%, Romania 56.3%).

As described by Wendt (2009), there are some others indicators to be considered in the transferability evaluation, such as the healthcare expenditure and financing, the healthcare service provision and the institutional regulation. Based on these indicators the Countries can be classified into three different clusters.

Cluster 1 shows a high level of total health expenditure, a high share of public funding and a moderate share of private out-of-pocket funding. The inpatient and outpatient indexes are respectively at a moderate and high level. The high level of autonomy of self-employed doctors and the high freedom of choice for patients characterise this cluster.

Cluster 2 is characterised by a medium level of total health expenditure. Private out-of-pocket funding is moderate, and the share of public health funding is high. Compared to Cluster 1, the level of inpatient healthcare providers is comparable, but the outpatient provider level is notably lower. Doctors face stringent regulations regarding their income opportunities and the access to doctors is highly regulated.

Cluster 3 reaches a notably low level of total health expenditure that is linked, except for the Finnish context, to the uncertain economic position of these European countries. The level of private out-of-pocket payments is high and institutional indicators reveal that the control of patients' access to medical doctors is high. The inpatient and outpatient indexes are respectively at a low and moderate level. GPs are characterised by more limited income opportunities, compared to Cluster 2, but they receive a fixed salary.

The DECI Countries cover all of these clusters. Indeed, we can consider in the cluster 1 Israel, because it includes all EU social insurance countries, in cluster 2, as reported by Wendt, Sweden and Italy and in cluster 3 Spain. In our view, to be applied the Business Model, the EU Country can be included in all of the clusters as the DECI Countries cover all the clusters.

7. CONCLUSIONS

Strengths of the adopted method are multiple because it utilises established frameworks (e.g. Business Model Canvas) and highlights common traits and differences among various Countries. It allows distinguishing between coherent and not coherent elements, and between high-priority and low-priority ones. It provides information about the impact of the different digital solutions and it is applicable in other Countries. It supports decision-making processes also after the pilot phases because, once the first most relevant needs are addressed, it will be possible to proceed with the actions to address the needs with a lower relevance. Furthermore, the approach was validated and refined through a Scientific Advisory Board with the involvement of external stakeholders. Finally, the approach is aimed to support the definition and implementation of a comprehensive and multifaceted BM in a complex and continuously evolving context. The main weaknesses of the method described in this paper are related to its high complexity. Indeed, it requires the contribution of a multitude of different actors (e.g. physicians, caregivers, technology providers) therefore it is highly time-consuming. Furthermore, the analysis of the Country-specific characteristics in the various settings requires huge efforts. The next steps of the DECI project are: (1) the implementation of the Pilot site (Italy, Sweden, Israel and Spain) adopting the proposed SMs and (2) the evaluation of key performance indicators considering different perspectives (e.g. economics, social) to highlight the potential benefits of the designed approach.

ACKNOWLEDGEMENT

This paper is based on DECI – Digital Environments for Cognitive Inclusion – a project (European Commission - Horizon 2020 program - grant agreement No 643588) that is aimed at improving a healthy lifestyle for elderly people affected by CI, passing through a system monitoring vital signs, treating and managing diseases (Locatelli et al. 2015).

DECI Consortium is led by Fondazione Politecnico di Milano (Italy) and involves partners from five different countries (Italy, Sweden, Spain, Israel and The Netherlands). Four pilots, involving 100 to 250 patients each, will allow assessing the feasibility and the effectiveness of the designed BM and related methodological approach to fit it in within real-life environments and local healthcare systems in Israel, Italy, Spain and Sweden.

The authors would like to thank the whole Consortium of the DECI project: Fondazione Politecnico di Milano, Consoft Sistemi SpA, Fondazione Don Carlo Gnocchi Onlus (Italy), Centre for Healthcare Improvement – Chalmers University of Technology, Västra Götalandsregionen (Sweden); Hospital Universitario de Getafe - Servicio de Geriatría (Spain); Maccabi Healthcare Services (Israel); Roessingh Research and Development (The Netherlands).

REFERENCES

Alexander, M., et al., 2015. Age-Stratified Prevalence of Mild Cognitive Impairment and Dementia in European Populations: A Systematic Review. *Journal of Alzheimer's Disease*, 48, pp. 355–359.

Alzheimer's association, 2016. 2016 *Alzheimer's disease facts and figures*. Alzheimer's & dementia, volume 12, issue 4, pp. 459–509.

Bharucha, A.J. et al., 2009. Intelligent Assistive Technology Applications to Dementia Care: Current Capabilities, Limitations, and Future Challenges. *The American Journal of Geriatric Psychiatry*, 17(2), pp.88–104.

Bouwman, H., de Vos, H., Haaker, T., 2008. *Mobile Service Innovation and Business Mod*els, Springer-Verlag Berlin Heidelberg.

Champy, J., 2002. *X-Engineering the Corporation: Reinventing Your Business in the Digital Age*, Warner Business Books. New York.

Hammer, M., 1990. Re-engineering work: don't automate, obliterate. *Harvard Business Review*, 68(4):104-112.

Kapadia, V. et al., 2015. Emerging ICT implementation issues in aged care. *International Journal of Medical Informatics*, pp.1–9.

Kerssens, C. et al., 2015. Personalized Technology to Support Older Adults With and Without Cognitive Impair-ment Living at Home. *American Journal of Alzheimer's Disease and Other Dementias*, 30(1), pp.85–97.

König, A. et al., 2015. Automatic speech analysis for the assessment of patients with predementia and Alzheimer's disease. *Alzheimer's & Dementia: Diagnosis, Assessment & Disease Monitoring*, 1(1), pp.112–124.

Locatelli, P., Restifo, N., Cirilli, F., Moser, R., 2015. DECI: Digital Environment for Cognitive Inclusion - Improving Elderly Citizens' Quality of Life Through an ICT-enabled Patient-Centric Home Environment. *Proceedings of the International Conferences on e-Health 2015- Part of the Multi Conference on Computer Science and Information Systems 2015*, IADIS.

Leutz, W.N., 1999. Five laws for integrating medical and social services: lessons from the United States and the United Kingdom". *Milbank quarterly*, vol. 77, pp. 77-110.

Lupianez, F., Maghiros, I. & Abadie, F., 2013. *Strategic Intelligence Monitor on Personal Health Systems, Phase 2 Citizens and ICT for Health in 14 European Countries: Results from an Online Panel* F. Abadie et al., eds.

Miranda-Castillo, C., Woods, B. & Orrell, M., 2013. The needs of people with dementia living at home from user, caregiver and professional perspectives. *BMC Health Services Research*, 13, pp. 43.

Osterwalder, A., Pigneur, Y., 2010. *Business Model Generation* (pp. 1–288). Hoboken, New Jersey: John Wiley & Sons, Inc.

Ógáin, E.N., Mountain, K., 2015. *Remember me*. pp.1–33.

Petersen, R.C., 2004. Mild cognitive impairment as a diagnostic entity. *Journal of Internal Medicine*, 256(3), pp.183–194.

Pistorio, A., Locatelli, P., Cirilli, F., Gastaldi, L., Solvi, S., 2017. A Business Model for Digital Healthcare Environments: An Organic Approach and a Use Case for Handling Cognitive Impairment. *Proceedings of the 10th International Joint Conference on Biomedical Engineering Systems and Technologies HEALTHINF*, BIOSTEC, pp. 340–347.

Restifo N., Cirilli F., Gastaldi L., Fugini M., Garavaglia G., Chiantore L. (2015) Health and Social Care Services for Frail People: ICT as a Sustainable Enabler of Integrated Care, *International Conference e-Health*, Las Palmas de Gran Canaria (Spain), July 21–24, pp. 193–197.

Reynolds, T. et al., 2000. Camberwell Assessment of Need for the Elderly (CANE) Development, validity and reliability. *British Journal of Psychiatry*, 176(5), pp.444–452.

Rizzi, L., Rosset, I., Roriz-Cruz, M., 2014. Global epidemiology of dementia: Alzheimer's and vascular types. *Biomed Res Int. 2014*; 2014:908915.

Robert, P.H. et al., 2013. Recommendations for ICT use in Alzheimer's disease assessment: Monaco CTAD Expert Meeting. *The Journal of Nutrition, Health Aging*, 17(8), pp.653–660.

Stroetmann, K.A., Stroetmann, V.N. & Westerteicher, C., 2003. Implementation of TeleCare services: benefit assessment andorganisational models. *Studies in Health Technology and Informatics*, 97, pp.131–141.

Wendt, 2009. Mapping European healthcare systems: a comparative analysis of financing, service provision and access to healthcare. *Journal of European Social Policy*, n. 19, pp. 432.

INTRODUCING PERSONALISED SELF-MANAGEMENT TO SUPPORT PHYSICAL ACTIVITY IN ELDERLY: A CASE STUDY

Jan-Willem van 't Klooster[1], Inge van Bruinessen[2], April Boessen[3], Loek van der Heide[3], Miriam Vollenbroek-Hutten[4] and Sandra van Dulmen[5]

[1]*Roessingh Research & Development, Enschede, The Netherlands*

[2]*Netherlands Institute for Health Services Research, Utrecht, The Netherlands*

[3]*Zuyd University of Applied Sciences; Maastricht University, Maastricht, The Netherlands*

[4]*Ziekenhuisgroep Twente, Enschede, The Netherlands*

[5]*Netherlands Institute for Health Services Research; Radboudumc; University College of Southeast Norway Utrecht, The Netherlands; Nijmegen, The Netherlands; Drammen, Norway*

ABSTRACT

Our population is aging, leading to great challenges in healthcare. A transformation to a pro-active system, support through technology, and self-management are regularly mentioned as potential solutions. In this context, the self-management program LIFE ("living independently functioning elderly") was started to promote physical activity in seniors.

A technology-supported personalized self-management program was developed. The aim of the program is to contribute to a physically active life style. LIFE offers various modules to elderly who are at risk of functional decline. These modules contain personalized advice, recommendations and suggestions how seniors can develop or maintain a healthy behaviour and prevent functional deterioration. To restrict functional decline, activities of the program are tailored to the needs of the user. The activities are delivered preventive instead of after the functional decline has been progressed to the extent that elderly have to be institutionalised. A main aspect of the concept of the program is that elderly can choose between the various provided services, making their own decisions. LIFE offers this in an easily implementable self-management program. In this paper, the program is presented, the care pathway of operationalizing the program is described, and evaluation results are discussed. As such, this paper demonstrates the feasibility of introducing an ict-mediated self-management program in elderly care.

KEYWORDS

Self-management programs, Physical activity, Elderly, Ehealth

1. INTRODUCTION

Our population is aging. This leads to great challenges in healthcare. In fact, the fastest growing age group of the western world population is elderly (> 65 years). In the Netherlands, 2.5 million of the population in 2010 was aged (above) 65 years and it is expected that in 2020 3.4 million of the population in Netherlands will be elderly (CBS, 2007). Elderly have a higher life expectancy compared to life expectancy of elderly in past decades (Moran, Cauwenberg, Hercky – Linnewiel, Cerin, Deforche & Plaut, 2014; Nelson et al., 2007). A decline of functional ability is often associated with increasing age. Much of the health care costs occur due to the patient's loss of functional independence. Also, the probability to suffer accidents or develop other problems rise with age (Cochrane, Munro, Davey, Nicholl, 1998). For these reasons, it is necessary to support elderly to maintain an adequate physical functioning that helps them to live longer independently (Van Holle, van Cauwenberg, Deforche, van de Weghe, Bourdeaudhuij & van Dyck, 2015). Physical activity has the potential to reduce the years of dependent living and improve health related quality of life. In addition to that, long – term physical activity is associated with postponed disability (Spirduso and Cronin, 2001) and also independent living in elderly (Paterson, Jones & Rice, 2007).

A transformation to a pro-active system, support through technology, and self-management are regularly mentioned as potential solutions. As aging leads to functional decline, self-management services become more and more important for active and healthy aging.

Yet, little is known about the working mechanisms and effectiveness of self-management programs to counter functional decline. (RVO, 2017) The question arises what makes such a program work in practice? To learn this, we developed and evaluated a self-management program for prevention of functional decline.

This program, called LIFE, is a technology-supported personalized self-management program. Its aim is to contribute to a physically active life style in a personalized way. LIFE offers various modules to elderly who are at risk of functional decline. These modules contain personalized tips, recommendations and suggestions how they can develop or maintain a healthy behaviour and prevent functional deterioration. The program offers personalized training exercises to this end and provides insight into a users' physical activity.

The goal of this paper is to present the self-management program and its implementation into elderly care. Researchers and healthcare professionals involved in promoting physical activity in seniors may benefit from the approach and lessons learned presented in this paper.

The paper is structured as follows. Section 2 describes the program and its components. Section 3 describes how the program was put to practice in a pilot case study in a nursing home. Section 4 describes the case study results. Section 5 describes the conclusions.

2. SELF-MANAGEMENT PROGRAM 'LIFE'

Following a series of focus group sessions with stakeholders, a requirement elicitation was conducted for the self-management program. The elicition approach is described in Boessen et al. (2016).

As a result, the program 'Life' was based on 4 pillars: screening, activities, exercise, and feedback. Section 2.1 describes these 4 pillars, then the operational usage of the program is described in Section 2.2. The program is available in Dutch and English at the moment at www.beweegportaal.nl.

2.1 Main Program Components

2.1.1 Screening

When starting the self-management program, a screening takes place, to obtain personal information necessary for tailoring. The user is requested to indicate personal preferences regarding physical activities. This information is used to match the preferences against available activities. The result of this match is presented to the user, to tailor the offer of activities to the individual preferences. Furthermore, screenings are offered for self-assessment, to give users insight in the current health status. This insight can be obtained, e.g. through filling out the PF-10 questionnaire measuring physical capabilities (van der Zee et al., 1993).

The program is based on the self-determination (SDT) theory (Deci & Ryan, 1985) in that users are offered a wide range of means to become more physically active, but the decision which actual activity is performed when is let to the user. As such, the program adapts the level of exercises to the capabilities of the user by advancing or decreasing the difficulty level.

2.1.2 Offline Activities

To support becoming active in a way that fits to the individual user, the program recommends 'offline' activities (e.g. outdoor activities in the neighbourhood) that correspond with the personal preferences. These activities are administered for a local setting such that when the program is used in a community, only local activities are offered.

The recommendation functionality used to suggest activities is based on two aspects:

- The intersection between users' interests and the interests that new activities are interesting for (a match of properties of a user and properties of an activity);
- Novelty of activities.

This way, the program presents matching activities, but also provides new potentially interesting novel activities.

2.1.3 Physical Exercises

The third part of the program consists of 'online' activities by means of over 65 video-based exercises. We use the scientifically validated Otago program to provide physical exercises (Campbell et al., 2005). These are offered as videos and contain spoken as well as written instructions, to enable home based exercises of physical fitness, strength, balance, and flexibility.

The program adopts adjusts to the level of the user by inquiring the perceived difficulty at the end of a 30 min. session, or by automatic advance to more challenging exercises after three weeks. A training session (which consists of a warming up, exercises sessions, and cooling down), automatically varies each time to keep the sessions interesting. Figure 1 shows the general concept; a movie with spoken instructions is played in which a recognisable actress shows the exercises; the instructions are also written in text. Strength, balance, flexibility, condition, agility *categories* are available, in both standing and sitting position. Users can follow a program with exercises from all categories, or choose to focus on one category. The portal measures time spent on each exercises page. Figure 2 shows tiles with different exercise categories for a given user.

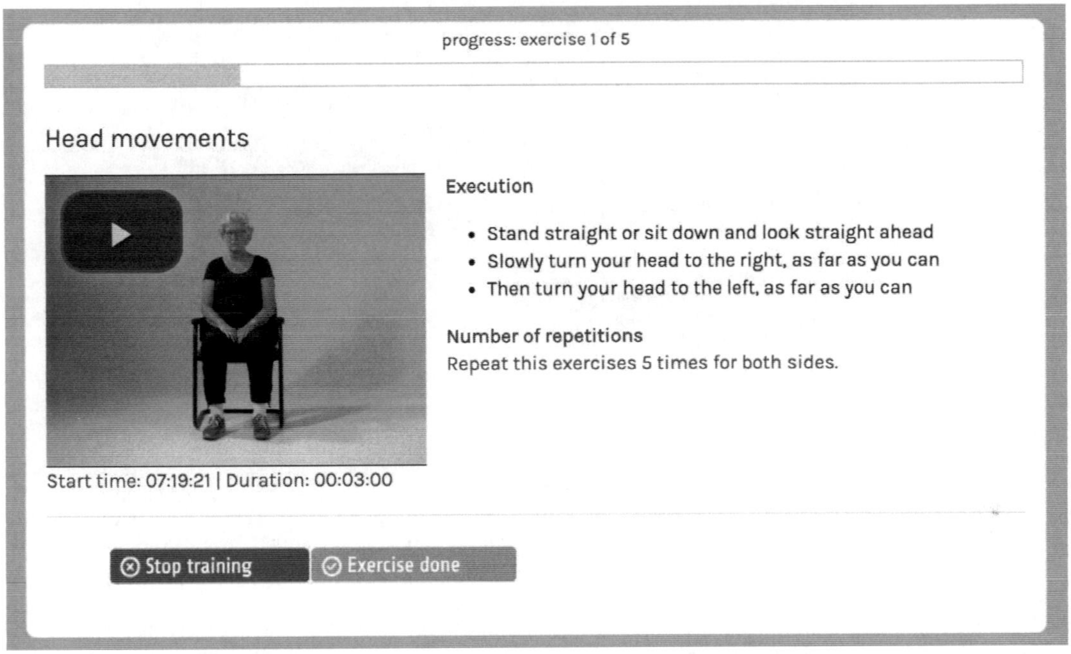

Figure 1. Exercise Page with Video and Instructions to Perform Physical Exercise

2.1.4 Result Overview

The final part of the program consists of a *dashboard* with an overview of activity metrics so that users can monitor their progress. The dashboard shows how much time is spent on performing activities and exercises, level or difficulty of exercise achieved, and what self-assessments are carried out. This is measured as mentioned in the above paragraph.

Optionally, an armband tracker measuring activity using accelerometers can be integrated. Then, both time spent on exercise webpages (only an indication that the exercises are in fact performed) but also actual daily physical activity are shown. The accelerometer addition is for the sake of brevity not further discussed in this particular paper.

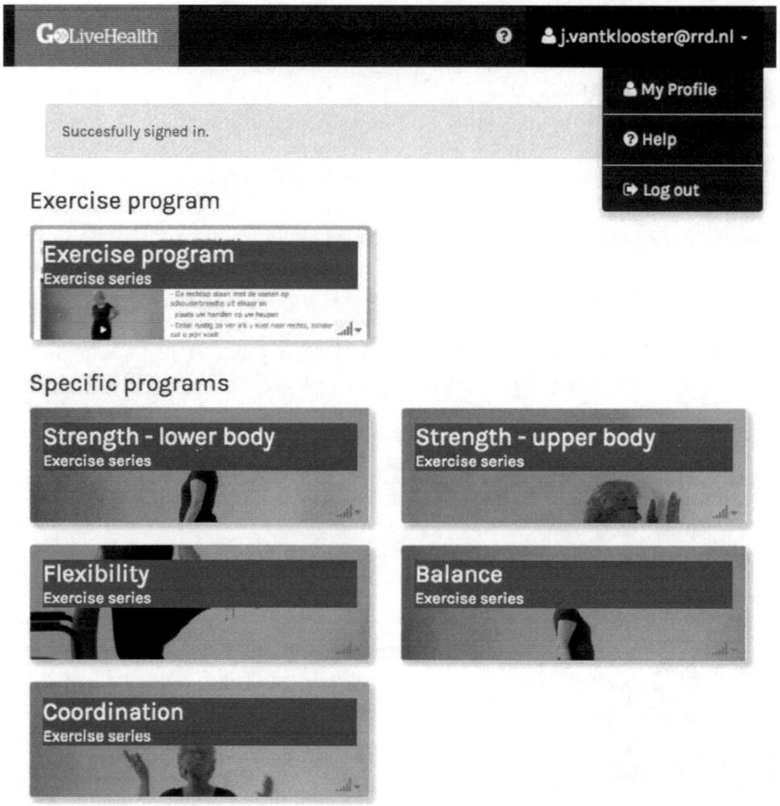

Figure 2. Different Exercise Categories (Mixed, Strength Lower / Upper Body, Flexibility, Balance, Coordination)

2.2 Embedding the Program in Practice

Based on interviews, focus groups sessions and literature reviews, a care pathway was crafted to structure the operational process regarding the self-management program. It is based on Boessen et al. (2016) and shown in Figure 3.

When embedding the program in practice in care institutions or nursing homes, we ought it to be crucial to have support of local organization staff. Hence, preparatory meetings with staff are paramount to be able to embed the service in the daily care pathways. Besides, local staff stimulate their clients to get to know the program. Finally, commitment and local contact such as ambassadors are essential to sustain usage of the program. The other option explored is elderly getting acquainted with the self-management program themselves through e.g. local news media.

Then, an instructional kick off session is organized to explain and to promote using the program in an adequate and informed manner.

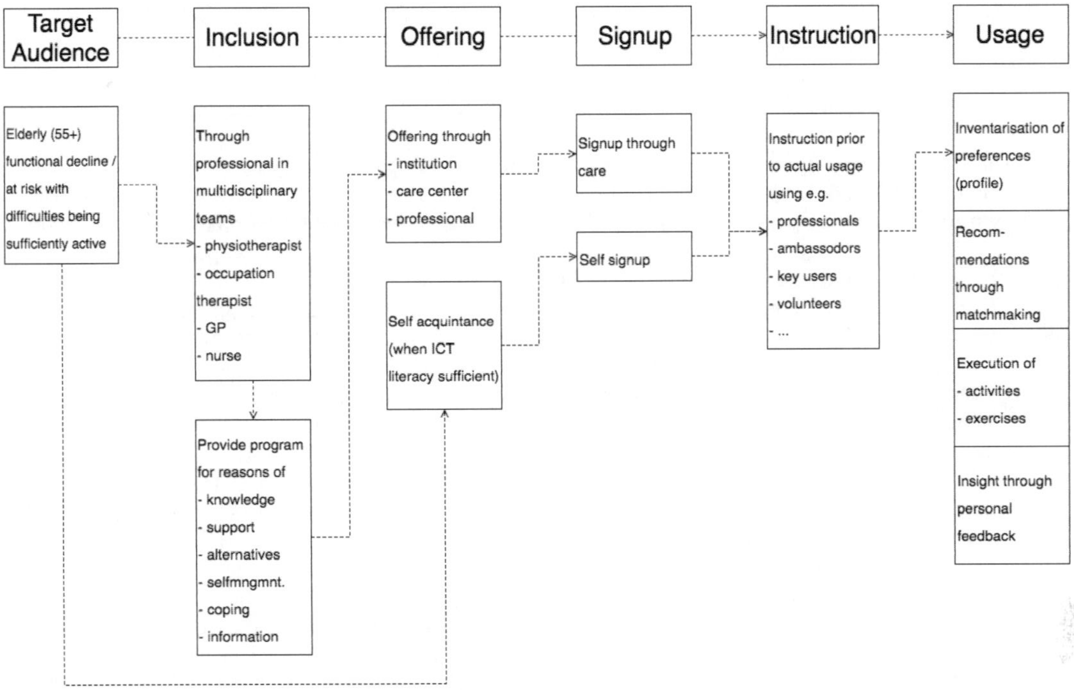

Figure 3. Care Pathway Self-Management Program Showing Process Flow for Elderly Working on Countering Physical Inactivity. Based on Boessen et al. (2016)

3. METHOD

Self-management programs for physical health are new and little is known about their working mechanisms (REF sm-programs). Therefore, we are interested in the working mechanisms behind the adoption and the uptake of the program.

Effects of the Otago program itself are already known (Campbell et al., 2005) as well as the effects of exercise and enough daily activity towards a person's health status.

Yet, it is unclear how web-based self-management programs contribute towards this end. Hence, we piloted this program and follow the usage and uptake both qualitatively (using interviews and focus groups) and quantitatively using log and database data.

After a series of lab tests and demonstrations, the program was embedded in a nursing home 'Parc Imstenrade' in Heerlen, The Netherlands. The approach taken was the upper approach in Figure 3. Approval from the regional medical ethical committee was obtained prior to rollout of this program. It was demonstrated at a kick off sessions with 26 elderly users, following a presentation on the motivation for maintaining a physically active lifestyle and a discussion. Then, the seniors were able to start using the program with assistance by students in personal hands-on sessions. Two follow-up focus group sessions were organized after a month.

4. RESULTS

As the goal of this paper is to present the self-management program and the implementation into elderly care, we limit ourselves here to discussing high-level results of the case study. More evolved results of end-user involvement in this case study are presented in (Bruinessen et al, 2017).

16 of the 26 potential participants registered to the program, both male and female. Their mean age was 83 and ranged from 74 to 91 years old. All were inhabitants of the nursing home. The participants tried

out both offline and online activities offered. They used their own laptop or tablet computer to use the program. Some asked the opinion or approval of their caregivers, showing that collaboration and communication with professionals before the introduction of a self-management program is paramount. There were 3 professionals involved: an activity manager, a physiotherapist and a district nurse.

The majority of the users felt that a weekly scheduled group to perform the physical exercises would be a good idea. Three reasons were mentioned: (1) because of computer literacy barriers, (2) to be able to perform the exercises under supervision, and (3) because of extrinsic motivation, as other, in many cases familiar seniors, are attending the group as well. A physiotherapist then added a weekly exercsise session asking a small fee of the participants, using the video-based exercise program. As expected, collaboration with a nursing home is indeed crucial to organize this.

Participants indicated that kick-off sessions are very important to get to know the relevance and ways of maintaining a physically active lifestyle and that it helps them think about their own health status. Otherwise, it would be difficult to see what a self-management program is about.

Interesting was that some activities mentioned in the system for demonstration purposes were indeed frequented, although not actually taking place. Other activities proposed by the users such as e.g. a weekly tai chi class were added.

There were no specific comments to the working of the recommender in personal contact or in focus group sessions. This 1) showed the screening mechanism for soliciting personal interests was stable and worked in practice and 2) meant that the system was successfully possible to present recommended events and activities matching to the user's interests.

Two follow-up focus groups took place two months after the kick-off session was organized. Here, reactions ranged from '*it really helps, after a few weeks I really started to feel something*' through '*the exercises provided are much too easy for me. I already have my own exercise program, every morning I wake up.*' The exercise group was especially appreciated, since it combined social and physical activity and served to promote discipline. This shows us there is a wide range of reactions to the program. Yet, the large difference in age and ICT literacy indicated that more pilot projects are necessary to pinpoint working mechanisms and effects of self-management programs for different types of users.

5. CONCLUSION

This paper presented Life, a novel self-management program to promote a physically active lifestyle in older adults. The paper demonstrates the feasibility of the ict-mediated program and described the content of the program. The LIFE program aspires to contribute to a physically active life style in a personalized way. LIFE offers various modules to elderly who are at risk of functional decline. These modules contain personalized advice, recommendations and suggestions how they can develop or maintain a healthy behaviour and prevent functional deterioration. To this end, the program offers screening, activities, exercise, and feedback.

Sharing knowhow on how to operationalize self-management programs in practice based on various sessions with end users, we crafted a care pathway (see Figure 3). The paper discussed two possibilities of implementing such a program in care, in a care pathway. It enables either (1) self-administered usage of the program (which supports elderly living at home), or (2) embedding in a nursing home (intramural setting). The case study involving the latter learns us that ICT literacy is important to consider and that it can be aligned with the program by offering activities together, such as an physiotherapist chairing sessions using the program in a group. This allows for social interaction and physical exercises at the same time. Participants indicated that kick-off sessions are very important to get to know the relevance and ways of maintaining a physically active lifestyle and that it helps them think about their own health status.

The screening mechanism for soliciting personal interests worked in practice; it was successfully possible to present recommended events and activities matching to the user's interests.

There is a wide range of reactions to the program. Yet, the large difference in age and ICT literacy signals that more case studies cq. pilot projects are necessary to pinpoint working mechanisms and effects of self-management programs for different types of users. Some users asked the opinion or approval of their carers prior to start using the self-management program, or needed them for performing exercises. This shows that collaboration and communication with healthcare organisations and professionals prior to introduction of a self-management program is of paramount importance.

ACKNOWLEDGEMENT

The Dutch agency for healthcare research ZonMw is acknowledged for funding this work. The authors would like to thank Thivvya Gugathas and Boris van Schooten for their contributions in this work.

REFERENCES

A.B.C.G. Boessen, L.A. van der Heide, J. Vermeulen, J.W. van 't Klooster, M. Vollenbroek, I. van Bruinessen, L.P. de Witte. (2016). A technology supported self-management program to promote physical activity in older adults *Eur J Public Health*. 26 (suppl_1): ckw175.029.

Campbell, A. J., Robertson, M.C., La Grow, S.J., Kerse, N.M., Sanderson, G.F., Jacobs, R.J., Sharp, D.M., Hale, L.A. (2005). Randomised controlled trial of prevention of falls in people aged >=75 with severe visual impairment: the VIP trial. *BMJ*, 331(7520), 817-0. doi:10.1136/bmj.38601.447731.55

Castaneda -Sceppa, C. (2007). Physical Activity and Public Health in Older Adults: Recommendation from the American College of Sports Medicine and the American Heart Association. *Medicine and Science in Sports and Exercise*.

Deci, E. L., & Ryan, R. M. (1985). Intrinsic Motivation and Self-Determination in Human Behavior. *doi:10.1007/978-1-4899-2271-7*

Eveleens et al. (2017). Een analyse van het innovatiesysteem ten behoeve van ondersteunende producten en diensten voor zelfmanagement in de gezondheidszorg. *RVO rapport,* 2017

Moran, M., Cauwenberg, J.V., Hercky-Linnewiel, R., Cerin, E., Deforche, B., Plaut, Pnina. (2014). Understanding the relationships between the physical environment and physical activity in older adults: a systematic review of qualitative studies. *International Journal of Behavioral. Nutrition and Physical Activity*, 11(79). doi:10.1186/1479-5868-11-79

Nelson, M. E., Rejeski, W. J., Blair, S. N., Duncan, P. W., Judge, J. O., King, A. C., Macera C. A., Spirduso, W. W., & Cronin, D. L. (2001). Exercise dose-response effects on quality of life and independent living in older adults. *Medicine and Science in Sports and Exercise*, 33(Supplement), 598-S608.doi:10.1097/00005768-200106001-00028

Paterson, D.H., Jones, G.R., Rice, C.L. (2007). Ageing and physical activity: evidence to develop exercise recommendations for older adults. *Canadian Journal of Public Health*, 32, 69-108. doi:10.1139/H07-111

Van Bruinessen IR, et al. (2017). Involving (elderly) end-users in the development and implementation of a web-based, physical activity platform. *Under review*

Van der Zee KI, Sanderman R, Heyink J. (1996). A comparison of two multidimensional measures of health status: The Nottingham health profile and the RAND 36-item health survey 1.0. *Qual Life Res* 1996, 5:165-174.

Van Holle, V., Cauwenberg, J.V., Deforche, B., Van de Weghe, N., Bourdeaudhuij, I.D., van Dyck, D. (2015). Do psychosocial factors moderate the association between objective neighboorhood walkability and older adults' physical activity? *Health & Place*, 34, 118-125. Retrieved from http://dx.doi.org/10.1016/j.healthplace.2015.05.004

WHO (2010). Global recommendations on physical activity for health. *World Health Organization*. Retrieved from http://whqlibdoc.who.int/publications/2010/9789241599979_eng.pdf

HUMAN-CENTRED DESIGN OF ONTOLOGY BASED CLINICAL DECISION SUPPORT SYSTEM

Alphonsine Mukabunani, Jan Pettersen Nytun and Ghislain Maurice Norbert Isabwe
University of Agder, Grimstad, Norway

ABSTRACT

Research and development of clinical decision support systems (CDSS) aims to support medical professionals in making the right diagnosis for improved outcome in patient treatment. However, the accuracy and technology acceptance of such systems can vary greatly depending on knowledge representation methodology, reasoning approach as well as the perceived usefulness and ease of use. In some cases, the system knowledge base may not be built using standard medical ontologies. Further on, some of the systems provide user interfaces with severe usability problems for users with average digital literacy. This work presents how an ontology and its generic tools can be used to overcome the above challenges. A human-centred design approach is applied in order to capture the needs of the medical personnel dealing with diabetes mellitus in Rwanda. A new ontology was created as an extension of the diabetes mellitus diagnosis ontology, and rules were created based on diabetes diagnostic criteria by using jena rule syntax and forward chaining inference. Testing and evaluation of the system proved that patient diagnosis, recommendation and decision explanation matched the results expected from a physician, hence proving that the designed CDSS is an expert system.

KEYWORDS

Clinical decision support; semantic web; HCD

1. INTRODUCTION

1.1 Background

Clinical diagnosis is a critical but often complex and error prone process. Healthcare professionals attempt to identify the cause and nature of disease by carefully examining and analyzing the information collected through patient's history, physical examinations, and laboratory test (Kiran 2014). Traditionally clinicians used to manually record all patient related information into paper (e.g. outpatient file/inpatient file/emergency file) and try to establish the necessary knowledge required for making a suitable decision. With rapid growth of information and communication technology in the field of medicine, different researchers have developed applications that can assist physicians and other healthcare professionals in their daily decision making tasks. These applications are called clinical decision support systems (CDSS) and have proven to be an efficient way to improve the quality of health care, patients' safety and the efficiency in delivering healthcare. These systems are designed to provide a variety of assistance (e.g diagnostic support, clinical guidelines, condition-specific order strategies, etc) and most of them focuses on diagnostic support. Diagnostic systems are intended to assist physicians in all processes involved in the diagnosis, that is, from initial consultation, diagnosis, treatment to follow up. They have to collect a huge amount of patient data (i.e manually inputted by clinician or from electronic medical records(EMR)), examine them, draw conclusion and send it to the clinicians in the form of alerts, recommendation or suggestions, diagnosis, and so on (Abdullah et al. 2014; Sherimon & Krishnan 2016). They are not intended to replace clinicians but rather to assist or guide them in taking fast and accurate decisions thus reducing the medical errors (both error of commission and omission) and improve the clinical practice (Weber 2011).

CDSSs come into two categories, that is, knowledge based CDSS and non-knowledge based CDSS (Dinevski et al. 2011). Knowledge based CDSS have 3 main components: knowledge base and inference engine and a way to communicate to the user (input and output) (Skjelvik 2008). Knowledge base is the main component of CDSS and contains all the information related to the domain of interest (e.g disease concepts, symptoms, etc.) in which CDSS works in. The information presented in knowledge base is obtained from domain expert and other literatures and need to be represented in a way that facilitate easy processing and retrieval. The clinician inputs the patient data, that is, information collected in patient history, physical examination (i.e signs and symptoms) and test results into the CDSS and inference engine applies rules stored in knowledge base to patient data and then produce the output for individual patient. The output can be the recommendation for the patient diagnosis, list of possible diagnoses, test ordering, the treatment if applicable, reminders (e.g preventive care), alerts (e.g drug- drug interaction) and so on (Skjelvik 2008; El-Sappagh & El-Masri 2014). Non- knowledge based CDSS does not contain the knowledge base. Rather, it relies on machine learning approach and other statistic pattern recognition to find hidden pattern in patient-specific parameters. Non-knowledge based CDSS are not widely applied to diagnosis because their reasoning process is done in so called "blackBox" which means that the rules used in their reasoning do not follow any logic which makes their results not trusted by the physician (Andrew 2016). Better understanding of the diagnosis process and the human reasoning when making diagnosis is important in the adoption and acceptance of CDSS. Similarly, knowledge representation, retrieval and sharing are also the key factors in the development of the CDSS which is beneficial to the health sector (Chang et al. 2011).

1.2 Problem Statement

Correct diagnosis is a key to ensuring the most appropriate treatment. Due to diagnostic errors, patients may suffer from many health problems including death, unnecessary tests and unnecessary side effects. This is because the methodologies used by many medical centers are not accurate and out dated. For instance, in different medical centers, like in Rwanda, they still record the patient information manually on the paper and try to establish the knowledge required to make the diagnosis. This knowledge which influences their decision can be from books (e.g. Guide therapeutic standard book), school, training, etc. In other words, the accuracy of the diagnosis depends on knowledge that a physician has on the patient case and may vary from one clinician to another. Additionally, clinician can fail to gather all patient medical history which also reduces the diagnosis accuracy. With the rapid grow of information technology, many applications have been developed to assist healthcare takers in their decision- making process, however, the methodologies and techniques used to build such applications is different and in turn it makes some of them not trusted by the physician. For instance, neural network approach which does not explain how the conclusion was reached. In addition, most of the existing applications face common problems, including poor designed interface, inability to let physician expressing their understanding on the patient case and they do not contain enough knowledge required for medical diagnosis. Furthermore, staff need to be trained before using such application which gives a burden to some countries with low income especially African countries. In this case, most of them are not interested in integrating these applications in their healthcare services.

Different technologies and methods have been proposed to support knowledge representation in CDSS (Kiran 2014). However, many of them have been proven to be not suitable in developing CDSS with higher accuracy and acceptance. Nowadays, semantic web technology is the promising solution for knowledge representation, sharing and reasoning. Furthermore, the ontology and its generic tools were adopted in semantic web as a means of representing a knowledge formally to support reasoning and understanding of the domain of interest, not only by people but also by machine (Malhotra & Nair 2015).

Additionally, the use of human centred design approach in the design and development of CDSS has been shown to be a best way of developing a usable and useful interactive system that meets user's needs which in turn increases the product adoption and acceptance rate in clinical practice as well as user satisfaction (McCullagh et al. 2014).

This work proposes a novel CDSS with emphasis on understanding the diagnostic process, diagnostic criteria, human reasoning on the diagnostic process and the physician's needs. The CDSS should be easy and effective to use by all healthcare providers including those without higher digital literacy. The investigations are carried out in an attempt to answer the following research questions:

RQ1: How to use ontology and its generic tools to represent different diseases, symptoms and diagnosis?
RQ2: How to formulate production rules based on the diagnostic criteria?
RQ3: How the system is to lead the dialog and expose the disease affecting a patient?

The next section presents a literature review on CDSS, followed by the design and development approach discussed in section three. The testing and evaluation of the new CDSS is presented in section 4, and finally the paper highlights main findings and conclusion in section five.

2. LITERATURE REVIEW

A CDSS is defined as any computerized system that provides an immediate and complete decision support to a physician after analyzing the individual patient data. A typical CDSS has three main components, that is, knowledge base, inference engine and mechanism to communicate with the users (Flores 2015). Having patient data (e.g clinical signs, symptoms, test results, etc), knowledge base containing medical knowledge mostly in form of if -then clauses, inference engine combines medical knowledge with patient data to produce an individual patient assessment or recommendation to a physician in form of alert (e.g. drug-drug interaction), recommendation (e.g., possible diagnoses), reminder (e.g., preventive care reminder) and so on (Kannry et al. 2015). Note that not all CDSS contain knowledge base, some use machine learning and other statistical pattern recognition to reason with clinical data, however, they are not widely used as diagnostic support.

CDSS has been proven to be the best solution to reduce adverse events that might occur in medicine such as medication errors, cost, test duplication and medication side effects, among others (Berner,2009). A CDSS is not designed to replace the physician instead to assist him/her in taking a fast and accurate decision that he/she may or may not take when working alone. In other words, CDSS is there to enhance clinician's performance and patient outcome. More specifically, a physician should not rely only on the CDSS decision instead he/she should sometimes accept or reject it based on his/her own diagnostic capabilities.

2.1 CDSS Classification

CDSS can be implemented using a variety of platforms based on a kind of problem being addressed and people's needs. Many factors can influence CDSS implementation such as security, clinical work flow, existing clinical systems and so on. (Velickovski et al. 2014) classify CDSS into four categories based on their architecture, that is, standalone, integrated, standard-based and service oriented.

In standalone system, the CDSS is built independent from Health Information System (HIS) or Electronic Medical Record (EMR) and physicians are required to enter clinical findings into system, thus, make it time consuming and user driven, however, it can be easily moved from one institution to another. Integrated system, on the other hand, CDSS is tightly coupled with HIS or Health Electronic Record (HER) and patient information is obtained from HIS thus makes the system to proactively provide decision support without requiring the physician to input findings and could avoid data duplication. However, it is difficult to transfer and reuse clinical knowledge across applications since they are tightly coupled with vendor specific HIS and sometimes, HIS information is (1) unavailable, (2) often incomplete and (3) represented in unstructured and non-machine-understandable form which hinders an accurate decision to be taken. Standard-based system uses standard formalism to encode, store, and share clinical knowledge to enable interoperability and scalability (Kawamoto et al. 2012). Finally, service-oriented system, CDSS and HIS are implemented separately and standardized, service-based interfaces (i.e Application Programming Interfaces) are used to facilitate communication between them. Each type of system has its own advantages and disadvantages and the choice depends on problem to be addressed and where the system is intended to be used. That's why, this work proposes to develop a standalone, standard-based application (rule & ontology based application) that can assist physician when making diagnosis of diabetes mellitus.

Different standards, methodologies and techniques are available for representing clinical knowledge in various forms such as logical condition, rules, graphs/networks and so on (El-Sappagh& El-Masri 2014) (Kiran 2014). Nowadays, ontology is being used as knowledge representation tool to deal with the complexity of the medical field, a huge amount of medical data and support data integration. Alharbi et. al. (2015) propose a diagnosis and treatment recommendation system for diabetes. The proposed CDSS is based on the use of domain ontology and rules. The rules are created in Semantic Web Rule Language (SWRL) based on clinical practice guidelines and executed by Jess engine. To generate decision, the system takes into account patient information, sign and symptoms, laboratory tests and diabetes risk factors (Alharbi et. al.

2015). This system is incomplete since it only modeled an ontology and rules but failed to show a user interface that user can use to get assistance. Additionally, the ontology does not extract its concepts from standard ontology. Sherimon et. al. (2016) propose a rule based CDSS for assessing and predicting the risk of diabetic patient and suggest treatment. Patient information such as smoking, alcohol, physical activity, etc are collected through adaptive questionnaire which is served by adaptive ontology. The reasoning was done by inference engine which uses SWRL rules encoded based on clinical practice guideline This system does have an interface but failed to explain how inference was reached and does not use standard ontology during ontology conceptualization. Chen Rung-Ching et. al. (2012) propose a rule based system for recommending antidiabetic-drug to diabetic patient. The proposed system uses a domain ontology and SWRL rule; jess rule engine for logical deduction This system is complete but failed to use standard ontology.

2.2 CDSS Effectiveness and Adoption

There are many factors that limit adoption and acceptance of clinical decision support system (Berner, 2009). Some of them includes the way data are inputted into the system; the development, maintenance, sharing and reuse of knowledge base; user interface; physician's computer literacy and time.

Patwardhan et. Al. (2009) proposed guidelines that every clinician should follow to ensure that the CDSS fit into clinical workflow and meet the requirement of its intended users. They have summarized them into 5 rights which are "provision of the right information, to the right person, in the right format, through the right channel, at the right point in workflow" (Patwardhan et al. 2009). In other words, CDSS intervention or recommendation should be provided to the right physician at the point of care (i.e., not before and after an encounter). It should be made for patient-specific data and presents information in a form that allow easy and unambiguous interpretation and should be justifiable (i.e., explaining how the conclusion was reached) (Hummel 2013). According to the systematic review conducted by Kawamoto et. al. (2005), 30 out of 32 clinical decision support system having these four features have proven to improve clinical practice.

Sim et al. (2001) also provides a list of recommendations that the current developer should follow to develop a CDSS with a higher adoption rate (Sim et al. 2001). These includes the use of standard vocabulary and knowledge representation standard to develop a machine-processable knowledge base and that knowledge base should be built based on clinical evidence and scenarios suitable for your system and son on.

3. NOVEL CDSS DESIGN AND DEVELOPMENT

In this work, a human centred design approach was adopted in which both qualitative and quantitative research methods are used. In addition, semantic web based approach was adopted in which ontology and its generic tools were used to develop a reliable, extensible, reusable and sharable knowledge base for our proposed CDSS. Our knowledge base extends Diabetes Mellitus Diagnosis Ontology(DDO) (El-Sappagh & Ali 2016) which was built based on Basic Formal ontology (BFO) (Holger 2017) and Ontology for General Medical Science (OGMS) (Barry 2013). In addition, jena rule engine with forward chaining mode was used to perform reasoning on patient clinical parameters based on production rules to infer diagnosis, recommendation and decision explanation. Production rules were created based on diabetes mellitus diagnostic criteria and formally represented using jena rule syntax.

The design and development of proposed system follows a human centered design principles and activities (Devi et al. 2012) and the ontology building guidelines proposed by Noy Natalya et al (2001) in which top-down approach was adopted. The ontology was developed in an iterative process that consists of 7 steps, that is, determination of ontology domain and scope, consider reusing existing ontologies, enumeration of ontology terms, defining concepts and concept hierarchies, defining object and data properties, defining the facets of the slots and creation of individuals (Noy et al. 2001). These steps were mapped into human centered design (HCD) activities as shown in Figure 1. The end users were identified, then involved from the early stages of HCD. Interviews were conducted involving 6 medical personnel based in Rwanda (doctors and nurses from both private and public clinics). The main goal of the interviews was to gather data for requirements. That include data on the users′ needs, clinical diagnosis process and their reasoning procedures to come up with diagnosis. Furthermore, the information was gathered regarding existing health information systems with a focus on their usability and the user experience, in order to identify potential areas for improvement.

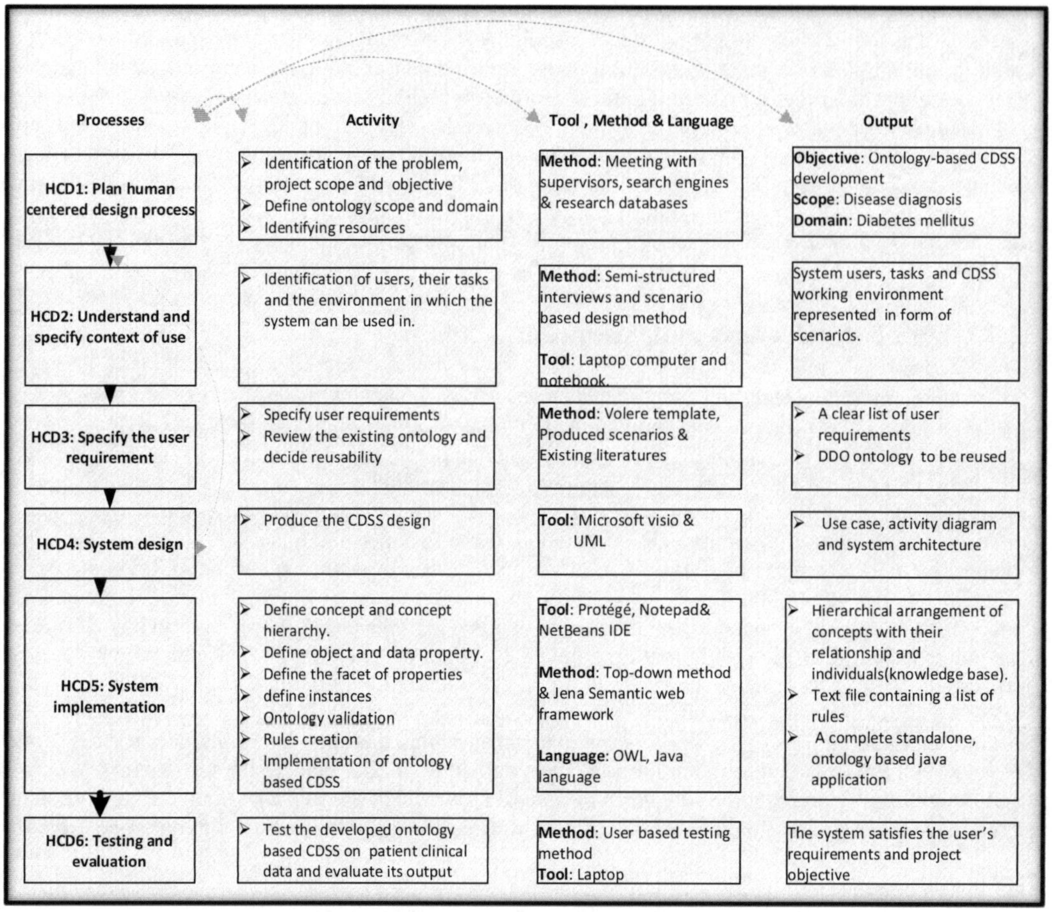

Figure 1. Solution approach and workflow processes

3.1 Use Case for proposed CDSS

Based on the requirements gathered through user studies and literature review, a use case and an activity diagram were developed as shown in in Figure 2 (a). The activity diagram describes a workflow involved in use case diagram along with all decisions and branching logics as shown in Figure 2 (b).

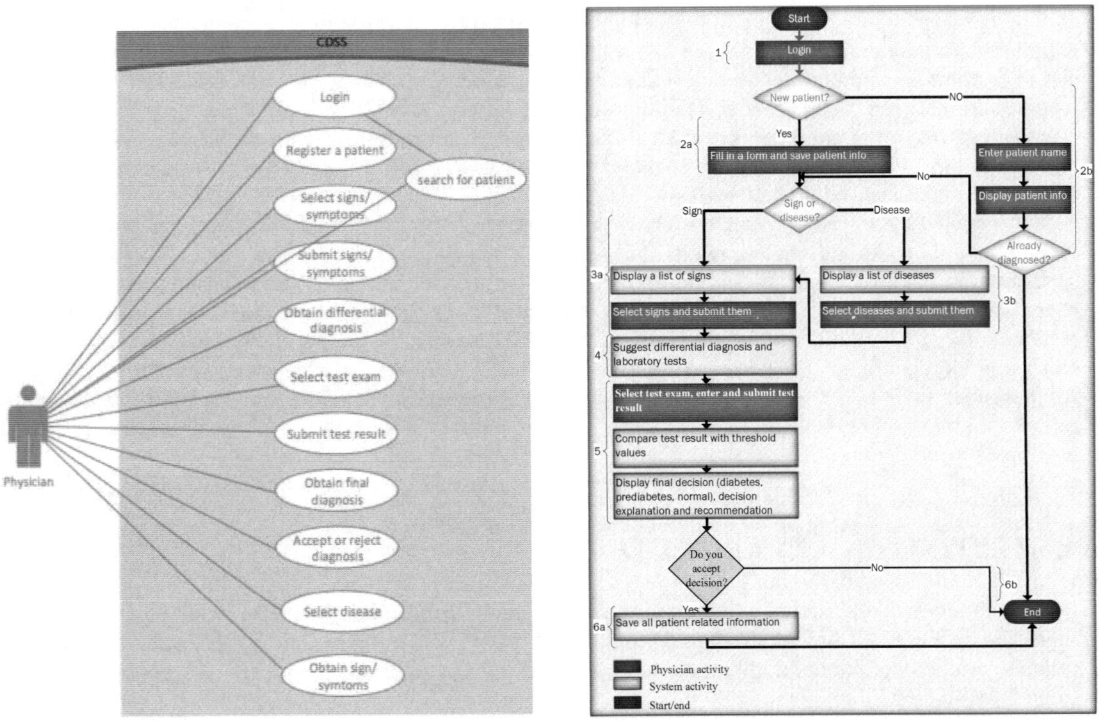

Figure 2. (a) Use case diagram and (b) activity diagram of the proposed system

3.2 CDSS System Architecture and Implementation

The proposed system consists of several components that works together to assist the clinician when making the diagnosis of diabetes mellitus. It was designed based on the human processes and reasoning when making the diagnosis. This is a multistep process that a physician goes through to come up with a right diagnosis. For example, taking patient history, physical examination, test result, and derive conclusion about disease affecting the patient after analyzing those patient data. The proposed components include database, CDSS user interface, inference engine, data loading and saving engine, search engine and knowledge base as shown in Figure 3.

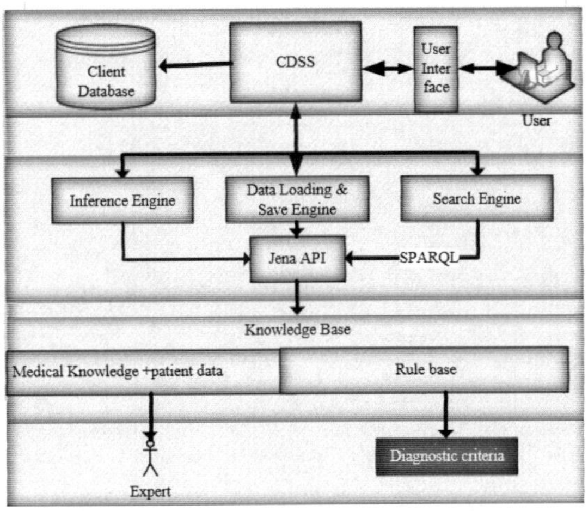

Figure 3. Overview of the system architecture

The ontology was built using web ontology language (OWL) which is a semantic markup language designed for a developing semantic web application and is based on the description logic. With OWL, one can represent a domain knowledge as a set of concepts (i.e classes), individuals, properties and defines the relationship between these concepts in a way that a computer can understand and reason with (Ian&Peter,2011). Owl ontology is written in xml syntax. In order to deal with the language syntax and complexity, protégé 5.0.0.0 (Stanford Center for Biomedical Informatics Research, 2017) desktop was used to intuitively create and edit OWL ontology.

To implement the ontology-based CDSS, this work used Java and Jena API, together with Simple Protocol and RDF Query Language (SPARQL). Jena is a free and open source java framework for building semantic web and linked data applications (Alves, Damásio and Correia, 2015). With jena, a user can create, read, write and manipulate RDF model and save it in memory or persistent storage (i.e database). Jena can read/write the file in a different format such as RDF/XML, N3, and N-triple and this file can be located in either a file system or be download from a given URL. SPARQL, on the other hand, is a query language recommended by W3C to retrieve information from an RDF data model (Eric and Andy,2013). Decision rules were created in reusable text files according to jena abstract syntax (Reasoners and rule engines: Jena inference support).

4. TESTING AND EVALUATION

In order to test and evaluate the system functionality, dummy patient data was used based on clinical data suggested by a person from the faculty of health and sport sciences at the University of Agder. In total, 21 patients´ profiles were considered for testing and evaluation. For illustration purposes, we present only one case of patient diagnosis:

"*Mr. John Tuyishimire, a Rwandan citizen, residing in Mbogo sector, northern province. He is a 27-year-old, single man. He is a student and uses "Mutuelle" insurance number 1234. He is allergic to eggs and has O blood group. The remaining patient information is shown in the filled form in Figure 4. He presents polyphagia, BlurredVision, tiredness and polydipsia. He has 2 tests: HBA1c and FPG with blood glucose level 6.9 % and 128 mg/dl respectively."* The Nurse inputs the patient details and vital signs into the system. Upon clicking diagnose button, the application infers that Tuyishimire suffers from Type2Diabete because he is having sign/symptom of diabetes and suggests that some tests are needed before confirming the diagnosis. The way the patient details and vital signs was entered into the system, their ontological representation and the obtained results are shown Figure 4."

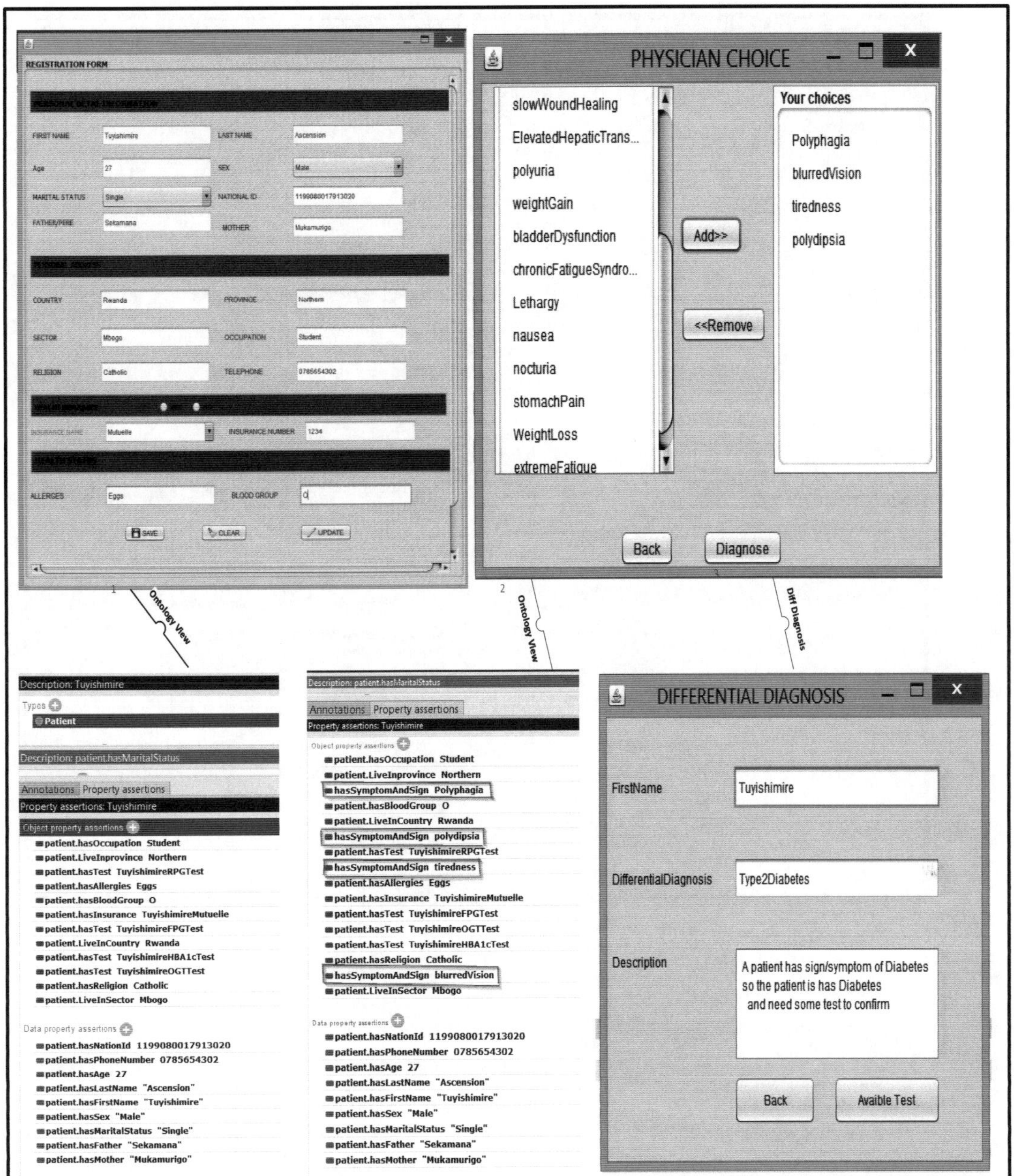

Figure 4. Extracting, formalizing Tuyishimire's data and retrieval of differential diagnosis

The nurse uses the available test button to check laboratory tests required for diabetes diagnosis. She selects HBA1c test and inputs 6.9% into the system. The application asks her for another test. At the second time, she selects FPG and inputs 128 mg/dl into the system. Upon submission, the application confirms that Mr. Tuyishimire suffers from Type2Diabetes. This is because Mr. Tuyishimire was having sign/symptom of diabetes and hemoglobin test with value greater than 6.5% and FPG test with value greater than 125mg/dl which is true. Furthermore, the system recommends that Mr. Tuyishimire should reduce calories, intake of dietary fat and is encouraged to take food containing whole grain and low-glycemic index foods and may take medication. The selected test, its value, its ontological representation and the obtained result is shown in Figure 5.

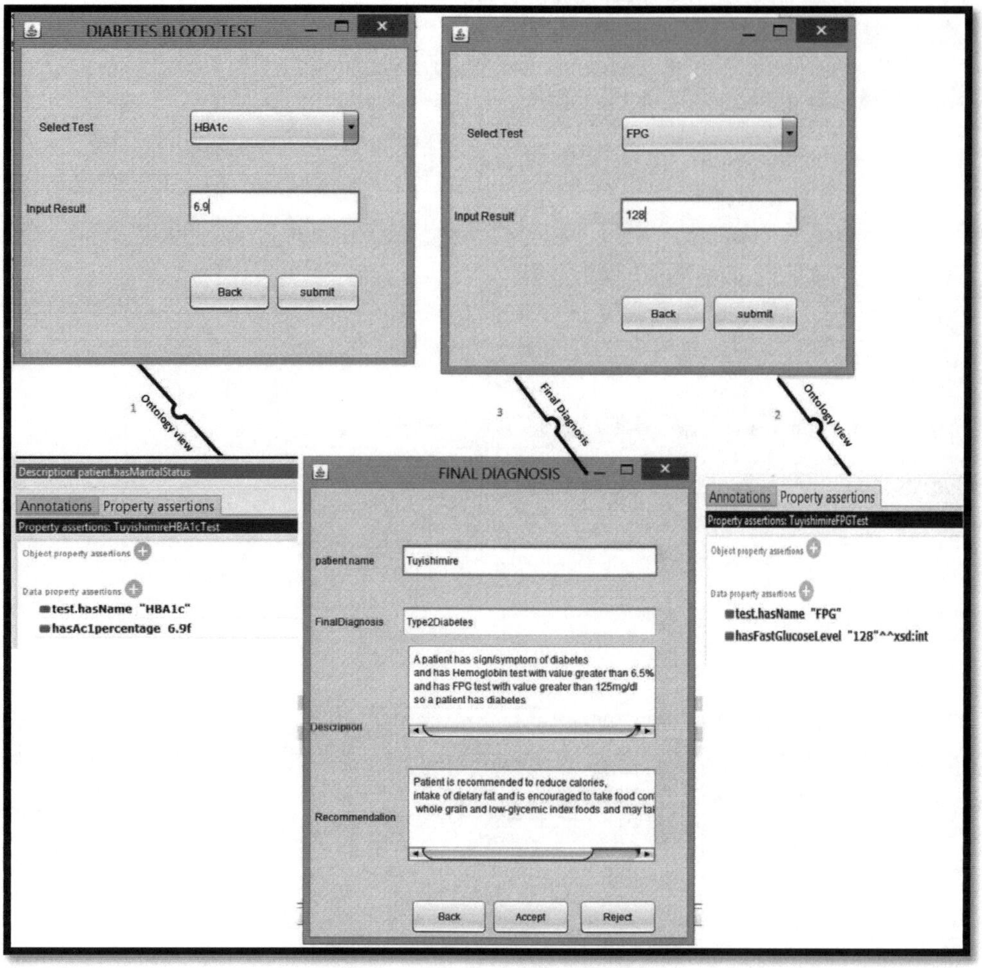

Figure 5. Patient1 test result extraction, formalization and final decision retrieval

5. DISCUSSIONS AND CONCLUSION

This work has presented an ontology based clinical diagnosis support system. In order to represent clinical data, medical knowledge and answer RQ1, the ontology was used in which diabetes mellitus related knowledge was encoded based on diagnostic criteria. Additionally, patient data was collected and formally represented in the ontology. This helped to maintain the semantic relationships between collected patient information in the ontology (e.g vital signs, tests and test results) which in turn makes them remain interpretable regardless of surrounding technology and software implementation (Bouamrane et al. 2008). The ontology extends diabetes mellitus diagnosis ontology (DDO) and contains key concepts and relationship required for the diabetes mellitus diagnosis, including patient and social role, symptoms, diagnosis, disease, recommendation, Patient decision explanation. This ontology can be easily reused within other ontology based applications; patient information recorded in heterogeneous systems can be reliably linked to this ontology and generate diagnosis, recommendation and decision explanation; it can be used for statistical reporting, for example the number of patients that use a given insurance, patient that are affected by diabetes etc. For the system to behave like an expert physician, it should mimic the reasoning process used by physician when making the diagnosis. This means that it should have a reasoning component and uses the problem-solving procedures to arrive to that conclusion. To achieve this and answer RQ2, decision rules were created and reasoning was performed by jena rule engine in such a way that the CDSS uses rules to derive diagnosis, recommendation and provide decision explanation about an individual patient's conditions. To produce the decision, the CDSS uses patient data contained in ontology file (this information is manually collected by a physician through a graphical user interface). The CDSS draws conclusion based on a patient vital signs and blood glucose test results. The conclusion is a diagnosis (diabetes, prediabetes, no diabetes), recommendation suitable for the obtained diagnosis and decision explanation (why the conclusion is like that). User testing of the CDSS proved that the system output was similar to results expected from a physician (the inferred results were correct in all test cases).

The designed CDSS is rule and ontology based. The kernel of the system comprises an adopted ontology that has been extended to fulfill the needs of the application. The ontology is handled in both Protégé (Ontology/Semantic Web tool) and in the application. The application has been built in Java using Jena (a Java Semantic Web framework). The user interface is perceived as easy to use and useful given that if has been designed according to the human-centered design principles and process. In the future, firstly, the proposed solution could be integrated with other electronic medical record systems to address the issue of manually entering patient´s personal information at different medical facilities. Secondly, the system will be tested (usability testing) in a hospital with real patient data. Lastly, the ontology can be further developed to consider other medical conditions and illnesses.

REFERENCES

Abdullah, A.L., Albeladi, K.S. and AlCattan, R.F., 2014. Clinical Decision Support System in HealthCare Industry Success and Risk Factors. *International Journal of Computer Trends and Technology (IJCTT)* –11 (4), pp.188-192.

Alharbi, R.F., Berri, J. and El-Masri, S., 2015, July. Ontology based clinical decision support system for diabetes diagnostic. *In Science and Information Conference (SAI)*, 2015 (pp. 597-602). IEEE.

Alves, M. B., Damásio, C. V., and Correia, N. 2015, September. SPARQL commands in Jena rules. *In International Conference on Knowledge Engineering and the Semantic Web* (pp. 253-262). Springer International Publishing.

Andrew, S. S. 2016. Mathematical foundations of decision support systems. *In Clinical Decision Support Syst*ems (pp. 19-43). Springer International Publishing.

Barry, S., 2013. "*The Ontology for General Medical Science,*" SlideShare. [Online]. Available: https://www.slideshare.net/BarrySmith3/the-ontology-for-general-medical-science. [Accessed 13 April 2017].

Berner, E.S., 2009. *Clinical decision support systems: state of the art*. AHRQ publication, 90069.

Bouamrane, M.M., Rector, A. and Hurrell, M., 2008. Using ontologies for an intelligent patient modelling, adaptation and management system. *On the Move to Meaningful Internet Systems: OTM 2008*, pp.1458-1470.

Chang, Y.J., Yeh, M.L., Lee, C.S., Hsu, C.Y., Li, Y.C. and Chiu W.T., 2011. Cross-domain probabilistic inference in a clinical decision support system: Examples for dermatology and rheumatology. *Computer methods and programs in biomedicine*. 104(2), p. 286–291

Chen, R.C., Huang, Y.H., Bau, C.T. and Chen, S.M., 2012. A recommendation system based on domain ontology and SWRL for anti-diabetic drugs selection. *Expert Systems with Applications*, 39(4), pp.3995-4006.

Devi, K., Sen, A. and Hemachandran, K., 2012. A working Framework for the User-Centered Design Approach and a Survey of the available Methods. *International Journal of Scientific and Research Publications*, 2(4), pp.1-8.

Dinevski, D., Šušteršic, O., Šarenac, T., Bele, U. and Rajkovič, U., 2011. Clinical decision support systems. INTECH Open Access Publisher.

El-Sappagh, S. and Ali, F., 2016, December. DDO: a diabetes mellitus diagnosis ontology. *In Applied Informatics* (Vol. 3, No. 1, p. 5). Springer Berlin Heidelberg.

El-Sappagh, S.H. and El-Masri, S., 2014. A distributed clinical decision support system architecture. *Journal of King Saud University-Computer and Information Sciences*, 26(1), pp.69-78.

Eric, P. and Andy, s. 2013, March. "*SPARQL query language for RDF*," W3C. [Online]. Available: https://www.w3.org/TR/rdf-sparql-query/. [accessed 22 April 2017].

Flores, B., 2015. Design and development of a decision support system for screening of Lynch syndrome using openEHR (Doctoral dissertation, Master thesis. Karolinska Institutet).

Holger, S., 2017"*Basic Formal Ontology*," Institute for Formal Ontology and Medical Information Science (IFOMIS. [Online]. Available: http://ifomis.uni-saarland.de/bfo/. [Accessed 25 April 2017].

Hummel, J., 2013. Integrating Clinical Decision Support Tools into Ambulatory Care Workflows for Improved Outcomes and Patient Safety. Rep. *Qualis Health*, pp.15-16.

Ian, H. and Peter, F.P., 2011. KR and Reasoning on the semantic web: OWL. In: D. Fensel., *Handbook of Semantic Web Technologies*. Berlin: Springer., pp. 365-398.

Kannry, J., McCullagh, L., Kushniruk, A., Mann, D., Edonyabo, D. and McGinn, T., 2015. A framework for usable and effective clinical decision support: Experience from the icpr randomized clinical trial. *eGEMs*, 3(2).

Kawamoto, K., Jacobs, J., Welch, B.M., Huser, V., Paterno, M.D., Del Fiol, G., Shields, D., Strasberg, H.R., Haug, P.J., Liu, Z. and Jenders, R.A., 2012. Clinical information system services and capabilities desired for scalable, standards-based, service-oriented decision support: Consensus assessment of the health level 7 clinical decision support work group. *In AMIA Annual Symposium Proceedings* (Vol. 2012, p. 446). American Medical Informatics Association.

Kawamoto, K., Houlihan C. A., Balas E. A. and Lobach D.F. 2005, March. Improving clinical practice using clinical decision support systems: a systematic review of trials to identify features critical to success. *BMJ*, 330(7494), pp.765.

Kiran R. 2014. *Developing Reliable Clinical Diagnosis Support System*. [Online] Available: http://www.kiranreddys.com/articles/clinicaldiagnosissupportsystems.pdf. [Accessed 03 January 2017].

Malhotra, M. and Nair, T.G., 2015. Evolution of Knowledge Representation and Retrieval Techniques. *International Journal of Intelligent Systems and Applications*, 7(7), p.18.

McCullagh, L.J., Sofianou, A., Kannry, J., Mann, D.M. and McGinn, T.G., 2014. User centered clinical decision support tools: adoption across clinician training level. *Appl Clin Inform*, 5(4), pp.1015-25.

Noy, N.F. and McGuinness, D.L., 2001. Ontology development 101: A guide to creating your first ontology.

Patwardhan, M.B., Kawamoto, K., Lobach, D., Patel, U.D. and Matchar, D.B., 2009. Recommendations for a clinical decision support for the management of individuals with chronic kidney disease. *Clinical Journal of the American Society of Nephrology*, 4(2), pp.273-283.

"*Reasoners and rule engines: jena inference support*" the apache software foundation. [Online]. Available: https://jena.apache.org/documentation/inference/. [Accessed 12 February 2017.

Sherimon, P.C. and Krishnan, R., 2016. OntoDiabetic: an ontology-based clinical decision support system for diabetic patients. *Arabian Journal for Science and Engineering*, 41(3), pp.1145-1160.

Skjelvik, D.V., 2008. GenSupport. A generic guideline-based clinical decision support system (Master's thesis, The University of Bergen).

Sim, I., Gorman, P., Robert A. G; Brian, R.H., Bonnie, K., harold, L. and Paul, C.T. 2001. Clinical decision support systems for the practice of evidence-based medicine. *Journal of the American Medical Informatics Association*, 8(6), pp. 527-534.

Stanford Center for Biomedical Informatics Research, 2017. Protege. [Online]. Available at: http://protege.stanford.edu/products.php. [Accessed 3 July 2017].

Velickovski, F., Ceccaroni, L., Roca, J., Burgos, F., Galdiz, J.B., Marina, N. and Lluch-Ariet, M., 2014. Clinical Decision Support Systems (CDSS) for preventive management of COPD patients. *Journal of translational medicine*, 12(2), p.S9.

Weber, S. (2011). Impacts of Clinical Decision Support Technology on Nursing and Medical Practice in U.S. Critical Care. *CJNI: Canadian Journal of Nursing Informatics*, 5 (4), Article Three. http://cjni.net/journal/?p=1094.

M-HEALTH PREDICTIVE DATA ANALYSIS OF DAILY ACTIVITIES AND PHYSIOLOGICAL CONDITIONS

Enkeleda Bocaj[1,2], Jonas Queiroz[3,4], Paulo Leitão[1,3] and Charalampos Z. Patrikakis[5]
[1]*Polytechnic Institute of Bragança, 5300-253 Bragança, Portugal*
[2]*Faculty of Automation Engineering, Piraeus University of Applied Sciences, Thivon 250, Egaleo 122 41, Greece*
[3]*Faculty of Engineering, University of Porto, Rua Dr. Roberto Frias, 4200-465 Porto, Portugal*
[4] *LIACC – Artificial Intelligence and Computer Science Laboratory, Rua Campo Alegre 1021, 4169-007 Porto, Portugal*
[5]*Faculty of Electronics Engineering, Piraeus University of Applied Sciences, Thivon 250, Egaleo 122 41, Greece*

ABSTRACT

The wearable devices technology has evolved dramatically in many respects over the last decade, e.g., in the accuracy and quality of the data provided, as well as the number of parameters measured. This created new opportunities not only in the fitness domain, but also in the well-being and general health. Indeed, each day, an ever-increasing number of people are interested in monitoring their daily habits and activities, as well as their physiological and psychological condition, aiming to improve their overall quality of life. Such tasks can be realized by the use of predictive tools that can guide and support individuals during their daily living activities. In this regard, wearable devices produce large volume of data, which should be properly analyzed in a fast and personalized manner. Furthermore, in order to provide the individuals with more effective and actionable information, other individuals and health professionals should be involved in the process. Having this in mind, this paper presents a smart health collaborative approach that considers the extensive analysis of the individual's wearable data, as well as a health social network to provide an infrastructure for the individuals to manage their data and easily interact with others individuals and physicians. The experiments focused on the data analysis module and considered data from four elderly individuals, wearing a Fitbit Charge HR. A clustering analysis was performed to identify and characterize patterns in their physiological behaviors and daily activities that were used for the prediction of the individuals' daily conditions and activities.

KEYWORDS

M-Health; Data analysis; Clustering; Prediction; Wearable devices; Fitness tracker

1. INTRODUCTION

The wearable technologies tend to be more sophisticated than the handheld ones, providing sensing and monitoring features not typically encountered on mobile devices, such as biofeedback and the tracking of physiological functions. Nowadays, the number of ordinary people using wearable devices (e.g., fitness trackers, health wristbands and sensors) and smartphones with health applications to monitor and track their vital signs (e.g., related to health and fitness conditions or even emotions) has been increased significantly. Moreover, such wearable devices include communication capabilities, which provide the wearer with real-time physiological measurements, alerts and information aiming to promote a healthier lifestyle.

M-Health (mobile health) (Istepanian, 2006) and wearable devices provide a significant opportunity for the future of medical treatments, both in terms of preventing and treating an illness, as well as promoting the well-being and healthy lifestyle. In many physical and mental diseases, the body starts showing signs, in the form of symptoms, to alert the patient to its deteriorating health, such as heart rate variabilities or progressive reduction in daily activities, as well as others that are not easily perceivable. In this regard, monitoring, analyzing and interpreting the body signals during the daily living tasks, in a proper time frame and considering the opinion of experts, can help to maintain the quality of life of the individuals, as well as detect diseases in advance or help to keep an existing one under control. In a broader sense, wearable devices are part of e-health (Eysenbach, 2001), which describes not only a technical development, but also an attitude and a commitment for networked and global thinking, whose goal is to improve health-care locally, regionally, and world-widely by using information and communication technology (ICT).

Nowadays, wearables can detect, measure and track a plethora of fitness activities and physiological signals (e.g., heart rate, steps, sweat, temperature, sleep, calories, blood pressure and glucose levels). Even if they present hardware and computational limitations, they can provide a high sampling rate with considerable accuracy and reliability. On the other hand, the ever-increasing amount of data provided by these devices, may confuse the individuals instead of effectively inform and support them in improving their lifestyle.

Aiming to overcome the lack of computational power to analyze data, aiming to increase of individual well-being and quality of life, external applications are required. These applications should be able to analyze the information from the wearables and to present it to the individual in a user-friendly way, highlighting the findings and conclusions. In this context, the predictive analysis of the individuals' habits, behaviors and physiological conditions, and posteriorly the reasoning about these predictions to provide alerts and advices, are essential tasks to provide individuals with decision-making tools to influence their behaviors. Such features can be realized by using analytical methods and logical reasoning, such those based on machine learning, data mining and data visualization (Witten, et al., 2016).

In this sense, this work proposes a smart m-Health collaborative approach that takes advantage of wearable devices' data and advanced data analysis algorithms to provide qualitative and personalized information to monitor and improve the individuals' well-being and health conditions. On the other hand, it considers a health social network to provide an infrastructure for the individuals to manage their data and easily interact with others individuals, e.g., physicians and nutritionists. Some preliminary experiments were performed considering a case study in the healthcare domain, using data from four elderly individuals, wearing a Fitbit Charge HR. In this work only the data analysis module was explored, considering two scenarios: i) identification and characterization of patterns in individuals' physiological behavior and daily activities using a clustering analysis, and ii) prediction of the individuals' daily conditions and activities.

The rest of this paper is organized as follows: Section 2 overviews the related work and Section 3 describes the proposed approach. Section 4 describes the case study and Section 5 presents the preliminary experimental results. Section 6 rounds-up the paper with the conclusions and highlights the future work.

2. RELATED WORK

Researchers have always been attracted to investigate the potential benefits and challenges of health-care systems (WHO, 2011). At the beginning of the new century, e-Health services had finally awakened and started to rapidly increase. This growing was analog to the rapid evolution of ICT infrastructures and the digitization, which provide access to patient data. The Web 2.0 concept and the emerging Web 3.0 have offered to health-care professionals conditions that never had been given before (Cheung, et al., 2008). In 2011, the World Health Organization (WHO) identified a compendium of emerging health technologies that present the potential for being low-resource solutions for the unmet medical needs (WHO, 2011).

A large number of telemedicine and e-Health systems are being widely and successfully produced, delivering health-care through different ICT. In this domain, data analysis has been widely used to support the realization of these systems (Raghupathi and Raghupathi, 2014). Currently, several e-health solutions are available, e.g., eHealthMonitor (http://www.ehealthmonitor.eu/) that offer individuals health services, ICT4Depression (http://www.ict4depression.eu/) that remotely connect patients and doctors using mobile technology, and also other approaches for treatment response monitoring systems (WHO, 2011). On the other hand, the wearable and m-Health technologies have provided novel ways to monitor individuals in an unobtrusive and inexpensive way. In the context of mobile application, there are several examples, such as, the use of a mobile phone to monitor the fetal heart rate (Lee, et al., 2009), to provide mobile health record for pediatric HIV (Paul, et al., 2009), an intelligent Augmented Quick Health monitoring system (Sharif, et al., 2016), and MobiGuide (http://www.mobiguide-project.eu/) that presents a mobile application comprising an intelligent decision support system for patients with chronic illnesses.

Hence, social network can contribute to m-health domain providing a wide social and collaborative environment where individuals can share information about their health conditions and experiences with each other (Swan, 2009). This can contribute to ensure the sustainability of the healthcare systems, unlocking the market for innovative solutions and delivering high-quality healthcare services (Deb and Srirama, 2013).

Besides the features covered by the previously reported works, regarding the support of individual's well-being and healthiness, this work focuses more on providing qualitative and personalized information for the individuals. On the other hand, it also intends to take advantage of the features provided by m-health, data analysis and social network technologies to provide an environment not only to analyze their data but also to interact and collaborate with other individuals.

3. SMART M-HEALTH COLLABORATIVE APPROACH

The proposed approach intends to combine the widely used wearable and mobile technologies with the features of a health-based social network to provide a smart and collaborative environment, where data mining and machine learning algorithms, in combination with experts' knowledge, can support and promote the individuals' general well-being and a healthier lifestyle, e.g., through actions' recommendations and advices. Figure 1 illustrates the architecture of the proposed smart m-Health collaborative approach, which comprises 3 main components: Data collection and Storage, Data Analysis, and Health Social Network.

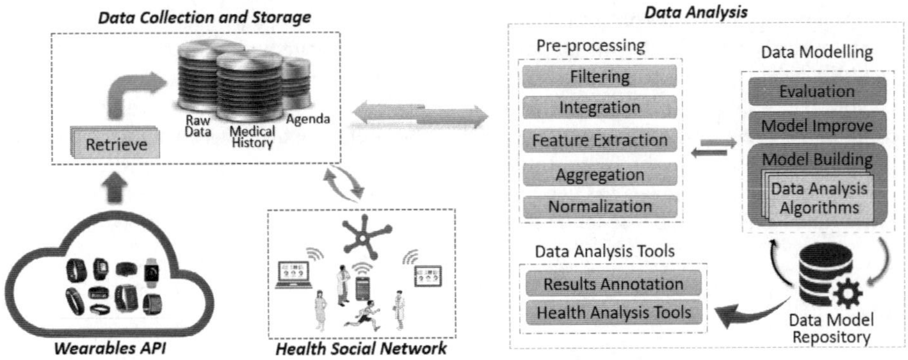

Figure 1. General architecture of the Smart m-Health Collaborative approach

Data collection and Storage

Wearable devices are used as the main source of data, complemented with some users' personal and also other external data. Depending on the device, the data can be sent directly or through a broker device (e.g., user's laptop or smartphone) to the wearable cloud or server. Most of the devices have specific apps and clouds that require the development of appropriate mechanisms to access and retrieve the user's data (de Arriba-Pérez et al., 2016). A local repository keeps a copy of the individuals' raw data to enable the offline data analysis, and also hosts the data analysis outputs and other background knowledge for further reasoning. In addition, the raw data and the data analysis outputs can be annotated with a simple metadata or a more sophisticated ontology, facilitating the interoperability and the automation of the data analysis process.

Data Analysis

This component is responsible to manage and provide data analysis features to attend the individuals' needs, mainly concerning their well-being. Such features are based on data mining and machine learning algorithms capable to summarize and identify structural patterns and relationships in the data, in order to build data models to be used in several tasks, e.g., monitoring, anomaly identification, prediction and recommendation. As depicted in Figure 1, this component comprises the following modules:

1) Pre-processing – responsible to process the raw data and prepare it for the data analysis, through the application of several filters (e.g., to eliminate noise and wrong measurements, or to correct them or impute missing values), feature extraction algorithms (e.g., to obtain other attributes that can enhance the data analysis outputs), data integration and aggregation procedures (e.g., based on the timestamp, integrate data from different sensors, or aggregate high frequency redundant samples) and normalization tasks (e.g., scale the values of all the attributes in order to have the same weight in the data analysis process). All these tasks have an essential role in this kind of application since they comprise many heterogeneous devices and sensors that may not provide accurate measurements or missing values.

2) Data Modelling – provides some tools and features to build, evaluate and improve the data models based on the data analysis algorithms (e.g., abnormally detection, classification and clustering). The built models should be stored in the *Data Model Repository* to be used by the *Data Analysis Tools*. The continuous evaluation and improvement of the data models should support the environment dynamics. In this sense, the output of the data analysis can be automatically compared with some feedback, measured or provided by the individuals, and if a degradation in the output is noticed, triggers can be activated to retrain the data models. These triggers can also alert domain specialists (e.g., physicians) that can manually evaluate the outputs to verify the needs for new models.

3) Data Analysis Tools – represents the application's health data analysis tools that are responsible to monitor and analyze the individuals' health and physiological conditions. They should support both, the individuals and health professionals, with several types of information, e.g., to aware the individuals' about their health conditions and guide their actions in order to keep or improve their well-being. Such tools use and combine several data models, as well as contextual information, to monitor and identify patterns and trends in the individuals' data, also performing tasks like prediction and recommendation. In addition, the data analysis outcomes can be enhanced with semantic information (e.g., medical ontology or vocabulary like SNOMED - http://www.snomed.org/) to improve their interoperability and interpretability.

Health Social Network

This component provides a social and collaborative environment that enables individuals and health professionals to easily and friendly interact and exchange knowledge and services. The connection among individuals and health professionals is through several monitoring and data analysis tools, following a patient-doctor relationship. In this sense, individuals will be able to monitor and control their everyday health related condition, receive alerts and advice from the health professionals. This component provides different tools and features according to the user's role, e.g., an individual has access to high-level information and monitoring tools, while a physician has access to the individuals' low-level data and data analysis tools that provide more detailed information, enabling them to check in depth the client's situation.

4. CASE STUDY

This work focuses in the data analysis aspects of the proposed approach, considering a case study in the domain of elderly people health-care. In this regard, mHealth applications based on wearable devices are able to provide personalized, remotely and faster monitoring and diagnostics. A social network can facilitate the interaction and communication among the health-care professionals (e.g., caregivers, physiotherapists), elders and their relatives. Hence, the objective of this case study includes the monitoring and analysis of the data collected from four older people (2 women and 2 men), living in an elderly home.

Fitbit Charge HR wristbands were used for the experiments, which provide a number of physiological and fitness measurements, such as heart rate value, activity level, sleep level, number of steps and climbed floors. The participants have been monitored during a period of one year (Dec-2015 to Jan-2017), meanwhile there is a lack of data between March and July. Through an exploratory data analysis, it was identified the presence of missing and erroneous values, probably caused by the device displacement, drastic movements of the hand, or not using the wristband during all the day. Besides the raw data provided by the wristband, some other parameters were extracted aiming to provide some kind of contextual information to enhance the accuracy of the data analysis. For instance, the individual's activities and habits usually depend on the *period of the day*, *weekday* or *season*. In the same sense, the heart rate value remains high for a while after intense activities. Table 1 describes all the extracted features used in the experiments.

Clustering and predictive data analysis were used to identify, characterize and predict different behaviors and physiological events, such as activities of daily living and the sleep quality. Two scenarios were explored:

1) Daily events and activities identification and characterization – This scenario comprises the analysis of individual's data to identify patterns in their daily habits, in terms of their physiological and fitness behaviors, for the active and sleep period of the day. This kind of information can be used to monitor, understand, maintain and enhance the individuals' well-being and health conditions. The recommendation, predictive and situation awareness systems can use such kind of information combined with external related data to explain a given event, predict the individual's activities and behaviors, or recommend several actions. For instance, in case of an outdoor walking exercise has been predicted and at the same time is expected rain, the individual can be advised in advance to reschedule this activity.

2) Characterization and prediction of the day periods – There are several studies discussing how the sleep affects the active part of the day and vice versa. In this scenario, the output from the previous one is used to characterize each period of the day and then predict the subsequent periods. The output of such prediction can be used to aware and recommend users about how will be the sleep or the active periods in terms of their physiological conditions. In this case study, this information can be used by the caregivers and physiotherapists of the elderly house to improve the elders' well-being, taking the proper actions to avoid or mitigate some condition, or even schedule a physician for future clinical exams.

Table 1. List of extracted features

Raw Data	Extracted Features	Description
Heart Value	sd 10/20	The Standard Deviation of a moving window of the previous 10 and 20 min.
	roc 10/20	The Rate of Change of a moving window of the previous 10 and 20 min.
	mean 10/20	The Moving average of the previous 10 and 20 minutes
	heart zones	The normal human's heart rate zones according to the age
Timestamp	weekday	The day of the week where the sample was measured
	season	The seasons of the year where the samples was measured
Sleep value	active part of day	Specify if the sample was measured when the user was awake
	sleep part of the day	Specify if the sample was measured when the user was sleeping

5. EXPERIMENTAL RESULTS

The experiments were performed using the use case dataset, stored in a MongoDB database. A simple simulation environment was developed to simulate the scenarios. For the sake of simplicity, it was considered that individuals update the data once per day, moments before sleeping, which triggers the simulation environment that retrieve the data from the database for the given period, integrate it with the data of the past periods and perform the data analysis process. The simulation starts after the first 30 days, which were used to build and train the data models that are updated after each day in a batch mode. Both, the simulation environment and the data analysis algorithms were implemented using the R environment (https://www.r-project.org/). The following sections describe how development and testing were performed.

5.1 Daily Event Identification and Characterization

The identification and characterization of the daily events ware performed based on two distinct periods, active and sleep since these periods present different types of activities and meaning for the same value of a given physiological parameter. For instance, a heart rate value of 90 bpm is considered normal in the active period (e.g., walking), while in the sleep period it may indicate some kind of stress (e.g., nightmare). Therefore, it was developed a method to separate the data in the two day periods based on the sleep information provided by the wristbands. Thus, every time new data is updated, two data sets were obtained, separating the individual's data in the sleep and active periods. For simplicity's sake, the sleep period contains the main sleep and the naps of the individual. The active period includes all the samples where the individual is physically awake. It is important to notice that the separation of the periods was made dynamically, rather than based on a fixed time period. For instance, an individual can have the sleep period split among two days (e.g., from 10pm to 6am) or inside only one day (e.g., from 2am to 10am).

An issue that had to be handled in this scenario regards the analysis of the individuals' unlabelled data provided by the wristbands, as well as the aforementioned noise and missing data. Considering the unlabelled nature of the available data, the identification of the daily events is performed based on the clustering of similar events in terms of the available physiological and fitness features. In this regard, as a preliminary experiment, the k-means clustering algorithm was used as a fast, robust and unsupervised learning approach. After several tests, 15 clusters were chosen to identify the events in the active period, since this configuration presents a good separation and level of detail. On the other hand, for the sleep period was used 10 clusters, since this period does not have many distinct events, and the physiological and fitness parameters (e.g., heart rate and a number of steps) are more stable rather than in the active period.

After the application of the k-means algorithm, each sample is labelled, i.e., identified with a cluster number, which represents a group of activities or events. Besides that, each cluster of events was characterized quantitatively and qualitatively. The quantitative characterization consisted in finding the average values ($\overline{x}$) and standard deviation (σ) of the physiological parameters among the samples of each cluster of events, while the qualitative characterization consisted of figuring out the set of events and activities that could be represented considering the quantitative characterization. In this context, Table 2 presents some of the parameters used to quantitatively characterize the data of Individual #1. Based on the features described in Table 2, the cluster of events with the label 1 of the sleep could be qualitatively characterized as deep sleep, while the label 9 could be characterized as light and stressful sleep, due to nightmares, in combination with some movements on the bed. In the same sense, the events of type 1 of the active period could represent like watching television or reading a book in a relaxed mood, while the label 15 could mean exercises that use the cardiovascular system with the predominance of steps and arm movements. It is important to notice that the qualitative characterization should be performed manually by a domain expert or automatically, based on rules and heuristics defined by a domain expert.

Table 2. Quantitative characterization of the events for active and sleep period of the individual #1

Cluster of events		1	2	3	4	5	6	7	8	9	10	11	12	13	14	15
Active period																
Heart rate	$\bar{x}$	55	61	63	66	64	67	71	84	89	70	80	88	79	90	104
	σ	3	4	2	7	11	5	3	6	17	5	12	9	13	11	11
Steps	$\bar{x}$	0	0	0	0	0	0	0	0	22	18	70	20	50	47	71
	σ	0	0	0	2	0	0	0	0	22	11	19	14	32	27	34
Activity level*		1	1	1	1	1	1	1	1	1,2	2	2	2	1,2,3	3	4
Sleep period																
Heart rate	$\bar{x}$	50	52	55	63	54	55	53	63	82	59	*Activity level: 1-sedentary; 2-light active; 3-fairly active; 4-very active **Sleep level: 1-asleep; 2-restless; 3-awake				
	σ	2	3	2	3	4	6	3	4	15	5					
Steps	$\bar{x}$	0	0	0	0	0	0	0	0	16	0					
	σ	0	0	0	0	1	2	0	2	28	5					
Sleep level**		1	1	1	1	1,2	1,2	2	2	2,3	3					

Figure 2 illustrates the distribution of the identified events along all the days for each period, where each dot represents the time duration of an event in a given day. The boxplot together with the weekday mean, illustrate that independently of the day of the week, the Individual #1 has the same behavior, presenting few exceptional days (outliers). This routine is characterized by the predominance of the events type 5, 6 and 10 for the active period and 1, 2 and 6 for the sleep period. The other events usually present none or few minutes during the days. Based on the Table 2, it is possible to say that this individual usually spend half of the time of the active period in a resting state (events 5 and 6), while the other half performing light activities (event 10). On the other hand, its sleep is usually based on peaceful and non-agitated moments.

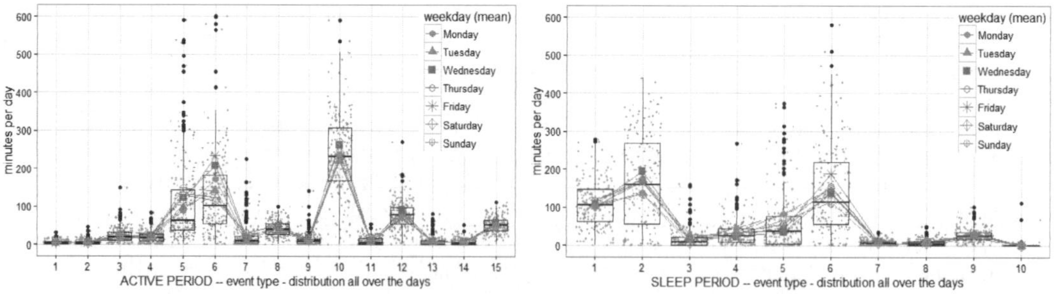

Figure 2. Distribution and weekday patterns of the identified events along all the days, for each period

5.2 Characterization and Prediction of the Day Periods

This experiment considered the identified daily events in order to characterize each period of the day and predict the future periods. It was assumed that a day comprises a sleep period followed by an active period, as well as the hypothesis that the events of the current period always affect the next period. In this sense, a day period is characterized considering its set of events and their respective time duration. Based on that, the k-means clustering algorithm was used to identify and group the similar periods. Each period of the day was clustered separately, where 10 and 5 k-means centers showed satisfactory results for the active and sleep period, respectively. The period characterization enables the identification of the similar days and week routines, in terms of a single or the pair sleep-active period, as well as the related periods, i.e., if a given pair sleep-active or active-sleep (next day) always occurs together. For instance, in the left chart of Figure 3, it is possible to notice that, based on the pairs sleep-active, the Individual #1 has 34 different types of day, which were observed all over the weekdays in the analyzed period. However, some of them are more frequent on specific weekdays, which can indicate a routine. For example, the type of day 16 present a high frequency on Mondays, Wednesdays and Sundays. On the other hand, in the right chart of Figure 3 is depicted the different types of the day among the winter and summer period. For instance, the winter period is characterized by the presence of some types of days, such as 28 and 29, that do not appear in the summer, and vice-versa. This means that the season affects the daily habits and activities of the individual.

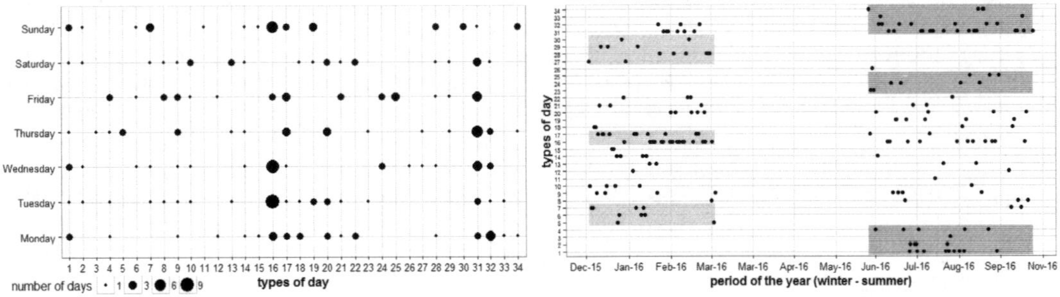

Figure 3. Distribution and patterns of the days along the weeks and year, based on the identified day periods

As in the first experiment, each period can be characterized qualitatively in order to generally describe how was the period, for instance a not active but stressful day or a poor and agitated sleeping. After this phase, the prediction of the day periods used the sleep characterization (the set of events and the respective time duration) to predict the type of the active period (given by the cluster analysis), while the active is used to predict the sleep period of the next day, and so on. In this regard, different algorithms were used, namely: J48, K-nearest neighbours (KNN, KNN1), Learning Vector Quantization (LQV1,2 and 3), Naïve Bayes classifier, Neural Net (Nnet), Sequential Minimal Optimization (SMO), Random Forest, Generalized Linear Model (GLM) and Support Vector Machine (SVM). Table 3 presents the results of the six most efficient ones, considering different sizes of the training set, i.e., during the simulation while in some experiments the models were updated with the data of the current day, in others experiments the oldest days were forgotten.

Table 3. Accuracy of prediction algorithms

	Prediction accuracy for different size of training period					
	sleep to predict active			**active to predict sleep (next day)**		
Algorithms	30	50	70	30	50	70
Learning Vector Quantization 3 (LQV3)	36.0%	40.0%	30.0%	66.0%	60.0%	70.0%
J48	28.0%	20.0%	50.0%	66.0%	53.3%	80.0%
1-Nearest Neighbour (KNN1)	28.0%	30.0%	60.0%	56.0%	50.0%	60.0%
Sequential Minimal Optimization (SMO)	36.0%	36.7%	40.0%	58.0%	50.0%	70.0%
Random Forest	38.0%	33.3%	50.0%	64.0%	63.3%	80.0%
Support Vector Machine (SVM)	36.0%	36.7%	50.0%	62.0%	56.7%	70.0%

The experiments showed better results for the sleep prediction, which can be explained by the larger amount of events during the active period that can be better associated with the sleep patterns. Better results were also obtained when more data was used for the training. The poor results obtained for the active period prediction may indicate that the sleep may not influence the complete active period. In addition, it was observed that the algorithms had a different response, depending on the predicted period. For instance, the J48 algorithm presents better results when predicting the sleep period rather than the active. The outcomes of the prediction algorithms could be used by caregivers to improve the elders' well-being, for instance, if the elder had a sedentary day period, characterized by few moments of walking or any other activity, it could be encouraged not to sleep many hours and also to perform some physical and social activities in the next days.

6. CONCLUSION AND FUTURE WORK

This paper presented a smart m-Health collaborative approach aiming to support and benefit individuals' health conditions and well-being by properly leveraging their wearable monitored data. This approach takes advantage of the ongoing fast progress in mobile and wearable technologies, illustrating the opportunities that the analysis of the data provided by these devices can bring to both, individuals and health professionals. In this sense, some experiments were performed, where the Fitbit ChargeHR wristbands were used to capture physiological conditions of four senior people during one year. Clustering and predictive data analysis were used to extract several kinds of information, which besides to support the simply monitoring and identification of the elders' daily events and routines, could be used to recognize functional degradation, deviation in normal behaviors, depression and stress conditions. In the context of elderly care, it could be used by caregivers to support the elders' independent living and a healthy and active aging.

The analysis of the wearable devices' data showed promising results. From the first experiment was concluded that the elders' daily life presented many similar events and activities, which were satisfactory identified by the k-means algorithm, providing a good basis for the second experiment. The characterization of the periods allowed the identification of similar routines on elders' lifestyle. The elder's sleep and active periods were predicted using different algorithms, where J48 and Random Forest presented better results.

Future work will be devoted to enhance the clustering and prediction analysis, considering other parameters (e.g., other devices, personal and external information), extending the experiments for different kinds of the population and develop the other components of the proposed approach.

ACKNOWLEDGEMENT

The authors would like to thank Jose Barbosa, Claudio Pereiros, the participants of the experiments and the team of Lar de Coelhoso in Bragança, Portugal, for all the support.

REFERENCES

Cheung, K.-H. et al, 2008. HCLS 2.0/3.0: Health care and life sciences data mashup using Web 2.0/3.0. *Journal of Biomedical Informatics,* Vol. 41, No 5, pp. 694-705.

De Arriba-Pérez, F. et al, 2016. Collection and Processing of Data from Wrist Wearable Devices in Heterogeneous and Multiple-User Scenarios. *Sensors,* Vol. 16, No 9.

Deb, B., and Srirama, S. 2013. Social networks for eHealth solutions on cloud. *Frontiers in Genetics, 4,* 171.

Eysenbach, G. 2001. What is e-health? *Journal of medical Internet research,* Vol. 3, No 2, e20.

Istepanian, R. et al, 2006. *M-health.* New York: Springer Science and Business Media.

Lee, C. et al, 2009. Advances in fetal heart rate monitoring using smart phone. *2009 9th International Symposium on Communications and Information Technology*. Icheon, pp. 735-740.

Paul, S. et al, 2009. A web-based electronic health care system for the treatment of pediatric HIV. *11th International Conference on e-Health Networking, Applications and Services (Healthcom 2009)*. Sydney, NSW, pp. 175-180.

Raghupathi, W., and Raghupathi, V. 2014. Big data analytics in healthcare: promise and potential. *Health Information Science and Systems,* Vol. 2, No 1, 3.

Sharif, S. et al, 2016. Augmented quick health. *International Journal of Computer Applications,* Vol. 134, No 11, pp. 1-6.

Subramoniam, S., and Sadi, S. 2010. Healthcare 2.0. *IT professional,* Vol. 12, No 6, pp. 46-51.

Swan, M. 2009. Emerging patient-driven health care models: an examination of health social networks, consumer personalized medicine and quantified self-tracking. *International journal of environmental research and public health,* Vol. 6, No 2, pp. 492-525.

Witten, I. et al, 2016. *Data Mining: Practical machine learning tools and techniques.* Morgan Kaufmann.

WHO. 2011. *World Health Organization - Compendium of new and emerging technologies.* Retrieved Mar. 1, 2017, from http://apps.who.int/iris/bitstream/10665/95786/1/WHO_HSS_EHT_DIM_11.02_eng.pdf

IMPLEMENTATION OF NATIONWIDE EHR SYSTEMS: A FAST EFFECTIVE APPROACH

Goran Velinov[1], Irena Skrceska[2], Marijana Neskovska[3], Miroslav Pevac[4], Dalibor Frtunik[5], Dragan Sahpaski[5], Margita Kon-Popovska[1], Leonid Stoimenov[6], Daniela Ivanova Panova[7], Berislav Vekic[8] and Boro Jakimovski[1]

[1] *Faculty of Computer Science and Enginereeng, Ss. Cyril and Methodius University in Skopje, Macedonia*
[2] *Faculty of Informatics., European University of Republic of Macedonia, Skopje, Macedonia*
[3] *Ministry of Health of Macedonia*
[4] *Ministry of Health of Serbia*
[5] *Sorsix International*
[6] *Faculty of Electronic Engineering, University of Nis, Serbia*
[7] *Medical Faculty, Ss. Cyril and Methodius University in Skopje, Macedonia*
[8] *Faculty of Medicine, University of Belgrade, Serbia*

ABSTRACT

Implementation of the e-Health or EHR systems at national level is a major challenge for any country in the world. There are numerous examples of projects for implementation of such systems that did not complete successfully. Funds spent for this purpose are also very significant. This paper provides a detailed description of the platform Pinga and comparison of two implementations of national e-health and EHR systems carried out in Macedonia (MK) and in Serbia (RS). It also provides a detailed description of the approach for the development and implementation applied, in terms of architecture and the development of technical solution and in terms of project management. Numerous challenges and difficulties are discussed that had to be overcome to achieve successful implementation of these systems. A review of some of the benefits and results of the implementation of the systems is presented. These results show that the platform enables rapid implementation of national e-health systems with positive effects on health systems visible as early as the final stages of the implementation.

KEYWORDS

Pinga Platform, National e-Health, National EHR

1. INTRODUCTION

Many countries in the world and almost all countries in Europe have perceived the benefits and need for implementation of national EHR system or national electronic health system. Different countries have chosen different system models and different approaches to their implementation (Bonomi et al. 2016).

Although research from the World Health Organization (WHO) in 2015 (WHO, 2016) shows that a higher percentage of European countries have implemented a national system of electronic health records, however in many cases these systems do not provide a complete EHR. In different countries the national EHR system is implemented at certain levels of care includes different part of national health institutions or covering only certain modules and functionalities. In other words small number of countries have managed to implement national EHR system at all three levels of health care and thus cover all health institutions at all levels.

A large number of countries had difficulties in implementation and have encountered a variety of problems that slow down or in the worst case temporarily or permanently stop the implementation process. Although as a barrier to implementation of national e-health system in up to 50% is considered (1) financing (WHO, 2016) or high planned budgets and most often their surpassing, the problems belong to one of the following categories: (2) problems in defining the objectives and scope of the system (France (Grady, 2012; MacDougall 2015), Britain (Bonomi et al. 2016)), (3) problems with the development team (Greece), (4) choice of implementation concept (Italy), (5) timeframe (Britain) - projects lasting a decade or more and (6) laws (Greece).

In MK in 2011 and RS in 2015 were initiated projects for the development and implementation of national e-health systems with included EHR systems within. Aware of the problems (1-6) in a number of countries, before starting the projects, i.e. in the process of creating a multi-annual plan for the introduction of e-health system at the national level, a comprehensive analysis was made of the health systems in both countries and were achieved all the necessary prerequisites for the start of the implementation. It was necessary to eliminate risk factors that could adversely affect the implementation of the system and then adversely affect the manner of using the system and thereby reduce the positive effects of its use. These factors are: a) Resistance to change by most stakeholders; b) Not very large capacities of the participants in the process; c) The complexity of the system and expectations - very fast results and great expectations.

To successfully overcome the noticed challenges from previous projects for implementation of e-health system in both countries, but also using the experiences from Europe and the world, it was necessary:

To provide strong political support. Throughout the period of implementation of the national e-health system strong political support from the Ministry of Health (MoH) should be provided. It should consist of continuous operational support to project teams to easily overcome the resistance to change. Also, it is needed to make changes in the laws governing the role and functionalities of the national e-health system, and to provide organizational and personnel resources to manage and support the national system.

To find a suitable national e-health model. A new concept of architecture was applied – model of adapted centralized system, which involves the integration of a central national system with existing local systems used in healthcare facilities, but also functional user interface for users in institutions that do not have an electronic system. Thus a functional ecosystem is formed where all information systems can function and develop and all members of that ecosystem can have certain benefits.

Apply an appropriate project methodology for implementation. To find an approach to successful implementation of such a complex system, an analysis was made of all factors that could affect the performance in the implementation process, whereby in both countries were applied different approaches, i.e. projects were organized on different ways and with different duration. In the rest of this paper is given a description of the systems implemented in MK and in RS respectively. In the description of the system in MK an emphasis is on the completeness of the system and on the key factors and solutions that have proven important to the successful implementation of the system. In the case of RS greater emphasis is given on the project management and on the speed of implementation, but are described some experiences and lessons learned from that project.

International recognition. The effects of the introduction of e-health systems are already high and affect almost all segments of the healthcare systems in both countries. MK national e-health system success story was identified and recognized by the wider European professional community. The country scored significantly high in the healthcare ranking made by European Healthcare Consumer Index (EHCI) in their 2014, 2015 and 2016 reports (Björnberg 2015, 2016, 2017). The success that the system achieved in MK is repeating in RS (Björnberg 2017). The positive effects of the national e-health system implementation in MK were also noted in the WHO eHealth report (WHO 2016).

The paper is organized as follows: section two describes the necessary preconditions to start the implementation of the systems in both countries. In section three is a description of the conceptual model of the system applied and a description of the projects to be implemented in both countries and in the section four is made discussion and some conclusions are presented.

2. PRECONDITIONS AND BACKGROUND WORK

In order to precisely define the business processes that would be covered by a national e-health system, such as for instance, the processes of scheduling, referral or prescription, it is necessary to make detailed analysis of health and e-health systems in both countries. Moreover, in order to provide functional integration of health systems in central state institutions, and to define the flow of data between them, it is necessary to analyze their roles and interconnectedness.

Introduction of Hospital Information Systems (HIS) in the health facilities in both countries is a continuous process that lasts from late '80, launched in early '90. As more important stages of computerization stand out the computerization of primary health care in MK, which took place intensively along with the privatization process - in the period 2001 - 2006. During that period, all private clinics on primary level acquired appropriate HIS. The core modules of these systems are: records of appointments, running a file, the admission of patients, examinations carried out (anamnesis, diagnoses, therapies, referrals etc.), creating referrals, drug prescription, dispensing ampullar therapy. The introduction of HIS in hospitals, specialized hospitals and clinics of Clinical Center (CC) Skopje (of second and third level of health care) happened independently, where only a small number of hospitals and clinics had already implemented information systems (IS). Computerization of the health system in RS in the period from 2006 to 2013 was performed through projects financed by the World Bank (SHP 2003, SHP-AF 2009 and DILS). Within the DILS project were developed and implemented health information systems in most health centers (on primary level of health care). Computerization of secondary and tertiary health care is at a very low level - hospitals that have HIS are rare and only one of the four CCs has HIS.

Numerous are attempts in the region, but also in Europe and the world, of the implementation of information systems at the national level that did not complete successfully. In the region, the projects are formally closed as successful, but most of them remain on the stage of delivery of technical solution which has little or no use. The World Bank report concerning the performance of projects financed trough foreign financial support: "Many public sector digital technology projects fail" (World Bank Group, 2016). In both countries there were attempts to establish integrated health information systems on national level.

In MK was organized a project for development and implementation of a centralized e-health system on national level. The system should have been used in all health facilities in public health in MK and should be integrated with systems in other central state institutions. The project had started in 2009 and for a period of two years only one module was partly implemented, while the rest did not even start. The project was stopped in 2011 by the MoH. Although there were some technical and organizational problems in the implementation, the main reason for project failure was the selected concept - in one project, in short deadline at national level to develop and implement almost all of the components of a complete e-health system. Taking into account the low technical knowledge of health professionals (doctors, nurses, administrative staff), the resistance to change of almost all of the parties involved, organizational and management capacities of the MoH and of health institutions, such projects could not have been successfully completed. In RS was also organized a project that should develop an integrated health information system. The system should have provided building EHR nationwide. The proposed model of building EHR was decenetralized with planned standards for interopreability and infrastructure for interconnecting the institutions. The project envisaged only a pilot implementation.

One of the key prerequisites to be fulfilled for successful implementation of national e-health system is adjusting legislation for inclusion the electronic system in the national health system, by defining the model of the electronic systems - functionalities, data sets, the manner of its use and others. In Europe, out of 27 countries in which EHR system is implemented nationwide, 18 countries have legislation that regulates the functioning and use of e-health and EHR systems (European Commission, 2014). In MK the issues related to e-health are regulated primarily by two laws (Health Care Law of MK, Law on health records of MK). A comparison of the legislation of the two countries with the EU countries in the region and beyond can give a few conclusions. For MK it is specific that the laws give very detailed description of the national e-health system, which is not typical to most EU countries. Moreover, besides the description of the set of data, there is a description of the processes required that should be completed through the system and envisages very strict penalties in case of misuse of the system. This means that changes in the laws are enacted which regulate the role and functionality of the national system for e-Health and prerequisites are created for providing organizational and personnel resources to manage and support the national system. In RS the work of e-health systems are regulated by two laws (Health Care Law of RS, Law on health records of RS). Using the experiences from MK, one of the basic requirements before starting the project for implementation of an integrated ehealth system at the national level, it was to analyze the legislation (laws and bylaws) and to propose changes in order to accommodate the system. Unlike in MK, in RS the regulation for the most part was done by preparing appropriate regulations (bylaws). This approach allows greater flexibility and more frequent changes, which do not depend on the Assembly.

Changes in the laws and bylaws in both countries have been made to meet the preconditions to start each subsequent stage of implementation pf electronic systems. The timeframe of implementation and the success of the implementation of reforms in the health sector in general, is closely linked to the dynamics of change of laws. The experience of both countries shows that the change in legislation should be made on time, so as not to slow down the implementation of elektonic systems, but also well defined to ensure successful change management and proper implementation of new electronic systems.

3. IMPLEMENTATION OF THE NATIONAL E-HEALTH SYSTEMS

3.1 National e-Health Ecosystem

Taking into account the risk factors and using the experience from previous implementations of e-health systems in the region, model of national e-health and EHR system was selected and then a technical solution was developed, which according to our estimates had the "best chance of success". So, concept of e-health system at the national level was elected, which had to build a functional ecosystem involving all health facilities and central government institutions of public healthcare - as providers and users of information in this ecosystem. The aim of the system is not only building functional EHR system, but rather a complete e-health system at the national level, that will play an important role in improving the operational management and the strategic planning of the reforms in public health.

It variation of the centralized e-health and EHR model was chosen. Electronic systems that were used in health facilities had to be integrated with the central system for all necessary functionalities. The functionalities that each facility had to use depended on the services that facility provides. E.g. the health centers use the modules for e-booking and e-referrals, whereas the hospitals use the module for hospitalization (HIS). All primary health level clinics who had their own E-Systems had to be integrated for functionality: e-Booking, e-Referral, e-Prescription etc. In addition, the integration provides bi-directional data exchange - local systems provide the necessary data to the central system and download the necessary data for storage into the local systems. Also, the selected model integrates all systems used in the central state institutions: The State (Republic) Health Insurance Fund (RHIF), the Medicines and Medical Devices Agency (MMDA), the Institute of Public Health (IPH) and others. E.g., for data retrieved from RHIF - insurance status of patients. The users from health facilities and central institutions that had no local hospital systems until, had to start using the functionalities of the central system via a web interface. E.g., it was planned the IPH to have access to all functionalities of the Business Intelligence (BI) module through an interactive web interface. Thereby several advantages were provided:

- Existing software systems continue to be used in the health facilities and government institutions, where they gain importance because the central system takes data from them, the need for their expansion, upgrading and improvement is created. Local systems are not merely providers of information; with the integration they receive data from the central system.
- For users of existing systems there is no change of the way they work or of the software system, thus avoiding resistance to change or the need for mastering new systems.
- For the new users that did not have electronic systems, intuitive user interface with simple and clearly defined operating procedures is developed.
- Great emphasis on data security, due to privacy and confidentiality.
- A model of integration is chosen which provides on-line operation of the system - all data are actualized when in the moment they are entered. All the existing systems (74 in MK, and 57 in RS different information systems) were integrated in a national eHealth system. Accurately defined API for integration. Enabling these advantages: no waiting for data synchronization, quick technical integration, minimizing technical errors and etc. The integration is based on interfaces that allow data exchange according to an internal XML based standard. Within the integration accepted international codification systems such as ICD-10 for diagnosis coding, ATC coding of drugs and DRG classification system for health services based on Australian Refined Diagnosis Related Groups, version 5.2 (AR-DRG, 2017), are used.
- System that is most suitable for users - agile approach to the definition, development and implementation of new functionalities. In the case of functionality that does not meet the real needs, fast repair and improvement.

The highest level architecture of the system based on the Pinga Platform is shown in Figure 1. The system consists of functional modules, grouped into four sections as follows:

- Healthcare: e-Referral, e-Prescription, e-Booking, Medical Daybook, Diabetes, E-Mother Card, HIS, Laboratory IS (LIS), Radiology IS (RIS);
- Information, monitoring and control: Reports and BI, SMS and E-Mail, Billing, Web & Mobile Public Portal, Payment for Performance (P4P), Security, Admin, Balanced ScoreCard (BSC);
- Health prevention: Immunology, Prevention Programs, Scheduled Checkups;
- Public health: Disease Registration, Code Lists, Registers, Human Resources (HR);

Central component of the system is EHR. All modules provide web user interface. Following modules enable integration with other systems via API: E-referral, E-prescription, E-booking, Medical Daybook, HIS, LIS, RIS, while others are used only through a graphical user interface.

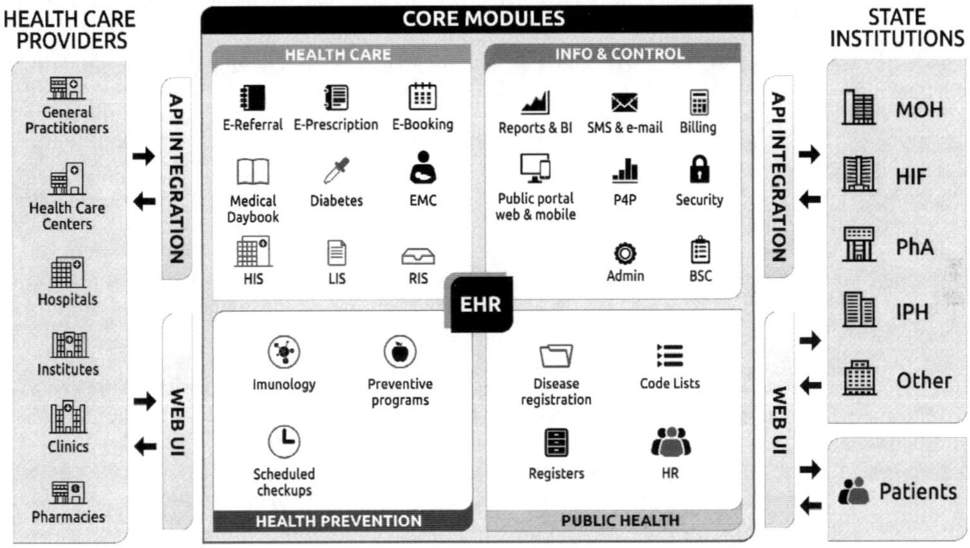

Figure 1. Architecture of national e-health system

3.2 Effective Implementation in Macedonia – MojTermin

In MK the system was developed and implemented in phases with gradual expansion, according to adapted methodology for iterative and gradual development (Larman and Basili, 2003) and implementation.

The first phase - initial success. At the end of 2011 the initial version of the system was developed within the project for development and implementation of Information system for electronic waiting lists on national level. The system was expected to allow booking for medical examinations, first only to healthcare institutions in Skopje, then it can be implemented in all public health institutions in MK, in order to create electronic waiting lists for all specialties i.e. for all types of interventions that have had to wait certain period (especially of interest to the MoH: Magnetic resonance imaging, Computed tomography, Colonoscopy, Gastroscopy, etc.). Within a short period of time electronic waiting lists were created for all specialties. According the core functionality of this system - scheduling of intervention in a given appointment slot (booking system), the implementation is named in MK - MojTermin (MyAppointment). The system is actually comprised of two modules - module for e-booking and e-referral module.

Second phase – on national level. In 2012 was organized a three-year project (2012-2014) for upgrading the System for electronic waiting lists to the National e-health system. Project includes extending existing system MyAppointment with new functionalities and involving several institutions as users of the system. As part of this project have been developed and implemented the following new functional modules: e-Prescription, E-Mother Card, Reports and BI, SMS and E-Mail module for notifications, Billing module, Web & Mobile Public Portal, Security, Admin, Disease Registration and Forms, Registers and Code Lists. The system was integrated with existing systems used in the MoH, in other governmental institutions or in public health facilities. As part of this project on 1st of July 2013 the system was launched on national level, which was the first version of the national e-health system. It is interesting to note that the system crashed on the first day of the launch due to failure of the service for integration with the RHIF. The system was restarted on 2nd of July2013, whereas the check of the insurance status of the patients continued by being carried out on a daily basis.

Third phase - completeness. In 2015 and 2016 the system was upgraded with new functionalities and modules in the scope of project to upgrade the National e-health and EHR system MojTermin. The existing modules of the second phase in this period were significantly advanced (improved and expanded). For e.g., a complete redesign was made of the module for e-referral. The system at this stage was upgraded with the following modules: Full hospital operations, Medical daybook, Diabetes. At this stage special modules were also developed: Laboratory IS (LIS), Radiology IS (RIS), Immunology, Preventive screening programs, Scheduled Checkups, Payment for Performance (P4P). Also it was developed special module Balanced ScoreCard (BSC) to measure and manage the performances of health facilities. At the end of 2016 in MK were implemented all modules of the system presented in Figure 1.

Factors of success. In all three phases adapted agile methodology for the development and implementation of information system was used. This implies that the development of the system was carried out in small iterations, but wherever functionalities were well defined, i.e. there was a precise and detailed description of the functional requirements, a sequential process of development, with elements of classic waterfall methodology, was organized. Here it should be emphasized that significant flexibility was expected from the implementer - to accept frequent change requests for change of the functionality, after finishing the stages of acceptance and putting it into production. Without considering them as change requests. Similarly, for development of functionalities that were not required in official technical documentation. In case when management of the two project teams assessed that some functionality is crucial for the successful use of the system, it was accepted and developed, regardless whether it was formally required in the functional requirements or not.

Another important factor influencing the success of the project was the established synergy between the project teams of the MoH and the contractors - developers and system implementers. This means that very often the list of open tasks was shared between the teams, with the aim of better or faster completion: both teams had the same goal - successful implementation, i.e. mass and quality using the system.

Throughout the whole period of implementation of the national e-health system, a strong political support was provided from the MoH. It consisted in continuous operational support to the project teams. Also, changes were made to the laws governing the role and the functionality of the national e-health system, as well as providing organizational and human resources to manage and support the national system.

Results and outcomes. The effects of using the system are shown in Figure 2 and 3. Figure 2 shows the average number of different patients who used the services, average number of prescriptions and referrals by months. It may be noted that these numbers are stabilized (very slightly increases), indicating that all patients users of the public health system are recorded in e-health system. Figure 3 shows the average waiting time from appointment to the actual examination and the average monthly number of realized regular (excluding control, urgent and laboratory) referrals. It may be noted that the average waiting time is stabilized, while the number of appointments slightly increases, indicating increased efficiency of doctors. As expected, in the summer months there are smaller realized referrals. The population of MK (2002) is 2.022.547 residents.

Figure 2. Avg. number of patients, referrals and prescriptions

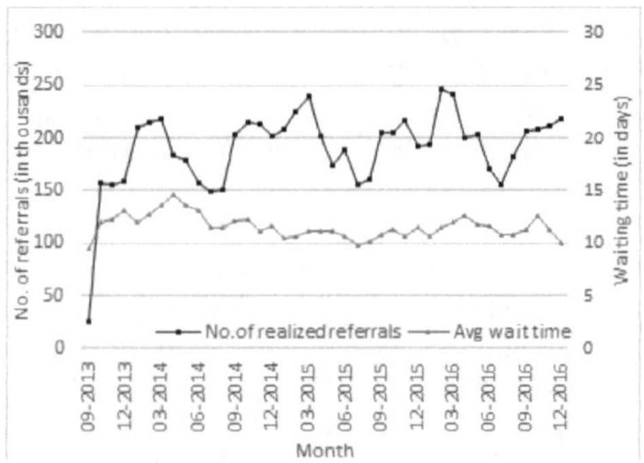

Figure 3. Avg. waiting time and number of referrals

3.3 Fast Implementation is Serbia - MojDoktor

In RS during 2015 project for implementation of Integrated Health Information System (IHIS, in Serbian - IZIS) was organized, which received the name MojDoktor (MyDoctor). It was precisely defined set of modules, which includes: e-Booking, e-Referral, e-Prescriptions, Medical daybook, Disease registers (for Birth, Cancer, Diabetes, Cardio-vascular diseases, death etc.), Reports and BI. The procedure for implementing the procurement lasted from June to August. Bidders had to develop a functional prototype till September and based on the evaluation of several offered prototypes, in November 2015 it was decided to implement a system that will be based on Pinga Platform, i.e. the concept of e-health system that was already being used in MK.

As the project conditions envisaged developing a prototype system, it was decided to apply the model for developing a functional prototype with adapted methodology Evolutionary prototyping (Hekmatpour, 1987). The developed prototype included the complete functionality of all modules and appropriate interfaces: web user interface and API for integration with the systems in health care facilities and central state institutions – RHIF, IPH and MMDA. Simulation of the functioning of interfaces for integration of the prototype with the other systems was made. The project for development and implementation of the system was carried out in two major phases. Methodology used was Adapted Prince II and ITIL V3.0 as a framework approach to the delivery of services envisaged in the project.

The first phase - development. This phase was organized in the period from November to December 2015. In this phase it was envisaged to analyze the health system in RS with emphasis on processes that should be automated with central e-system as well as analysis of the technical equipment of the institutions - network infrastructure and connectivity to the Internet, work stations, medical information systems. As a result of the analysis documents were prepared with recommendations for technical equipping of the health facilities and changes in laws and regulations, extending medical documentation. For example, extending the content of referrals with mandatory fields - the exact time of the examination envisaged and name and surname of the doctor, or the clinic to which the patient is referred. Also, changes of workflows within and between health facilities are proposed. For example, all doctors are obliged to create calendars of planned activities for the following month, their managers approve them and the administrators publicize the public part of the calendars. Second example: Changing the path of referral in one episode of treatment – starting with referral always being made by the GP to the path in which doctors specialists can refer the patient, without patient having to come back / visit GP to just draft and sign the referral.

It was also envisaged the existing prototype to adapt to recommended functional changes, to import reference data according to the current situation, to deliver technical functioning system and run training for the key users of the system from MoH and from a number of selected health institutions.

Second phase - dissemination. This stage was organized in January 2016 - June 2016. In this phase it was planned to disseminate of the system at the national level - in all institutions, and functional use of all modules. For this purpose, two parallel processes were planned: 1. Manage the integration of the local hospital information systems - for users in institutions that will continue to use existing systems and 2. Inclusion of the work of the institutions lacking adequate hospital information systems - for customers of institutions that will directly work on the national system.

The integration of local systems took place in sub-stages by incorporating groups of the envisaged modules. 2A.1: e-booking and e-referral, 2A.2 e-prescription, 2A.3: e-daybook / medical protocols. In parallel was organized implementation in institutions, with planned introduction of the system to be in regions that gravitate to the CCs - Southeast Serbia to CC Nis, Central Serbia to CC Kragujevac, the Region of Belgrade to CC of Serbia and Vojvodina to CC in Novi Sad, and by functional modules. The division of the territory in 4 regions that gravitate towards CCs was most appropriate because very few patients are referred from one region to another. Thus the implementation, i.e. the introduction of new functionalities was carried out in sub-stages 2B.1-2B.3, for the same groups of modules as in the sub-stages of the integration. It meant incremental (but fast) introduction of new functionalities. In 2A.4. implementation sub-stage was envisaged the integration with the central state institutions. In the fourth 2B.4 sub-stage was implemented the module Disease registration and the modules used by the MoH – BI, Admin and others. Table 1. shows the dates of commencement of sub-stages for the implementation of the system by regions.

Table 1. Beginning dates of sub-stages implementation

Sub-stage \ Region	Southeast Serbia	Central Serbia	Region Belgrade	Vojvodina
2B.1:e-Booking, e-Referrals	28.03.2016	25.04.2016	16.05.2016	30.05.2016
2B.2: e-Prescriptions	25.04.2016	16.05.2016	30.05.2016	13.06.2016
2B.3: e-Daybook / Protocols	16.05.2016	30.05.2016	13.06.2016	27.06.2017
2B.4: Registers / BI, Admin	27.06.2017	27.06.2017	27.06.2017	27.06.2017

Promotion and trainings. One important step in the implementation was the system promotion, i.e. informing the users of the purpose and benefits of the system. The first step was to inform the managers and IT administrators from each health facility. For each of the four regions was jointly organized presentation, to present the objectives to be achieved using the system and presentation of the basic functional characteristics of the system. After these initial presentations, followed the series of training the system users.

Within the development phase, in Dec. 2015, five-day training was carried out for a group of 20 users - super users of the major health facilities and of the MoH. Training model train the trainers was planned, and these users had to train administrators of the facilities. From the previous experience it was concluded that each facility should have at least one person with technical education or with high level of knowledge in using computer, who will assume the role of system administrator of the facilities (a role with the highest privilege on facility level). He is in charge of providing training and support to end users of the system. Larger facilities should have more than one administrator. At the beginning of the dissemination phase it was concluded that the training is not sufficient and that it is necessary the implementer to directly train the administrators. Region by region, in all four regions were first organized two-day trainings for administrators of facilities. Although at this stage the idea was to adopt train the trainer principle, i.e. to train persons in institutions that will continue the training of end users of the system (e.g. doctors, nurses, technicians, etc.), it was however decided to also organize two-day groups in the health facilities. In some facilities, where the change caused by the system introduction was difficult to accept, individual training was held, or training directly of a doctor in the clinic while he works with patients. Some users of the system in this period attended more than 3 trainings before beginning using the system. The most common reasons for organizing additional training directly in facilities was a reference of inadequate staff to be trained as administrators, e.g. employees without sufficient knowledge of the work processes and of the functioning of the health system, or without sufficient technical knowledge etc. Such persons could not carry out the training of users and could not take the expected role in the further implementation of the system in their own health facilities.

In the phase of the system dissemination 18 two-day trainings were held for administrators of facilities, over 1000 individual trainings in clinics. In the CC of Serbia alone were held 60 group trainings and additional presentations intended for software companies. One training and three additional presentations for employees in the call center and trainings for Pharmaceutical chamber were also held. In this period alone over 5.800 hours of training for various users of the system were invested. In the period until 31.12.2016 the system was under warranty maintenance. And in this period were made further efforts to improve the use of the system - through additional training and assistance in the work on site, but also through minor changes in functionalities, and in order to adapt to the real needs of the users.

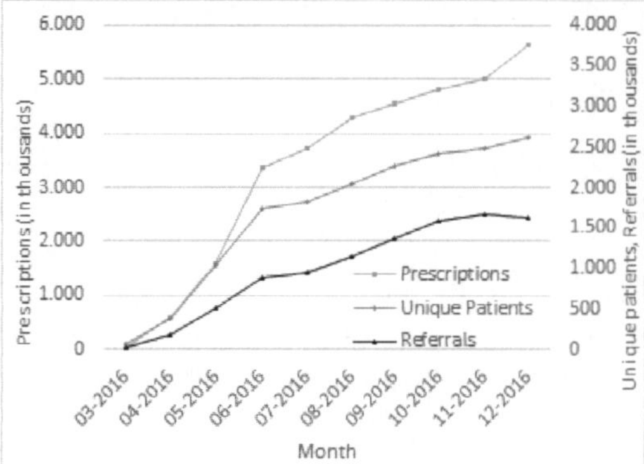

Figure 4. Avg. number of patients, referrals and prescriptions

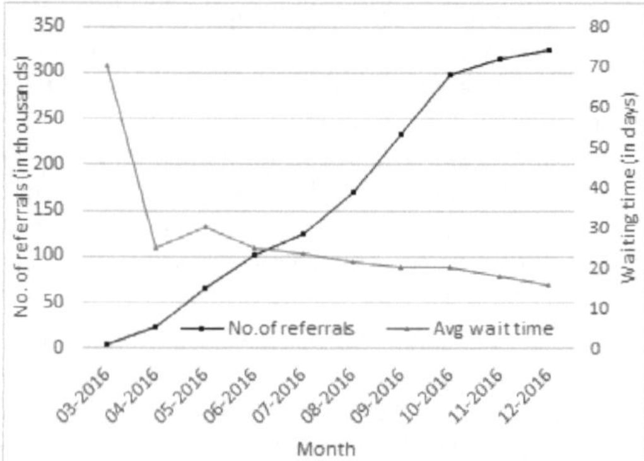

Figure 5. Avg. waiting time and number of referrals

Results and outcomes. Figure 4 shows the average number of prescriptions, patients, referrals monthly. As it can be noticed, the system began to be intensively used in a very short period of time. The total number of individual patients in the system at the end of 2016, including GP's examinations, was 4.400.910, 2.617.804 of them were referred to specialists. Figure 5 shows the average waiting time from appointment to the actual examination and the average monthly number of regular (excluding control, urgent and laboratory) referrals. According to the census in 2011, the population of RS is 7.106.862 residents.

4. DISCUSSION AND CONCLUSION

Importance of application of modern information technologies to improve the implementation of effective policies of public health management at the state level is undoubtedly great. On the other hand, the implementation of complex information systems in the health sector is not a simple task. It is even more difficult in countries in the Balkan region for many reasons, some of which are unknown in the countries of Western Europe or North America. Such causes and aggravating factors are for instance non-cooperative and non-constructive behavior by some of central institutions; congenital personal and collective resistance to change and the built-in skepticism that any change will lead to improvement, and opportunism of significant number of involved persons. In such conditions, the successful implementation of large systems is very difficult. That is why previous attempts in this segment weren't very successful, but in general in this part of the world in almost all areas, the successful implementation of information systems is really rare.

However, in both countries a "magic solution" was discovered through appropriate technical solution, applicable implementation methodology, proper planning of activities - by gradually increasing the scale of operation, shortening the deadlines for implementation and tightening (the introduction of stricter conditions and rules) of the manner of using the system and thus relatively successfully overcome many challenges. Thereby the following conclusions can be made:

- Applied is an incremental way of development and implementation of the system. The development and the implementation of the system were organized in phases - gradual introduction of new functionalities and modules (in MK) and gradual introduction by regions by functional modules (applied in RS). Gradual change processes of functioning of the health system by introducing rules and patterns of using the system - the gradual change in the work of users doctors, from the existing way of working towards the planned.
- Quick and appropriate legislative change was made, before or during the process of implementation of the system, change of all laws pertaining to e-health system (in MK) detail and precise definition of a health system and manner of using it.
- Timely and appropriately informing the users of the system on the benefits of its proper application (managers, doctors, nurses and etc.). Training for proper use of the system of all system users. Often repeat the same training, and for certain user groups on-job training while working with patients.
- Strong management. In both countries there was strategic commitment of the governments to reform the public health system and strong support of the implementation of e-health system, as the main tool for implementing many of the reforms in the health system. Direct (and operational) involvement of the ministers was extremely important.
- Synergy and competence of project teams. Collaborative work of the teams of the implementer and of MoH. By accepting the suggestions of implementer on all the important issues. Clear understanding of the goals and expectations by the MoH and by the implementer. Flexibility in accepting the change of objectives and appropriate adjustment of the system model and the procedures for implementation. Hiring a suitable professional team of experts in the field (users and developers of e-health systems).

REFERENCES

AR-DRG (2017), Australian Institute on Health and Welfare, Australian refined diagnosis-related groups (AR-DRG) data cubes, http://www.aihw.gov.au/hospitals-data/ar-drg-data-cubes/ [15 March 2017]

Björnberg, A., (2015), Health Consumer Powerhouse, European Healthcare Consumer Index Report 2014, http://www.healthpowerhouse.com/files/EHCI_2014/EHCI_2014_report.pdf;

Björnberg, A., (2016), Health Consumer Powerhouse, European Healthcare Consumer Index Report 2015, http://www.healthpowerhouse.com/files/EHCI_2015/EHCI_2015_report.pdf;

Björnberg, A., (2017), Health Consumer Powerhouse, European Healthcare Consumer Index Report 2016, http://www.healthpowerhouse.com/files/EHCI_2016/EHCI_2016_report.pdf

Bonomi, S., Badr, N.G., Zardini, A., Rossignoli, C., (2016). Improving the Introduction of Electronic Health Record: Lessons from European and North American Countries. In: Borangiu T., Dragoicea M., Nóvoa H. (eds) Exploring Services Science. IESS 2016. Lecture Notes in Business Information Processing, vol 247. Springer, Cham

European Commission, (2014). Overview of the national laws on electronic health records in the EU Member States and their interaction with the provision of cross-border eHealth services. Final report and recommendations

Grady, A., (2012). Electronic Health Records: How the United States Can Learn From the French Dossier Medical Personnel. *Wisconsin International Law Journal*, Vol. 30, No. 2, pp.374-400.

Hekmatpour, S., (1987). Experience with evolutionary prototyping in a large software project. ACM SIGSOFT Software Engineering Notes, Volume 12 Issue1, Pages 38-41, doi:10.1145/24574.24577, ACM New York, USA

Larman, C., Basili, V., (2003). Iterative and Incremental Development: A Brief History, *IEEE Computer*, volume 36, issue 6, page 47-56, doi: 10.1109/MC.2003.1204375, IEEE Computer Society Press Los Alamitos, CA, USA

MacDougall, J., (2015). France still seeks an electronic health record, [website] http://www.healthcare-in-europe.com/en/article/14069-france-still-seeks-an-electronic-health-record.html, [10 February 2017]

Official Journal of the Republic of Macedonia No. 43/2012, 145/2012, 87/2013, 164/2013, 39/2014, 43/2014, 188/2014, 10/2015, 64/2015, 154/2015, 192/2015, 17/2016, 37/2016 Закон за здравствена заштита на Р.Македонија (Health care Law Republic of Macedonia). Available from: http://mz.gov.mk/wp-content/uploads/2012/12/zakon za zdravstvena-zastita-2_12_2012.pdf, [01 March 2017]

Official Journal of the Republic of Macedonia No. 20/2009, 53/2011,164/2013, 150/2015, Закон за евиденција во областа на здравството (Law on records in the field of health), Available from: http://zdravstvo.gov.mk/wp-content/uploads/2015/05/ZAKON-ZA-EVIDENTSIITE-VO-OBLASTA-NA-ZDRAVSTVOTO-konsolidiran-tekst-2013.164.pdf, [01 March 2017]

Official Journal of the Republic of Serbia No. 106/15, Zakon o zdravstvenoj zashtiti (Health Care Law of Serbia), Available from: http://www.zdravlje.gov.rs/downloads/2016/Januar/Januar2016ZakonOZZ.pdf [15 March 2017]

Official Journal of the Republic of Serbia No. 123/14, Zakon o zdravstvenoj dokumnetaciji i evidencijama u oblasi zdravstva (Law on health records of Serbia), Available from: http://www.rfzo.rs /download/zakoni/Zakon%20o%20zdravstvenoj%20dokumentaciji%20i%20evidencijama%20u%20oblasti%20zdravstva.pdf. [15 March 2017]

World Bank Group, (2016). Digital Dividends, World Development Report 2016, p 165 Available from: http://documents.worldbank.org/curated/en/896971468194972881/pdf/102725-PUB-Replacement-PUBLIC.pdf, [03 February 2017]

WHO, (2016). Regional Office for Europe, From Innovation to Implementation, eHealth in the WHO European Region, ISBN 978 92 890 51378, Available from: http://www.euro.who.int/__data/assets/pdf_file/0012/302331/From-Innovation-to-Implementation-eHealth-Report-EU.pdf [12 February 2017]

"DON'T MAKE ME AN ORPHAN, MOM": A MOBILE GAME TO SUPPORT SMOKING CESSATION

Olga Shabalina[1], Vitaliy Aleynikov[1], Aleksandr Davtian[2], Ann Matokhina[1] and David C. Moffat[3]
[1] *Volgograd State Technical University, 28 Lenin Ave., Volgograd, 400005, Russia*
[2] *Moscow Institute of Physics and Technology, 9 Institutsky Lane, Dolgoprudny, 141701, Moscow region*
[3] *Glasgow Caledonian University, Cowcaddens Road Glasgow G4 0BA Scotland, UK*

ABSTRACT

Quitting smoking is one of the biggest challenges of our time. Smartphone technology appears to be ideally suited to provide tailored smoking cessation. Analysis of existing mobile games shows three smoking secession approaches: intimidating the user through the threat of loss of life and health, motivating him to stop smoking by staying healthy, saving money, etc.; or providing smoking cessation support.

The games, based on the idea of intimidation of the user, intimidate the user himself and make him feel uncomfortable. But the uncomfortable feeling of the smoker leaving behind his loved ones (especially kids) to suffer is much stronger than the fear to die; and it is hardly possible to get used to such anxiety. The paper presents a mobile game implementing a virtual dialogue of the smoking user with his child. Several times a day the user receives a virtual message from his child with a question on how many cigarettes the user has smoked during the last period of time. At the end of each day the user receives the emotional photo of his child with the text comments demonstrating the child attitude to the current smoking activity of the parent.

To analyze the current state of the user in terms of his smoking activity the data on the number of smoked cigarettes is represented by a two-parameter random time series variable. Two indices reflecting the user smoking dynamics and smoking behavior are calculated as a function of this variable. The combination of the current values of indices is interpreted in terms of the smoking activity of the user. To organize a virtual dialogue of the user with his child, a nonlinear scenario is used. Some examples of the dialogue in the game are shown.

KEYWORDS

Smoking cessation, Mobile game, Virtual dialogue, Emotional photo, Smoking dynamics index, Smoking behavior index

1. INTRODUCTION

Quitting smoking is one of the biggest challenges of our time. Many different strategies can be used for quitting without assistance to behavioral counseling. There exist different smoking cessation methods intended to help motivated smokers who are ready to quit and using special computer applications is one of the most promising among them.

The wide proliferations of smartphones lead to the growth of the mobile apps developed to help people to stop smoking (Abrams et al, 2011). Smartphone technology appears to be ideally suited to provide tailored smoking cessation (Heppner et al, 2015). The growing interest in the development of mobile smoking cessation apps is reflected in the regular appearance of various top-lists of the best quit smoking mobile apps, eg. "The Five Best Quit-Smoking Apps" with the most effective habit-kicking apps for the iPhone, Android and Windows Phone (Bell, 2017), the "Best Apps to Help You Quit Smoking" top-list with the best in 2011 iOS apps (Men's Fitness, 2017), and the latest one with the best quit smoking apps in 2016 (Healthline, 2017).

Different qualitative studies and researches aimed at examining a content of mobile apps (Abrams et al, 2013), analyzing the approaches to smoking cessation in the apps (Heppner et al, 2015) and their effectiveness for helping smokers (El-Hilly et al, 2016) prove the great potential of mobile apps to support smoking cessation and encourage game companies, academics and hobbyists to conduct new research and to find new practical solutions for smoking cessation support.

2. MOBILE APPLICATIONS FOR SMOKING SECESSION: DEVELOPMENT APPROACHES AND TECHNIQUES

Existing mobile apps use different approaches and techniques for persuading the user to stop smoking, from intimidating by using the fear of death, to motivate him to save money; and even to fulfill a cherished dream on the money saved.

Thus, the game "Get Rich or Die Smoking"(Captain-droid.com, 2017) shows the user how much money he can save by not buying cigarettes and what he can buy with that money instead. The same idea is implemented in the game "Quit Smoking" (QuitNow!, 2017). The game keeps the track of the amount of cigarettes the user didn't smoke, and shows how much money he has saved. The both games also tell the user the health benefits he gained.

Such games as "Smoke Free"(Crane, 2017),"Quit Pro" (Quit-pro.com, 2017) track the smoking activity of the user and help to develop a quitting strategy. The game "LivestrongMyQuit Coach" (LIVESTRONG.COM, 2017) is a virtual coach that allows the user to create a personalized plan for quitting. The "Quit Smoking Slowly" app also helps to create a stop smoking plan and controls its implementation (Sameapk.com, 2017). The Antismoke app is an example of statistical applications intended to control the time the user spends without smoking and to support the process of quitting smoking in economic and health terms.

Another approach is implemented in such games as, for instance, "Quit Smoking: Cessation Nation" (Appcrawlr, 2017). The games involve the user with a social community of quitters and give the them encouraging messages and share the achievements of each user with fellow quitters.

Stop Buddy [4] includes a counter that shows the functions of the body compared to a non-smoker, from the point of view of a doctor.

In the game "Stop Smoking " (Roxoft.hr, 2017) the user can set his personal goal (for instance, a voyage to Maldives), monitor how many days he needs to reach it and get a notification when he reaches it.

Summarizing, the following smoking secession approaches can be distinguished in the implementation of mobile games:

- intimidating the user through the harm to health, fear of death, harm to the health of people around, etc.;
- motivating the user to stop smoking by keeping his health, saving money, etc.;
- smoking cessation support (collecting and visualizing smoking statistics, psychological advising, planning a smoking cessation program, providing the help of community, etc.).

3. SMOKING SECESSION MOBILE GAME BASED ON VIRTUAL EMOTIONAL PARENT-CHILD DIALOGUE

The existing games, based on the idea of intimidation of the user, implement different game mechanics to intimidate the user himself and to make him feel uncomfortable. In its most explicit form, this idea is implemented as frightening inscriptions or images on cigarette packs. But the long-term smokers are not so easy to intimidate: they tend to get used to those images and don't pay attention to them.

But the uncomfortable feeling of the smoker leaving behind his loved ones (especially kids) to suffer is much stronger than the fear to die and it is hardly possible to get used to such anxiety. Parents never feel comfortable when their kids are scared to lose them.

In 2011, research was conducted in England (Gov.uk, 2017) on how children are worried about their parents' smoking. The research conducted on behalf of the Department of Health and polled 1,000 children between the ages of 7 and 13, revealing that children are so concerned about the impact of smoking on their parents' health that they would go to considerable lengths to get them to give up. The key findings of the research included among others the following: almost all (98%) children with a smoking parent wish that they would quit; almost three quarters (73%) of children with a smoking parent worry about the risk of their parent dying, a further 58% worry about the risk of heart disease; 42% of children surveyed thought smoking was dangerous.

The idea of the mobile game developed by the authors was inspired by the results of this research. The game implements a virtual emotional nonlinear dialogue of the smoking user with his child.

Before using the game the user sees the following "child's initial massage" with the description of the game rules (Figure 1):

Hello! You're a heavy smoker, aren't you... You do know how dangerous that is, don't you?
I love you and I don't want you to die and to make me orphan.
If you quit smoking I will be the happiest child in the world!

Please, do it for me! I will talk to you and help you to quit smoking.
Every two hours I will ask you how many more cigarettes you have smoked.
Please be honest with me!

I need some information from you.
Do you want to see me when I'm talking?
Then please upload then some emotional photos of me.

If the user agrees to follow the rules he is asked to indicate his relationship with the child (father, mother, grandfather, grandmother, etc.) and to upload a set of emotional photos of the child demonstrating three ranked positive (pleasure, joyfulness, happiness) and three ranked negative emotions (upset, offence, sorrow) (Figure 2).

After running the game, seven times a day the user receives a virtual message from his child with a question on how many cigarettes the user has smoked during the last period of time. To give the answer, the user pushes the corresponding digit on the screen (Figure 2).

To analyze the smoking activity the data on the number of smoked cigarettes is used. The number of smoked cigarettes (*NoC*) is represented by a two-parameter random time series variable ξ. The implementation of the random variable ξ is the number of cigarettes smoked by the user between (i-1) and i-th virtual massages from the child during the j-th day. An example of the smoking activity of the user for the previous k days is shown on the Figure 3.

Two indices are used for the assessment of the user smoking activity:

- smoking intensity index,
- smoking behavior index.

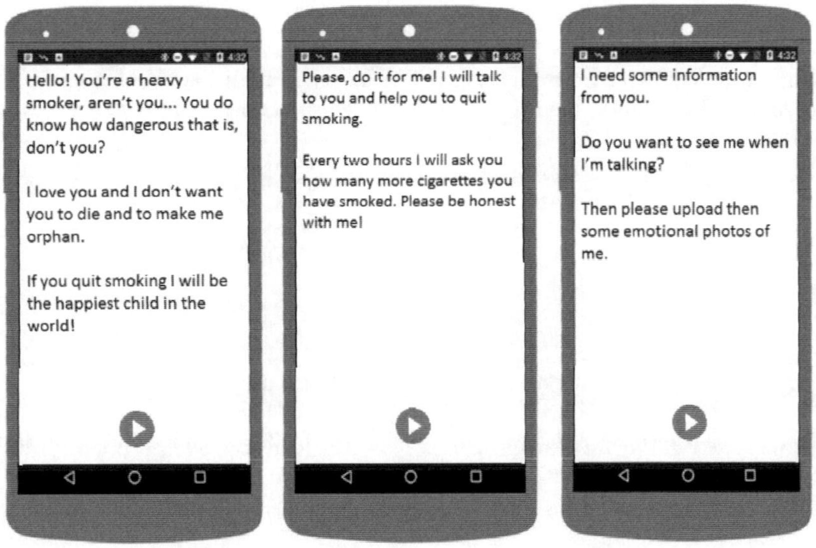

Figure 1. Screenshots "Introduction to the game"

Figure 2. Screenshots "User settings"

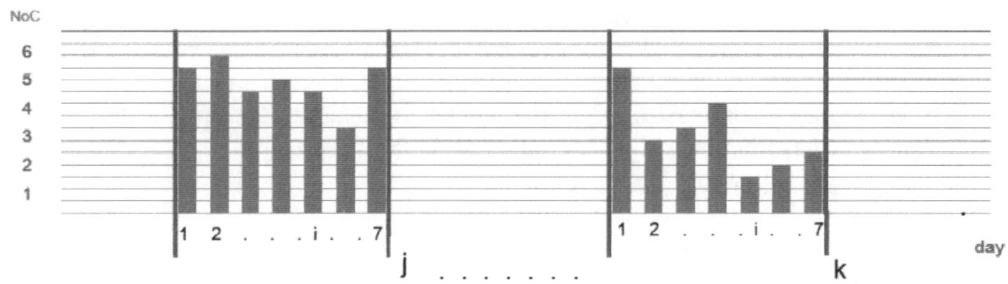

Figure 3. Smoking activity chart

Both indices reflect the changes in smoking activity of the user for a certain period of time and are calculated as the ratio of two ensemble averages. For the period for the ensemble average a week is taken as adequately reflecting the human life cycle. The first index shows the changes in the user smoking intensity during the last two weeks:

$$SmokingIntensity = \sum_{k-6}^{k} \xi_j \Big/ \sum_{k-13}^{k-7} \xi_j ,$$

where $\xi_j = \sum_{1}^{7} \xi_j^i$ – the number of cigarettes smoked during the j-th day.

The smoking behavior index reflects the changes in user smoking evenness during the last two weeks:

$$SmokingBehavior = \frac{\Delta\xi_j(Q_2)}{\Delta\xi_j(Q_1)},$$

where $Q_2 = (\xi_{k-6},...,\xi_k)$ – a set of numbers of cigarettes, smoked per day during the last week including the current day *k*,

$Q_1 = (\xi_{k-13},...,\xi_{k-7})$ – a set of numbers of cigarettes, smoked per day during the previous week,

$$\Delta\xi(Q) = \frac{1}{|Q|} * \Sigma_{j,i\in Q}\left|\xi_j^i - \xi(Q)\right|,$$

$$\xi Q = \frac{1}{|Q|} * \Sigma_{j,i\in Q}\xi_j^i,$$

$|Q|$ – cardinality of Q.

The combinations of the current values of indices are interpreted in terms of the user smoking behavior. Some examples are shown in Table 1.

The question about the current smoking activity is asked seven times a day. During the first week the information is just collected without any "feedback" to the user. Starting from the 8-th day at the end of each day the user receives the emotional photo of his child with the text comments demonstrating the child's attitude to the current smoking activity of the parent. During the second week ($k\in$[8-13]) a truncated set is used for calculating the both indices.

Table 1. Interpretations of the smoking activity indices

Indices values	Description	Interpretation
$SmokingIntensity \cong 1$ $SmokingBehavior \cong 1$	The user tends to keep smoking habits	The user doesn't take the game seriously
$SmokingIntensity < 1$ $SmokingBehavior \cong 1$	The user smokes fewer cigarettes per day but his smoking behavior has been still the same	The user tries to smoke less but he still hasn't changed his smoking behavior
$SmokingIntensity < 1$ $SmokingBehavior > 1$	The user tends to smoke less and he smoked more unevenly the last week in comparison to the previous one.	Seems the user really wants to stop smoking but he couldn't succeed so far

For organizing a dialogue with the user a nonlinear scenario is built. The scenario consists of the text messages. Each message corresponds to the current smoking status of the user, defined by the combination of values of indices and the frequency of repetition of the combination. Each message is matched to the most suitable emotional photo of the child chosen from the set provided by the user.

Depending on the values of the indices and the frequency of their repetition, the text of the message and the photo of the child become more and more emotional. Some examples of the game dialogue are shown in Figures 4-5. The values of smoking activity indices and corresponding emotions are shown in Table 2.

Table 2. Emotional interpretations of the smoking activity indices

Emotion	Indices values		Frequency
	SmokingIntensity	*SmokingBehavior*	
Upset	$\cong 1$	$\cong 1$	5-10
Anxiety	$\cong 1$	$\cong 1$	11-20
Sorrow	$\cong 1$	$\cong 1$	>30
Joyfulness	<1	>1	1-5
Pleasure	$\xi_k = 0$		1
Happiness	*0*		1

a) Emotion "Upset" b) Emotion "Anxiety" c) Emotion "Sorrow"

Figure 4. Screenshots with the virtual dialogue in the game

d) Emotion "Joyfulness" e) Emotion "Pleasure" f) Emotion "Happiness"

Figure 5. Screenshots with the virtual dialogue in the game

The game also provides the user an option of monitoring his smoking activity (it is hoped that it is the smoking cessation activity!). If the user choses the "Results" option he sees the chart demonstrating his smoking intensity (for seeing the results for a certain period if days he can swipe the screen horizontally). By touching a bar for a certain day the user sees the chart with the smoking behavior for every two hours of the chosen day (Figure 6).

Figure 6. Screenshots with the user statistics

4. CONCLUSION

The present study describes an approach for smoking cessation based on a virtual dialogue of the smoker with his loved one in a mobile game. The aim of the dialogue is to persuade a smoking user to stop smoking to make his child happy. In the current version of the game a dialogue with a limited number of smoking statuses, demonstrating the suggested approach, is implemented. The game includes functions to display data on the user's smoking history, calculation of his current smoking status, and visualization of the dialogue.

By now a group of smoking volunteers (the real smoking users) have installed the game on their mobile phones. The results of the real use of the game will be collected and analyzed in terms of an effective of the game to help people to stop smoking.

ACKNOWLEDGEMENT

The authors express their sincere gratitude to Lena Matoknina for her participation in the development of the game layouts and to her parents Andrey Matokhin and Anna Matokhina for giving their permission to use the photos of their daughter in the paper.

The reported study was funded by RFBR according to the research projects No. 16-07-00611a.

REFERENCES

Appcrawlr. (2017). Quit Smoking: Cessation Nation. [online] Available at: http://appcrawlr.com/android/quit-smoking-cessation-nation [Accessed 11 Feb. 2017].

Abroms, L., P. (2013). iPhone Adds for Smoking Cessation. American Journal of Preventive Medicine, 40(3)(279-285).

Bell, K. (2017). Best Apps to Help You Quit Smoking [New Year's Resolutions] | Cult of Mac. [online] Cult of Mac. Available at: http://www.cultofmac.com/75269/best-apps-to-help-you-quit-smoking-new-years-resolutions/ [Accessed 11 Feb. 2017].

Captain-droid.com. (2017). Get Rich or Die Smoking — Get Rich or Die Smoking скачать на Андроид бесплатно. [online] Available at: http://captain-droid.com/apps/health-and-beauty/get-rich-or-die-smoking/ [Accessed 11 Feb. 2017].

Crane, D. (2017). Smoke Free - Quit Smoking Now. [online] Smokefreeapp.com. Available at: http://smokefreeapp.com/ [Accessed 11 Feb. 2017].

El-Hilly AA, I. (2016). Smoking Cessation Through the Gamification of mHealth: A Longitudinal Qualitative Study. JMIR Serious Games, 4(2).

Gov.uk. (2017). All children really want this Christmas is their parents to quit smoking - News stories - GOV.UK. [online] Available at: https://www.gov.uk/government/news/all-children-really-want-this-christmas-is-their-parents-to-quit-smoking--2 [Accessed 11 Feb. 2017].

Healthline. (2017). The Best Quit Smoking Apps of 2016. [online] Available at: http://www.healthline.com/health/quit-smoking/top-iphone-android-apps [Accessed 11 Feb. 2017].

LIVESTRONG.COM. (2017). Calorie Tracker and MyQuit Coach Mobile Apps | LIVESTRONG.COM. [online] Available at: http://www.livestrong.com/mobile-apps/ [Accessed 11 Feb. 2017].

QuitNow!. (2017). Quitting smoking made easy!. [online] Available at: http://quitnowapp.com/ru [Accessed 11 Feb. 2017].

Quit-pro.com. (2017). Quit Pro - Smoking Cessation App for iOS and Android. [online] Available at: http://www.quit-pro.com/ [Accessed 11 Feb. 2017].

Sameapk.com. (2017). Quit smoking slowly 3.1.3 APK by MotiveBite Details. [online] Available at: https://sameapk.com/quit-smoking-slowly/ [Accessed 11 Feb. 2017].

Roxoft.hr. (2017). *Roxoft.com.* [online] Available at: http://www.roxoft.hr/index_en.html [Accessed 11 Feb. 2017].

THE T2ROL ACCESS CONTROL MODEL FOR MOBILE HEALTH SYSTEMS IN DEVELOPING COUNTRIES

Jane Katusiime[1,2] and Niels Pinkwart[1]
[1]*Department of Computer Science - Humboldt Universität zu Berlin, Unter den Linden 6, 10099 Berlin- Germany*
[2]*Department of Computer Science-Mbarara University of Science and Technology, P.O.Box 1410, Mbarara- Uganda*

ABSTRACT

In resource constrained settings faced with scarcity of health practitioners and poor infrastructure, coupled with the high penetration of mobile technology, use of mobile technology seems to be a feasible way of improving health care service delivery especially in developing countries. However, mHealth systems are faced with security and privacy challenges such as third party attacks and eavesdropping among others. Much as the available security models such as RBAC, TMAC and TBAC have been successfully used in mHealth systems, security and privacy issues still persist. In addition, these models may not be applied in some contexts in developing countries such as in situations where mobile devices are shared and where some users are illiterate among others. This paper presents a hybrid model based on role-based, team-based and task-based models specifically tailored to the context of mobile health in developing countries. In this paper we discuss the formal description of the model and give an application example.

KEYWORDS

Security Models, Access Control, Mhealth Systems, Developing Countries, Mobile Phones

1. INTRODUCTION

Mobile health (mHealth) systems are gradually gaining popularity in regards to patient follow-up, communication, and lifestyle management among others. This can be attributed to the increased penetration of mobile devices due to their easy mobility, low costs, convenience and ability to be used in remote areas where infrastructure is poor (Napoleon & Bhuiyan 2010). Moreover, in resource constrained settings faced with scarcity of health practitioners, use of mobile technology seems to be a feasible way of improving health care service delivery. However, privacy issues such as eavesdropping and third party attacks among others remain a challenge to mHealth systems. Social technical factors such as cultural differences and low literacy levels among others also contribute to the privacy and security issues. Due to the sensitivity of health information, there is an ethical need to equip mobile health systems with adequate security measures to safeguard patient's information. Existing health systems attempt to safeguard client's information by implementing access control security models.

However security/ privacy issues still persist because health systems present a new set of privacy and security requirements such as the inevitable need for shared access of patients information. For example, a patient may be examined in one hospital, her case reviewed by experts in another health facility and then treated by health practitioners in yet another different hospital depending on where the required expertise is available. This may be across health facilities within a country or facilities across different countries or continents. This makes health systems largely distributed and complex. The complexity is even more in mHealth systems that introduce the location component thus raising the need for more reliable security models to ensure consistency and accuracy of information. In this paper we propose an access control model that enables hierarchical structuring of tasks, roles and teams and introduce the component of location.

2. USAGE CASE FOR MOBILE TECHNOLOGY IN DEVELOPING COUNTRIES

Penetration of mobile technology is on a continuous rise especially in developing nations. This can be attributed to reduction in prices among other factors. There is an increase in the number of people who own cell phones and much as the coverage of smart phones is still low in developing nations, research shows that there is a continuous increase in the number of people who own smart phones in these countries. However, according to the world development report(Version 2016), much as more people are acquiring mobile phones globally, there is still gender divide whereby women are less likely to own phones let alone smart phones compared to their male counterparts. This is even worse in developing countries where trends show that even with the increasing acquisition of cell phones, the number of women that own cell phones is still low and the number of those with smart phones is even much low (Poushter 2016).Use of internet is also on increase but it is also affected by the gender divide (James 2011). This in most cases forces women to share mobile phones with their male counterparts (James 2011). This is attributed to cultural influence and gender insensitive resource distribution among others.

Despite increase in ownership of mobile phones, the sharing phenomenon may take long to gradually reduce because some of the cultures in these nations are more characterized by sharing resources as a cultural aspect rather than scarcity. In other words, there is communal ownership of resources including technology especially at family level. This poses privacy and security challenges to mobile systems because users are skeptical about using systems that capture sensitive information due to the fear of having the information accessed by the people with whom they share the devices (Jennings et al. 2013). In some communities, to overcome these challenges, individuals resort to owning personal simcards which they use every time they have access to the shared mobile phones. This however leads to quick wear and tear of both the mobile phones and the simcards.

Available mobile health systems face privacy and security issues as a result of challenges discussed above. Much as privacy and security are vital for systems that handle sensitive information such as banking systems among others, lack of privacy in health systems may present life threatening consequences. For instance, absence of privacy may prompt patients to provide false information about their illnesses and worse still avoid seeking healthcare in an attempt to avoid stigmatization, embarrassment, loss of insurance and jobs among others. This may result into provision of wrong medications since the diagnosis is based on inaccurate information and in some cases death may result. There is a need for access control models that put into consideration the attributes of phone sharing and literacy among other aspects.

We propose a Team-Task-Role and location based access control (T^2RoL) hybrid model for mHealth systems that will ensure privacy and security of users including those that share mobile devices and are illiterate. The model is applicable to two categories of users i.e. literate health practitioners who share mobile devices during health care service delivery and the patients who share mobile phones and may be illiterate or literate. It is also important to note that the proposed model may be applied in other mobile systems that deal with sensitive information such as banking. However it is specifically applicable in mHealth and more specifically maternal health due to the vulnerability of women in cultures especially in developing countries that are characterized by male dominance, whereby males control resources. Therefore women end up relying on men for resources such as mobile devices, since they cannot afford to buy them for themselves. In some cases, men may even prohibit women from owning mobile devices, and this forces them to share with their male partners. Furthermore, pregnant women and nursing mothers are less mobile, and therefore, are most likely to be in settings where mobile devices may be shared. It is also important to note that this model can be useful everywhere but it is more applicable to developing countries due to the contexts such as mobile phone sharing.

3. SECURITY MODELS USED IN HEALTH CARE SYSTEMS AND REQUIREMENTS FOR THE PROPOSED MODEL

If patient information is to be kept private, it is paramount to have a strict mechanism of limiting access permission in health care systems. It is a requirement in access control models to limit access permissions based on roles, tasks, teams and location among others. Research shows that there are no models that grant access permission based on all the four components (roles, tasks, teams and location) while considering developing countries contexts like device sharing as discussed below.

Security models implemented in health systems are mainly access control models. Access control models are more concerned with limiting the behaviour and operations of the user(Zhang et al. 2006). Commonly used models are Role-based Access Control (RBAC) model (Sandhu et al. 1995), (Ferraiolo et al. 2001) Team-based Access Control (TMAC) model (Thomas 1997) and Task-based Access Control (TBAC) model (Zhang et al. 2006). However, the first access control security models were Discretionary Access Control (DAC) and Mandatory Access Control (MAC). Access control models utilize various access control techniques such as access control matrix, access control lists constrained user interfaces, content and context dependent access control and rule based access control (Hu et al. 2014).

MAC enforces access control independent of user operations and controls disclosure of information by assigning and limiting access to objects and subjects at various security levels. It is more concerned with issues of confidentiality than integrity (Hu et al. 2006), (Ausanka-Crues 2011). MAC is considered suitable for military systems and commercial systems such as financial management systems which are highly prone to attacks and therefore are more concerned with confidentiality. However it is less suitable for healthcare systems because it limits the user's actions and restricts users from controlling their data. On the other hand, DAC controls access basing on the object permission level. It grants users access to objects/ information they own. However, allowing this kind of access makes the system vulnerable to attacks. For instance limited control of copying privileges by DAC opens way for Trojan attacks. The mentioned limitations of MAC and DAC led to the development of RBAC and later TBAC and TMAC among others.

RBAC incorporates features from both DAC and MAC. It encompasses both integrity and confidentiality but puts more emphasis on integrity.

RBAC assigns roles to users, permissions to roles and users get permissions by playing roles and the whole process is managed by a security administrator. Much as users are granted access to roles, they have no rights to transfer permissions assigned to them to other users. With RBAC, access permission is associated to a role and then the role is associated with the user. The key strength of this model is that it enables separation of duties(Ferraiolo et al. 2001). RBAC promotes system integrity and easy access control in organisations with many users since multiple users can be allocated a single role. However, the need for customised privileges and role inheritance may make administration in large systems based on RBAC unmanageable.

Managing roles and users is difficult especially in cases where roles fluctuate in an organization due to varying organizational needs. In addition, some users may sometimes half-fill multiple roles. Furthermore, RBAC may not easily and quickly subdivide roles into new permissions to new users in cases of emergency. For instance, in a healthcare setting where a particular doctor is assigned specific patients, absence of this doctor due to emergency situations such as accident would necessitate another medical personnel to immediately take up some or all the roles of the absent doctor. This may call for access of private and sensitive information such as passwords and this would breach the privacy and security component of RBAC which is based on roles. To control crime in such scenarios, some systems are configured to monitor users and permissions they access so as to keep track of who did what and when. This further interferes with privacy and security of users of such health systems.

TMAC model is mainly used in collaborative environments and access control is based on teams whereby access rights are given to groups of users. In this case, a team is a collection of users with individual roles who collaborate with the aim of achieving a specific goal/ task. In TMAC, a user can only access resources allocated to a team in which they belong. However, permissions are granted based on the roles the individual users are assigned to in the team and the activity the team is working on at that moment.

The main advantage of TMAC is that it allows for dynamic management of permissions as tasks progress to completion (Thomas 1997). It can activate permissions for a particular user based on situation at hand and it is therefore referred to as an active security model (Georgiadis et al. 2001). However, the limitation of TMAC is that it does not have self- administration capabilities.

TBAC model is based on tasks and permission control is dynamic. When authorisation is activated, the permissions associated to it are activated too and then the user can then use the permissions to run the task. The user can not use the permissions unless they have been activated. Tasks in TBAC have time restrictions and therefore the users to have time limitations on the permissions granted to them. Permissions assigned to the user during task processing are withdrawn from the user when the task is stopped or ended.

The advantage of TBAC is that it is dynamic and therefore supports real time processing of tasks, and supports least privilege processes(Zhang et al. 2006). Access control is not static and it may vary depending on the situation of the task. However, in large systems where processes are many, processing time will increase.

With the persistence of privacy and security issues, more new access control models are being proposed. Most of these models are an extension or combination of RBAC, TBAC and TMAC. They include Situation, Team and Role based Access control (STRAC), Context-based Team access control (C-TMAC), Task Role-based Access control (TRBAC), Spatial Role-based access control (SRBAC), Object relationship- based access control (RoBAC), Attribute-based Access control (ABAC) among others. It should however be noted that most of these models are relatively new and have not yet been deployed on a large scale.

STRAC introduces the concept of situations to RBAC and TMAC such as emergencies. In addition to assigning access permissions to users depending on roles and teams, STRAC further assigns situations to users and assigns access permissions to users based on the situations (Kawagoe & Kasai 2011). However STRAC does not specify the hierarchy structures of situations, teams and roles.

On the other hand, C-TMAC(Georgiadis et al. 2001) integrates and extends RBAC and TMAC by introducing contextual information such as location where access is requested, time of access, location of the object to be accessed, etc.

TRBAC combines RBAC and TBAC by appointing tasks to roles and permissions to tasks (Zhang et al. 2006). In other words, the user is appointed to a role, and then the user acquires tasks to carry out based on the role. On the other hand, unlike other access models, RoBAC (Krishnamoorthy et al. 2016) is based on the relations held among the users and the class relations in the java programming. It is meant for a cloud environment.

SRBAC extends RBAC by adding a spatial component of utilising location information in the definitions of the security policy (Hansen & Oleshchuk 2003). In this model, assignment of permissions is dependent on location and therefore a user assigned to a role could have different permissions depending on their location.

ABAC (Hu et al. 2014) is based on attributes associated with the subject, objects and requested operations. When a user requests access, the access is granted or denied basing on the attributes assigned to that user, attributes of the object and attributes associated with the operation being requested and in some cases the environment conditions. We summarise the limitations of the current security models in the table below.

Table 1. Limitations of the Current Security Models

Access permission	RBAC	STRAC	C-TMAC	TBAC	TRBAC	TMAC	SRBAC
Access based on roles	√	√	√		√	√	√
Access based on tasks				√	√		
Access based on teams		√	√			√	
Access based on location			√				√

Based on the above analysis of the models, it is evident that the available models have limitations in addressing privacy and security challenges. RBAC, TMAC and TBAC which are commonly used attempt to solve these challenges but they are limited. RBAC for instance, tries to bridge the security gap by assigning roles to users and granting permissions based on the roles. This implies that all users with the same role have the same permissions. However this is not practical and makes the model less unusable in real life especially in healthcare settings. For example, even if two nurses have the same role, they may not have access to the same patient records. On the other hand, TMAC tries to solve the collaborative challenges by combining roles and teams permissions. In this model, members in the same team are assigned the same set of permissions. This is problematic because even if users belong to the same team, they may not play the same role. For example a doctor may play the role of team manager in one team and a team member in another team.

Mobile health systems pose even more privacy and security challenges to the available access control security models because they are affected by location of users, an attribute most of the available models are unable to address. This is made more complex in situations where the mobile devices are shared. There are new access control security models such as Context Team- based Access control (C-TMAC) and Spatial Role-based Access Control (SRBAC) that try to address contextual challenges such as location and time. However, they do not specify the hierarchy structures of situations, teams and roles which is a vital component in healthcare.

There is a need to develop more reliable security models for healthcare systems since according to research (Abou et al. 2003), (Xiao et al. 2010) they are prone to attacks. To address some of the challenges discussed above, we propose T^2RoL access control model that will facilitate sharing of sensitive information while enhancing security of mobile healthcare systems by enabling access permission based on a concatenation of task, role, team and location of the user while taking into consideration of factors like sharing of mobile devices and literacy level of the user.

3.1 Integrating RBAC, TBAC, TMAC and Location

In RBAC, a user can have access to several permissions assigned to a role which that user is assigned to whereas in TMAC, users have access to permissions available to the team in which they belong. On the other hand, in TBAC, users have access to permissions based on the tasks they are assigned to. As earlier discussed in section 3, these models face challenges. In T^2RoL, we integrate RBAC, TBAC and TMAC while including location information in the security policy definitions as illustrated in figure 1 below.

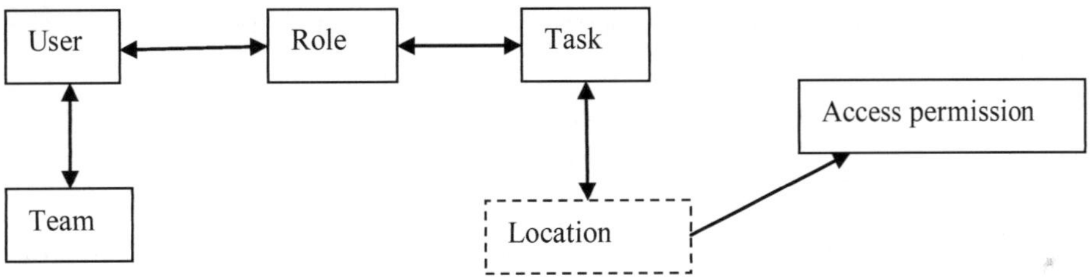

Figure 1. Illustration of T^2RoL

3.2 Formal description of T^2RoL

The new model consists of seven components namely users, tasks, roles, teams, permissions, locations and sessions. A user (U) is an employee that utilizes the system and is considered to be a mobile subject. A task (T) is a unit of work flow and it may have sub-tasks whereas a role (R) is a job function associated with the responsibility and qualifications of a user to perform tasks. On the other hand, a team (Tm) is a group of users with a goal of achieving a given task and permission (P) is an approval to access data objects and to execute operations. A location (L) represents an area identifiable by the system. In this model, we assume that the location of the user can be identified and verified by the network based on the underlying network architecture. A session (S) is a duration during which a user activates a role. A user can be assigned to roles, teams and location but the roles assigned to the users are based on the tasks that they are to complete. Based on the task, role, team and location, access permissions are assigned to a user in a given session.

$\{u_1, u_2, u_3, u_4 \ldots\ldots\ldots u_n\} \in U$

$\{t_1, t_2, t_3, t_4 \ldots\ldots\ldots t_n\} \in T$

$\{r_1, r_2, r_3, r_4 \ldots\ldots\ldots r_n\} \in R$

$\{tm_1, tm_2, tm_3, tm_4 \ldots\ldots\ldots tm_n\} \in Tm$

$\{p_1, p_2, p_3, p_4 \ldots\ldots\ldots p_n\} \in P$

$\{l_1, l_2, l_3, l_4 \ldots\ldots\ldots l_n\} \in L$

$\{s_1, s_2, s_3, s_4 \ldots\ldots\ldots s_n\} \in S$

Flow element relationships

- UTA $\subseteq$ UxT and is a many-to-many user to task assignment relation (A denotes assignment)
- URA $\subseteq$ UxR and is a many-to-many user to role assignment relation
- TRA $\subseteq$ TxR and is a one-to-many task to role assignment relation
- UTmA $\subseteq$ UxTm and is a many-to-many user to team assignment relation
- ULA $\subseteq$ UxL and is a one-to-many user to location assignment relation
- UPA $\subseteq$ UxP and is a many-to-many user to permission assignment relation
- TPA $\subseteq$ TxP and is a many-to-many team to permission assignment relation

Model functions

- Session-user (SU): S $\rightarrow$U is a function mapping session s $\in$ S to a user
- Session- role (SR): S $\rightarrow 2^R$ is a function mapping session s $\in$ S to roles whereby SR $\subseteq$ {r| (u,r) $\in$ URA }
- Session- task (ST): S $\rightarrow 2^T$ is a function mapping session s $\in$ S to tasks whereby ST $\subseteq$ {t| (u,t) $\in$ UTA }
- Session- team (STm): S $\rightarrow 2^{Tm}$ is a function mapping session s $\in$ S to teams whereby STm$\subseteq${tm|(u,tm)$\in$UTmA }
- Session- location (SL): S $\rightarrow 2^L$ is a function mapping session s $\in$ S to location whereby SL$\subseteq${l|(u,l)$\in$ULA }
- Task- role (TR): T $\rightarrow 2^R$ is a function mapping task t $\in$ T to roles whereby TR $\subseteq$ {r| (t,r) $\in$ TRA }
- Team- user (TmU): Tm $\rightarrow 2^U$ is a function mapping team tm $\in$ Tm to users whereby TmU$\subseteq${u|(u,tm)$\in$UTmA }

The user needs to access a combination of permissions based on his role, the task at hand, the team she belongs to and the location.

- Role based permission for a user = Session-role permission + Team-role permission + Task-role permission where "+" denotes combination
- Location based permission = Role based permission + Location based location

3.3 Application Example of T²RoL

Due to poor infrastructure that make it hard for women to frequently travel long distances to the hospital to access maternal health related services, a referral hospital decides to temporality extend its maternal health services to remote villages by operating mobile clinics. The hospital dispatches a team of gynecologists and medical lab scientist but realizes the need for the teams to have access to the health records of the patients (women in the villages they are going to) which are securely kept on the server in the hospital. The teams decide to carry mobile devices that have an mHealth app installed to enable them access the records but there is a need for a secure mechanism to access the records. We explain how the new model achieves this. It is however important to note that the current models have to some extent been successful in securing patient's information but most of the systems that employ these models are based in hospitals where access permissions are based on the locations within the hospital premises. Also, much as mHealth systems enable the patient and health practitioners to be virtual, this may require complicated authentication procedures that illiterate people may not be able to accomplish.

In this example John and Sarah are Mary are users belonging to different collaborating teams and with different tasks and roles. In this example, they are operating outside hospital premises in what we may refer to as a mobile clinic and using mobile devices to access patient data from the hospital. John is a gynecologist while Mary is a medical lab scientist.

U= {John, Mary, Sarah}

R= {Gynecologist, medical lab scientist}

T= {Treat patient, order lab test, perform lab test}

P= {Access patient records, Fill lab results form}

Tm= {Gynecology team, medical lab team}

Patient record: Patient(code, name, contact, due date, medical condition)

URA= {(John, Gynecologist), (Medical lab scientist)}
UTm={(John, Gynecology team), (Sarah, Gynecology team), (Mary, medical lab team)}
TRA= {(Treat patient, Gynecologist), (Order lab test, Gynecologist), (perform lab test, medical lab scientist)}
ULA= {(John, mobile clinic), (Sarah, mobile clinic), (Mary, mobile clinic)}
UPA= {(John, (Read(Patient code, name, age, due date, contacts, medical condition))), (Sarah, (Read(Patient code, name, age, due date, contacts, medical condition))), (Mary, Read patient code)}

Session assignments

Session 1:
User (s1)= {John, Sarah}
Session role (s1)= {Gynecologist}
Session team (s1)= {Gynecology team}
Session location= { mobile clinic }

Session 2:
User (s2)= {Mary}
Session role (s1)= {Medical lab scientist}
Session team (s1)= {Medical lab team}
Session location= {mobile clinic}

The assignment process

Step1: Detecting task and role- from John's task of treating patient and his role as a gynecologist, permission privileges for task and role are detected in session 1.

Step 2: Detecting team- from John's team (gynecology team), privileges for the team are detected.

Step 3: Detecting location- John's location and patient's location are detected and in this example they are in a location outside hospital premises. John's location and the patient's location must be the same in order for the location privileges to be accessed.

Step 4: Access privilege concatenation- Privileges from step 1,2 and 3 are concatenated and assigned to the user (John). In other words, John must be assigned a task of treating a patient A, a role as a gynecologist, assigned to the gynecology team and be in the same location as patient A before any access privileges are granted to him. The same applies to Mary in session 2. However, for step 3, Mary's location must be the same as the doctor's and patient's location and the doctor must have performed the task "order lab test".

Sarah is trying to access records of patient B, whom she had actually treated before in the hospital. However Sarah is unable to access the records of the patient because this patient shares her mobile phone with the husband (who is at the moment in possession of the phone and not at the mobile clinic) which implies that the system is picking the location of the patient's husband. This means that Sarah's location and the patient's location are perceived to be different and thus access permission is denied. On day two, due to the increasing number of patients, Allen- one the doctors from the hospital decides to spend her day off by volunteering at the mobile clinic. Allen is assigned a task of treating patients and a role as a gynecologist in the hospital but since she is not assigned to the team of gynecologists working on the mobile clinic, then she is denied access to records of patients handled in the clinic. At the end of the day, Mary who is the only medical lab scientist in the clinic seems to be remaining with many tests to carry out. John who was a medical lab scientist before becoming a gynecologist decides to help Mary to do some of the lab tests. However John is denied access to permissions meant for medical lab scientists such as results entry forms because he was not assigned the task of performing lab tests and the role as medical lab scientist.

It is important to note that access control and denial of access permissions is crucial in health care systems that capture sensitive patient information. However, if strict access control is not carefully handled, it may slow down work flow processes. To address this trade off, we shall enable remote assignment of tasks, roles, teams and locations by an administrator in the hospital.

It is also important to note that data is encrypted to prevent unauthorized people from intercepting and accessing information. Furthermore, patient consent is sought and granted by acceptance to share current location and other vital information such as date of birth and mobile phone number. This patient information is captured in the hospital system during registration and is checked together with the location before access is granted.

4. CONCLUSION AND OUTLOOK

In this paper, we propose a hybrid model called T^2RoL. This model is a combination of the existing TMAC, RBAC and TBAC with addition of a location component. This model allows flexible permission activation in mobile environments. We believe that T^2RoL will be a good starting point for further research into security models for mHealth systems especially in developing countries where circumstances like epidemic outbreaks may necessitate some doctors to operate mobile clinics. In our future work we will evaluate the model by implementing it using a health care system. We will do extensive empirical studies and evaluate the impact of the model implementation on security and usability of mHealth systems. In the implementation, we shall take into account cases of "possessive husband" by creating double login mechanisms whereby a user can login into the same system but access different forms of data.

ACKNOWLEDGEMENT

We are grateful to all the stakeholders (KAAD, Humboldt university of Berlin and Mbarara University of Science and Technology) for the financial support and collaboration.

REFERENCES

Abou, A., Kalam, E. & Deswarte, Y., 2003. SECURITY MODEL FOR HEALTH CARE COMPUTING AND COMMUNICATION SYSTEMS. *springer Science Business Media new york*, Security a.

Ausanka-Crues, R., 2011. Methods for access control : Advances and limitations. *Harvey Mudd Colledge*, pp.1–5.

Ferraiolo, D.F. et al., 2001. Proposed NIST standard for role-based access control. *ACM Transactions on Information and System Security*, 4(3), pp.224–274.

Georgiadis, C.K., Pangalos, G. & Thomas, R.K., 2001. Flexible Team-based Access Control Using Contexts. *SACMAT.*

Hansen, F. & Oleshchuk, V., 2003. SRBAC : A Spatial Role-Based Access Control Model for Mobile Systems. *NORDSEC'03. Proceedings of the 8th Nordic Workshop on Secure IT Systems*, pp.129 – 141.

Hu, V.C. et al., 2014. Guide to attribute based access control (abac) definition and considerations. *NIST Special Publication*, 800.

Hu, V.C.V., Ferraiolo, D.F. & Kuhn, D.R., 2006. Assessment of access control systems. *Nist interagency report 7316*, p.60.

James, J., 2011. Sharing mobile phones in developing countries: Implications for the digital divide. *Technological Forecasting and Social Change*, 78(4), pp.729–735.

Jennings, L. et al., 2013. Exploring the use of mobile phone technology for the enhancement of the prevention of mother-to-child transmission of HIV program in Nyanza, Kenya: a qualitative study. *BMC public health*, 13, p.1131.

Kawagoe, K. & Kasai, K., 2011. Situation , Team and Role based Access Control. , 7(5), pp.629–637.

Krishnamoorthy, G., Umamaheswari, N. & Venkatesh, R., 2016. RoBAC — A New Way of Access Control for cloud. *Circuits and Systems*, 7(May), pp.1113–1119.

Napoleon, A.E. & Bhuiyan, M.S.H., 2010. Contemporary Research on Mobile Government. *Scandinavian Workshop on e-Government (SVEG)*, pp.1–13.

Poushter, J., 2016. Smartphone Ownership and Internet Usage Continues to Climb in Emerging Economies. *Pew Research Center*, pp.1–5.

Sandhu, R.S. et al., 1995. Role-Based Access Control Models. *IEEE Computer*, 29(2), pp.38–47.

Thomas, R.K., 1997. Team-based access control (TMAC): a primitive for applying role-based access controls in collaborative environments. In *Proceedings of the second ACM workshop on Role-based access control*. pp.13–19.

Version, W., 2016. World Development Report 2016. , (91877), pp.1–18.

Xiao, L. et al., 2010. A knowledgeable security model for distributed health information systems. *Computers & Security*, 29(3), pp.331–349.

Zhang, C., Zhang, Y.H.U.G. & Chin, P.R., 2006. Task-Role Based Dual System Access Control Model. *IJCSNS International Journal of Computer Science and Network Security*, 6(7), pp.211–215.

PRE-COMMERCIAL PROCUREMENT OF PERSONAL HEALTH SERVICES – INTEROPERABILITY CONSIDERATIONS

Jaakko Lähteenmäki[1], Juha Leppänen[1], Anna Sachinopoulou[1], Jean Patrick Mathieu[2], Rossana Alessandrello[2] and Suzan Ikävalko[3]

[1] *VTT Technical Research Centre of Finland - Tietotie 3, FI-02650 Espoo, Finland*

[2] *Agency for Health Quality and Assessment of Catalonia (AQUAS) - Carrer de Roc Boronat, 81-95, 08005 Barcelona, Spain*

[3] *Nordic Healthcare Group - Vattuniemenranta 2, FI-00210 Helsinki, Finland*

ABSTRACT

Public healthcare providers are increasingly guiding their patients to using personal health services to support self-care. The provider is typically in the role of specifying the required functionalities and purchasing the technologies to be used by the patient. A new pre-commercial procurement (PCP) model has been introduced by the European Union with the objective of increasing use of new innovative technologies and interaction between the procurers and technology suppliers. The model is well fitted for personal health services where there is a high potential for exploiting advanced information and communication technologies (ICT). When applying the PCP model it is important to ensure that the developed prototypes can be integrated to the existing health IT infrastructure. This is particularly important when the developed service needs to exchange information with Electronic Health Record (EHR) or Personal Health Record (PHR) systems. Since the relevant interfaces are still largely missing from existing EHRs and PHRs it is important to provide test interfaces, which enable the developed services to be tested for interoperability during the PCP process. This paper provides background for the interoperability needs of personal health services and describes the test server solution developed in the context of the DECIPHER PCP project. Based on feedback from the supplier companies the test server was an acceptable and useful solution for the development phase as actual PHR interfaces have not yet been implemented by the procurers.

KEYWORDS

Pre-commercial procurement, personal health services, cross-border health, interoperability, interface testing

1. INTRODUCTION

ICT (Information and Communications Technology) based services and applications have shown potential in supporting self-care and health maintenance. Patients with chronic diseases may carry out blood glucose, blood pressure and other measurements at home and share the results with their care providers (Klersy et al., 2009; Orsama et al., 2013). Services and applications may motivate individuals for healthy life styles by tracking physical activity and eating habits. Although a large variety of personal health services is already in the market, there is a high potential for new innovations with impact on personal health and healthcare efficacy.

The exploitation of new technology is currently suboptimal due to the fact, that development of new innovations takes place in companies without either sufficient connection to healthcare provider organizations or knowledge about healthcare domain and its regulatory constraints (e.g. the Medical Device Directive, 93/42/EEC). This often leads to services not matching with the needs of the procurer organizations and end-users. Pre-commercial procurement (PCP) has the potential of combining the R&D work of innovative companies with public procurers' need for new services (Hommen & Rolfstam, 2009). The European Commission has invested in several projects with the objective of developing and demonstrating viable PCP practices in a variety of industry sectors, including robotics, traffic, boarder security, firemen security and education[1].

This paper addresses the application of PCP to personal health service development in a setting where three procurers from different countries are involved. In such case the interoperability challenges are particularly high, as the developed services and applications should be connectable with existing distributed and fragmented national system infrastructures. Moreover, the related data contents are highly confidential, sensitive and heterogeneous, including structured and unstructured data. At the same time, the services are provided by a diverse group of companies. The paper addresses the PCP process and focuses on the related interoperability challenges, which are especially high in a cross-border setting. We will describe the test server approach set up in the DECIPHER project for ensuring a minimum level of interoperability. DECIPHER is among the first PCP projects initiated in the 7th Framework Programme of the EU.

2. PRE-COMMERCIAL PROCUREMENT

Public healthcare providers have an important role in recruiting patients to self-management programs, monitoring their progress and providing feedback. In many countries it is widely accepted that self-management tools and related costs should be completely or partly subsidized by the society. In such case, the services need to be purchased via public procurement processes.

Pre-commercial procurement refers to the situation where a public body is buying research and development work from companies. The European Union has proposed a model for applying PCP in harmony with the existing public procurement legislation (Figure 1). The model highlights the difference of “pre-commercial” and “commercial” part of the total procurement process. In the start of the pre-commercial development activity companies are selected to participate based on a public tendering process. The pre-commercial tendering process does not fall under WTO’s (World Trade Organization) Government Procurement Agreement (GPA) nor the national procurement legislation and the new EU public procurement directive (2014/24/EU). Therefore, it can be carried out along a lighter and faster process as compared with the conventional public procurement process. The pre-commercial development process involves parallel development of ideas by multiple companies. After the initial awards, the development process is carried out in three phases with evaluations at the end of each phase. During the process the number of companies reduces as only part of the companies qualify to continue to the next phase. The interactive and iterative development process of the PCP model is particularly intended to produce new innovations applicable to real-world problems. The model helps to steer the development of solutions towards the concrete needs of the procurers and end-users. IPRs (Intellectual Property Rights) are left partly or completely with the supplier companies to ensure further exploitation. Following with the risk-benefit principle, own investment to the R&D work is required from the suppliers. After the pre-commercial part the procurer shall organize a commercial tendering process in order to implement the R&D results as an operational service.

[1] https://ec.europa.eu/digital-single-market/en/pre-commercial-procurement

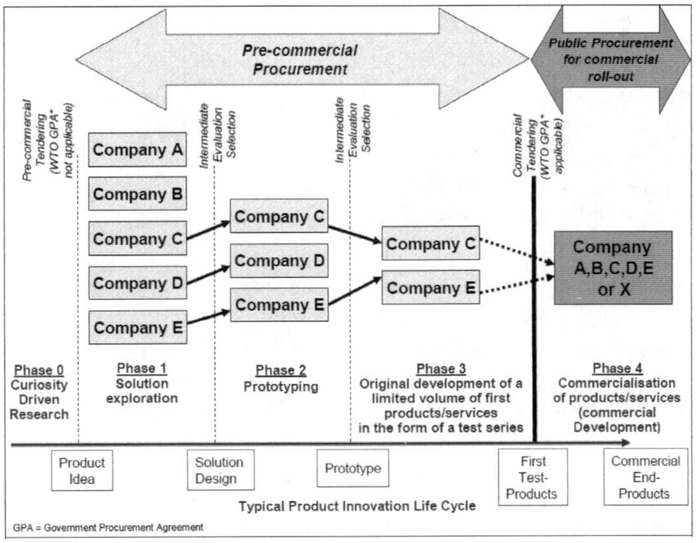

Figure 1. Pre-commercial procurement model proposed by the European Union (EU COM 2007:799)

3. PERSONAL HEALTH SERVICE INTEROPERABILITY

The PCP model referred above is well fitted for personal health service development where there is a high potential for exploiting advanced ICT. New technology enables monitoring of health parameters with minimal user effort and with automatic feedback based on intelligent analysis of monitoring data. Advances in natural language processing (e.g. automatic language translation) provide a basis for intelligent cross-border health applications. IoT-technologies (Internet of Things) enables health related data to be effectively collected from devices and sensors. These developments hold the promise of empowering the patients for self-care and thereby reducing the demand pressure towards conventional healthcare services.

The PCP-model is expected to produce disruptive innovations as it leaves considerable freedom for the companies to develop new solutions. It is left to the companies to select which technologies they apply in the service development. However, it is the procurers' responsibility to define the interfaces for connecting the services with the rest of the service system and the clinical processes. The healthcare provider has an EHR system (Electronic Health Record) which the clinicians intensively use in the clinical process to access and enter patient data (Kalra, 2006). Additionally the health provider may maintain a PHR system (Personal Health Record) where the patient can access and enter patient data (Jones et al., 2010). Various types of applications and services are used for collecting health monitoring data and for supporting health delivery in the case of acute illness. For example, a service may help the care givers to access the essential health history of the patient as depicted in Figure 2. The service should be able to retrieve such information from the EHR or PHR system. Also in the case of supporting chronic disease management the exchange of data with electronic health records is crucial (White et al., 2016). Integration of monitoring systems with EHR and PHR systems would allow self-measurement data to be directly made available to the clinicians. Unfortunately the interface for data exchange is rarely available: many EHR and PHR systems still lack the required capabilities to connect with external services.

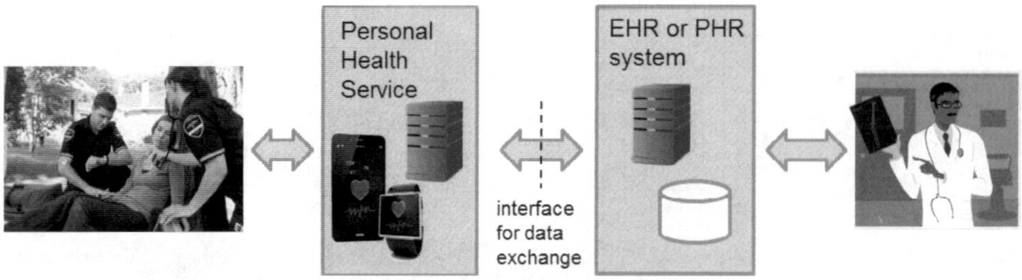

Figure 2. Personal health service exploits an open interface in providing access to patient's critical health history in the context of acute illness

Another challenge arises from the differences of healthcare system infrastructures between countries. Although interoperability standards exist and are adopted by many EHR systems there are national differences in the way standards are implemented. Therefore, personal health systems intended for international markets should be capable of using variable standards and clinical coding systems in order to connect with local EHR and PHR systems. This capability is especially important when the application shall support cross-border health scenarios. For example, in the case of acute illness abroad a personal application should be able to support the care process in the visited country.

4. CASE: DECIPHER PCP

The PCP process carried out in the DECIPHER[2] project was aimed at the development of a mobile service supporting cross-border health. The objective was to support chronic disease management and acute care episodes faced during travelling or living abroad. The PCP was a joint action of three procurers: NHS/Trustech (Manchester/UK), ESTAR (Toscana/Italy) and TicSalut (Catalonia/Spain). The process was led by AQUAS (Spain) and supported by Anci Innovazione (Italy), Eurecat (Spain) and VTT (Finland).

The process followed the model depicted in Figure 1. In the public tendering process, nine companies were selected to participate phase 1. In subsequent phases, the number of companies was reduced to six and three respectively. The development work carried out in the project was guided via the requirements and evaluation criteria set out in the challenge brief of the invitation to tender (ITT). The intention was to avoid detailed specifications, and instead formulate problems to be solved, thereby leaving room for participating companies to propose innovative solutions. Along with this freedom came the need to monitor and evaluate the outcomes of the development activity during the PCP process. In line with Figure 1, the development of technical solutions took place in three consecutive steps. During each phase the companies were requested to provide a Interim Outcome Report (IOR) which included the relevant service descriptions and demonstrations reflecting the current status of development. In the subsequent phases the companies were requested to provide service concept descriptions (phase 1), initial prototypes (phase 2) and final prototypes (phase 3). The MOR provided a way to follow the progress and give feedback to the companies before the end of the phase. The final results were evaluated after each phase by expert groups consisting of project partners and external experts. Based on the evaluation the companies granted for next phase were selected.

All resulting applications of the PCP process included basic functionalities related Diabetes management and the functionality to support quick access to essential health data in the context of urgent health episodes. Typically the applications included sections for inserting and viewing important health related parameters such as medication, physical activity, encounters, nutrition, etc. (Figure **3**a). Additionally the applications included functionalities for guiding the patient for self-care and providing feedback (Figure **3**b). In most applications it was possible to define a subset of data to be quickly available in the user interface in the case of emergency (Figure **3**c). Also the idea of providing automatic emergency calls was presented (Figure **3**d). Companies addressed the cross-border aspect by claiming support to standard interfaces for data exchange and support for language translations of static and dynamic contents.

---

[2] http://decipherpcp.eu

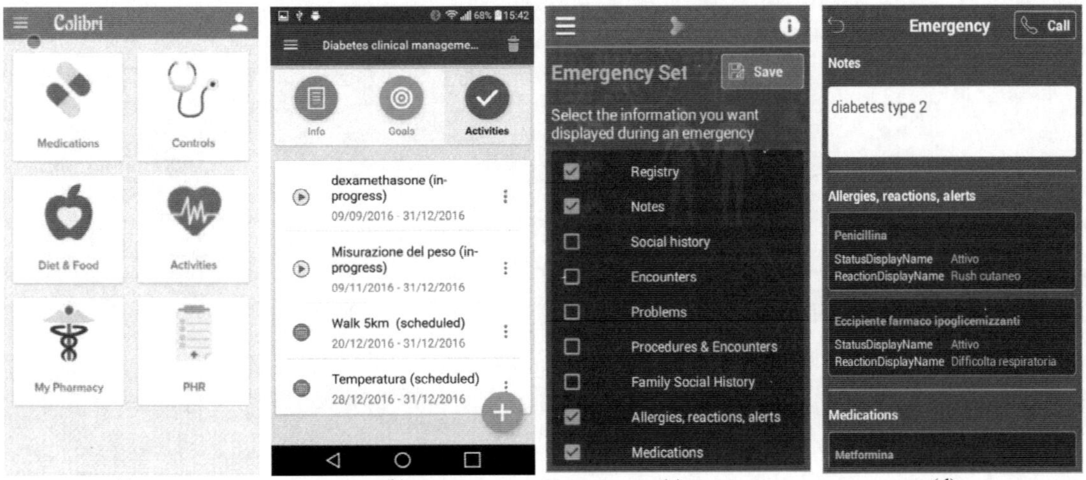

(a) (b) (c) (d)

Figure 3. Examples of application screenshots by PCP supplier companies.
(a) Nextage/Camelot[3], (b) GNOMON[4], (c-d) eResult[5].

5. ENSURING INTEROPERABILITY

The use cases targeted by DECIPHER are chronic disease management and unplanned care episodes abroad. As discussed in Section 3 such use cases evidently benefit from a connection between the personal health service and the local EHR or PHR system. Unfortunately, such connection was not possible during the project lifetime for two main reasons. PHR interfaces were included in future development plans of the procurers, but were not available for use in the project. On the other hand, access to either live PHR or copies containing real patients' data was not possible in the context of the technological research and development activity due to privacy related reasons. In addition to the DECIPHER procurers, a similar situation prevails in many other countries and districts. In such case, it is important to ensure that the solutions being developed in the PCP process are compatible with international standards and can be integrated with the EHR or PHR at a later stage.

The DECIPHER project took the approach of defining the compatibility with HL7 CCD (Continuity of Care Document) content specification as a minimum requirement (Benson, 2016; Gordon et al., 2012). This choice follows the approach adopted also for the cross-border patient summary in the epSOS[6] project. The objective of DECIPHER was not to be dependent on epSOS infrastructure, since it is still unclear if it will be implemented and largely available. However, it was considered useful to adopt a similar CDA-based (Clinical Document Architecture) data structure to facilitate possible epSOS integration in the future. The ITT also required the solutions to be flexible, allowing additional standards to be supported as needed. For example HL7/FHIR (Benson, 2016) (Fast Healthcare Interoperability Resources) has received wide interest and may become a dominant EHR/PHR interoperability standard in the future.

The monitoring and evaluation mechanism described in Section 4 already enabled to follow how the companies complied with the interoperability requirements. In order to support the development of standard-based applications, the project also provided a test server enabling the participant companies to store and retrieve personal health data in standard form. The DECIPHER test server (DTS) provided an open service interface towards the companies' applications thereby simulating a PHR connection. The overall architecture of the server is depicted in Figure 4.

[3] http://nextage-on.com/, http://www.camelotbio.com/
[4] www.opendecipher.gr
[5] http://www.eresult.it/en-us/
[6] www.epsos.eu

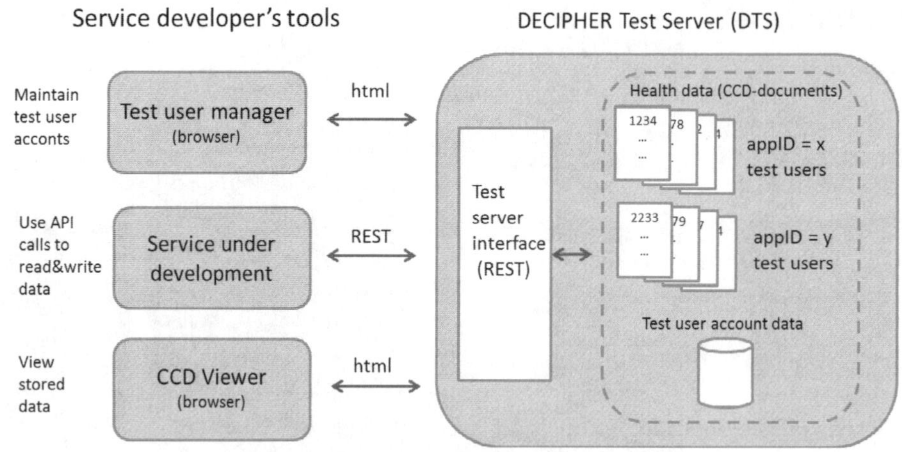

Figure 4. DECIPHER Test Server architecture

The test server maintains a collection of test user ("patient") accounts and corresponding personal health data in the form of CCD document files. The test server includes a "test user manager", which enables the developers of the companies to create test user accounts and corresponding security credentials. The application under development can access the test user's health data via REST API calls (Application Programming Interface). The REST API functionality enables the application to read and write data items managed by the CCD document file. The DTS enables read and write operations focusing on particular entries or the complete record. Figure 5 illustrates the CCD file operations and the standard entry types.

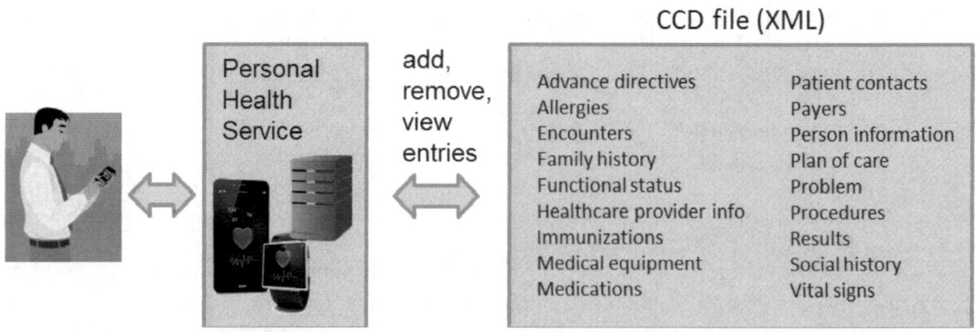

Figure 5. The CCD document file simulates a personal data storage for the needs of service testing

The DTS provides only the data storage and related management functionality. It depends on the application how it displays the stored information for the user and which information is collected from the user and stored in the DTS. For testing purposes, the DTS provides a web viewer for showing users' stored data as depicted in Figure 4.

Initially 9 companies were selected to the DECIPHER PCP process based on the tenders received in response to the ITT. The DTS was used by 7 companies. Although, the platform was available already in phase 1, it was more useful in phases 2 and 3, where actual implementations were developed. The companies participating in these phases were: Nextage/Camelot (phases 2&3), GNOMON (phases 2&3), eResult (phases 2&3), Linkcare (phase 2), Nissatech (phase 2) and alterAid (phase 2).

A questionnaire was made to the companies after phase 2. It revealed that the companies were in general happy with the DTS. They clearly expressed the wish to have access to open APIs and sandboxes enabling the exchange of data with the real PHR and EHR systems of the procurers. In the absence of such access, the DTS was considered to be a viable solution. In addition to testing the standard-based data exchange the companies expressed the need to test with other standards (especially FHIR) and with different authentication and authorization protocols, besides the basic authentication provided by the DTS.

6. DISCUSSION AND CONCLUSIONS

During the past decades considerable efforts have been focused in ensuring connectivity of clinical systems. Recently, the importance of interoperability between personal health services and clinical data storages has attracted increasing attention. As interconnected health ecosystems are emerging the needs for testing the interoperability of health applications is increasing. Major health record manufacturers are now developing new functionalities, which enable personal health services to be connected with EHR/PHR systems[7]. The ecosystems are increasingly being built based on the HL7 FHIR draft standard. FHIR is especially appreciated by developers as it employs modern web technologies and enables faster application development. FHIR defines base resources, frameworks and APIs. Thereby, it enables a "platform-based" architecture (Benson, 2016), which is particularly well-suited for supporting connected ecosystems. One example is, national PHR of Finland, which is currently being set up aside with the national "Kanta EHR archive".

The ecosystem is currently providing an open FHIR test environment ("sandbox") with OAuth 2.0 authorisation for supporting companies in the development of connected applications[8]. The implemented PHR exploits the open source HAPI-FHIR reference implementation[9].

Interoperability is a major challenge especially in the context of cross-border health solutions. In the DECPHER PCP project the standard HL7 CCD structure was adopted as a common tool to describe the health history of a patient and transfer it between systems. The CCD was selected, since in the beginning of the PCP process, FHIR was not yet available and CCD matched best with the intended functionalities of the applications.

The project provided a test server, which enabled application developers to test their solutions for PHR connectivity over a REST API. The objective of the DECIPHER test server was to provide a testing tool for the companies to be used in parallel with other testing methods. This approach was appreciated by the companies, as revealed by the feedback collected from the companies. Some of the companies participating the PCP used their own test servers or those freely available[10] to test with FHIR. The DTS is planned to be exploited and further developed in the framework of follow-on research projects.

ACKNOWLEDGEMENT

The paper is based on work carried out in the DECIPHER project jointly funded by the European Commission and the project participants Anci Innovazione, AQUAS, ESTAR, Eurecat, NHS/Trustech, TicSalut and VTT.

REFERENCES

Benson, T., 2016. *Principles of Health Interoperability*. Springer, Switzerland.

Franz, B. et al, 2015. Applying FHIR in an Integrated Health Monitoring System. *EJBI,* Vol. 11, No. 2.

Gordon P. et al, 2012. Processes and Outcomes of Developing a Continuity of Care Document for Use as a Personal Health Record by People Living with HIV/AIDS in New York City. *International journal of medical informatics*, Vol. 81, No. 10, e63-e73.

Hommen, L. and Rolfstam, M., 2009. Public Procurement and Innovation – Towards a Taxonomy. *Journal of Public Procurement*, Vol. 9, No. 1, 17-56.

Jones, D. A. et al, 2010. Characteristics of personal health records: Findings of the medical library Association/National library of medicine joint electronic personal health record task force. *Journal of the Medical Library Association: JMLA*, Vol. 98, No. 3, 243–249.

[7] https://open.epic.com/
[8] http://fhirsandbox.kanta.fi/kanta-phr-sandbox-ui/
[9] http://hapifhir.io/
[10] http://fhirtest.uhn.ca/

Kalra, D., 2006. Electronic health record standards. *IMIA Yearbook 2006: Assessing Information – Technologies for Health*, Vol. 1, No. 1, 136–144.

Klersy C et al, 2009. A meta-analysis of remote monitoring of heart failure patients. *J Am Coll Cardiol*, Vol. 54, No. 18, 1683-1694.

Li, Y. C. et al. (2012). A global travelers' electronic health record template standard for personal health records. *Journal of the American Medical Informatics Association: JAMIA*, Vol. 19, No. 1, 134–136.

Orsama, A. L., et al, 2013. Active assistance technology reduces glycosylated hemoglobin and weight in individuals with type 2 diabetes: Results of a theory-based randomized trial. *Diabetes Technology & Therapeutics*, Vol. 15, No. 8, 662–669.

White, H. et al., 2016. Requirements and access needs of patients with chronic disease to their hospital electronic health record: results of a cross-sectional questionnaire survey. *BMJ Open,* Vol. 6, No. 10.

FALL DETECTION METHOD USING SINGLE AXIS ACCELERATION AND ANGUALAR VELOCITY

Daniel Badran[1], Kabalan Chaccour[1], Amir Hajjam El Hassani[2] and Emmanuel Andres[3]
[1] *Ticket Lab., Université Antonine, Hadat – Baabda, Lebanon*
[2] *Nanomedicine Lab, Univ. Bourgogne Franche-Comté, UTBM, F-90010 Belfort, France*
[3] *Universit´e de Strasbourg, Centre Hospitalier Universitaire, 67000 Strasbourg, France*

ABSTRACT

Falls of elderly people are a major public health issue. For the victims and their surroundings, the resulting health expenses can be a heavy burden, largely because of the long recovery periods and the potential of co-morbidities that arise. Research efforts in fall detection have produced a wide range of solutions. These are classified as wearable and non-wearable systems. Fall detection algorithms running on these systems are being tested by young volunteers inside lab environment taking out the impact of real-life scenarios and real elderly people. Unlike other algorithms that use three-axial acceleration and angular velocity to detect a fall, our algorithm uses one single axis. The algorithm was validated with 8 elderly aging above 65 years and with either a minor walking disorder or coping from either fear of fall or previous fall injuries. Results showed 99% sensitivity and 94.8% specificity. The system has a registered accuracy of 97.5%.

KEYWORDS

Ageing; Fall detection; Body posture; Wearable systems; Inertial sensors

1. INTRODUCTION

Ageing affects all living species. In humans, it is characterized by the decline of physical, cognitive and affective capacities. On the physical level, loss of muscle strength induced by the increased frailty escalates the risk of falling. In this context, falls are a serious public health problem for the ageing population. It is the second leading cause of accidental or unintentional injury deaths worldwide (Unit, et al., 2008). There are four main risk factors for falls, these are categorized into four aspects: biological, behavioral, environmental and socioeconomic.

Aside from physical injuries, studies show that falls of elderly people have drastic psychological and behavioral consequences (Evitt, et al., 2004); Psychological trauma and fear of falling can produce a downward spiral of self-imposed reduced activity, leading to a loss of strength, flexibility, and mobility, thereby increasing the risk of future falls and injuries (Tamura, et al., 2009); Roughly 28-35% of senior people above 65 years of age fall each year and that percentage increases to 32-42% for those above 70 (Unit, et al., 2008). Moreover, a wider problem related to psychological side effects are socioeconomic risks. These impact the social status of the elderly making engagement in the social activity and one's community no longer pleasant and consequently leading to a lack of social interaction, loneliness and depression. These consequences are detrimental for an elderly's health. Fearing a fall or coping with it after one that happened from one hand and suffering from isolation or depression from another hand, reduce the effectiveness of the immune system and increase the risk of pathologies (Penninx, et al., 1998). Alongside physical and behavioral factors, environmental factors present in the elderly's surrounding may also increase the risk of falling. For instance, narrow steps, slippery surfaces, looser rugs and low lighting turns any place whether it's public or the elderly's home into a hazardous environment (Unit, et al., 2008).

Despite their inevitable risks, falls could be managed and detected if proper means were administered to the patient. This requires both medical and technological interventions. For instance, researchers and medical technologists working in the field of healthcare, can develop devices that detect a fall. Such devices can contribute to alleviate the consequences of falls (e.g. long lie, fear of falling) by reducing the response time to detect a fall. In order to be adopted by elderly, these devices must be efficient (minimum false positives and maximum true positives) and compliant to real-life scenarios. In this context, the present research proposes a fall detection algorithm with refined traits deducted from combining standard fall detection parameters such as acceleration, orientation and body posture. The algorithm uses the acceleration and the angular velocity provided solely by the axis of motion. The proposed method addresses people with either a minor walking disorder or coping from either fear of fall or previous fall injuries.

The rest of the paper is structured as follows: Section II pro-vides a state of art on existing methods developed for fall detection using wearable and non-wearable systems. Section III outlines the elaboration of the fall detection approach using the acceleration and the angular of the axis of motion. Section IV presents the experiments conducted to determine the efficiency of our proposed approach based on daily activity analysis to determine fall detection thresholds. Finally, section V concludes the paper.

2. RELATED WORK

Research efforts in the fall detection track is abundant. Over 300 research studies were found while searching the web of knowledge describing devices and algorithms for fall detection. Commercial products have also started to appear. These algorithms use one or more input parameters based on which falls are detected. These parameters are often collected using sensors. (Chaccour, et al., 2016), provided a generic classification of fall detection systems based on their sensor deployment. They classified fall detection systems as wearable and non-wearable. Non-wearable systems include ambient and vision based; in their review paper, algorithms running on these systems can use either analytical or machine learning processing techniques to detect falls. The current state of art provide a general overview on methods used by wearable and non-wearable fall detection systems.

2.1 Algorithms used by Non-Wearable Systems

These systems usually answer the need of protecting an elderly who refuses to use a wearable device or in some cases to eliminate environment-related risks. Devices such as wall or ceiling mounted cameras (e.g. video or thermal) and ambient sensors (e.g. acoustic, inertial, etc.) are able to monitor the elderly's daily activities and detect fall incidents.

2.1.1 Vision Based Methods

Methods used in such systems benefit from temporal images captured by ambient cameras. These images are run through a specific image processing algorithm that identifies obstacles and help the elderly avoid them or they simply recognize when the elderly falls. Many types of algorithm can operate a large variety of cameras; while some systems depend on multiple fixed cameras with an algorithm that connects the images attempting to eliminate blind spots, others use more sophisticated methods like the one used by (Greiffenhagen, et al., 2001). In their paper, they proposed a surveillance system that combines a CCD camera and a convex mirror to capture panoramic scenes. (Miaou, et al., 2006) used an Omni-camera to capture 360° images simultaneously. The algorithm will detect a fall after using a threshold based on the difference in ratio between height and width of the standing state and the fall state. While this method is well thought of and the experiments show promise, the documented results showed a success rate of 79.8% which means 1/5 of all falls where not detected properly.

Some methods based their fall detection scheme on temporal contrast vision where the algorithm manages the data from two or more cameras located on different sides of the room. (Fu, et al., 2008) used the technique of moving-average that enables the detectors to quickly compute motion vectors and trigger an alert when a fall incident happens with low computational effort. The proposed technique is impressive particularly with such lightweight algorithm, yet it holds major drawbacks. For example, if the sensor is blocked in any manner, it will not detect a fall or provide the algorithm with faulty data, and therefore the use of multiple sensors is required which greatly increases the cost. Moreover, this type of detection is light sensitive which means some variations in certain light specters might reduce the efficiency of the whole system.

2.1.2 Thermal Imagery Based Methods

Tracking a person's heat signature is a very effective detection method. An algorithm will run the data from a thermal sensor to trace every movement inside a room. Unlike normal cameras thermal cameras do not require light and cannot be blocked by objects. (Wong, et al., 2010) constructed a fall detection system using a thermal camera, a laptop runs the algorithm which assesses the thermal images by converting them into a gray scale version then into a binary image using minimum body temperature threshold. After that, the algorithm processes the binary form by removing the smallest body size represented by a number of pixels within the image. Following noise filtering, it outlines the region of boundaries to finalize an image and determine the positioning of the body thus determining a fall situation. The method does not require ambient light which gives it an advantage over other camera based solutions; however solutions that distinguish thermal scenes have a few disadvantages such as the algorithm being unable to differentiate between a large pet and a small human being. Moreover, thermal devices have high costs.

2.1.3 Acoustic and Vibration Based Methods

Falls have drastic speeds which potently increases the force at impact. (Tamura, et al., 2009), measured the falling time while mimicking a fall. The computed falling time interval is between 0.177 and 0.387s with an average of 0.249s. In addition, the force at impact is also affected by the height and the weight of the person which is detectable by the sound amplitude. Some solutions thought of reducing false detection by using an algorithm that capture data from an acoustic sensor. (Popescu, et al., 2008), conceived a method to determine falls by acquiring and analyzing sound height from a linear array of acoustic sensors; a digital signal processing algorithm is used to compute the energy and sound height in a particular window of N samples. In this study, the algorithm filters sound signals using Weiner filter then the height is concluded by a correlation in time of the signals from the two microphones. A fall is detected when an event is present in two consecutive windows. By reducing false positives, this study takes fall detection using ambient sensors one step ahead, regrettably it has few setbacks since the thresholds used by the algorithm are not dynamic and they are changed according to noise removal needs reducing the efficiency of the whole system.

Floor mounted solutions are adequate for large monitoring demands. Algorithms running these systems have an advantage over others by having less computational power particularly in distributed sensor networks. Due to a wide physical system distribution, accuracy increases noticeably but on the detriment of the cost since the number of deployed sensors become large. (Werner & Diermaier, 2011), developed an algorithm that detects physical vibrations on the floor. The algorithm applies feature extraction from each sensor that picked up a signal. After a data fusion process, the algorithm reduces the amount of data to one set per potential fall, those potential fall events are eliminated depending on the user's next activity. Fall detection is then performed by setting adequate thresholds. This method distinguished 80% of all sound impacts, while similar algorithms showed better results. For instance, (Litvak, et al., 2008), demonstrated laboratory performance of 100% specificity and sensitivity and (Alwan, et al., 2006), registered a 98.5% specificity and 97.5% sensitivity. All these methods have shown better results, but the experiments were conducted on a maximum of five floors plates and since the results and performance of the algorithm is dependent on the floor holding, the system leaves a margin of error which demands a wider range of testing to accurately confirm these results.

All previous algorithms had a major setbacks tied to the system running them. These exhibit physical limitations and environmental problems. While these algorithms showed exceptional sensitivity and specificity, they are, in most cases, being susceptible to a dimensional area or being affected by light or humidity which render the system vulnerable to restrictions that can be easily avoided in wearable systems.

2.2 Algorithms used by Wearable Systems

Non-wearable systems can be applied to elderly who are required to stay in a safe environment such as hospitals or elderly-care facilities. Controversially, other people are considered in a safer state giving them the privilege of to perform normal daily life activities in various environments; (Fuke, et al., 2012), classified subjects with BBSs under 45 as high-risk which require a care taker to watch over them, while others with higher BBSs are classified between caution-needed and safe class entitling them more freedom in their daily activities. The latter group of people make better candidates for a wearable fall detection system. The opt for a wearable systems require higher efficiency in terms of sensitivity, specificity and response time.

2.2.1 Accelerometry Based Methods

Common solutions in the field of fall detection use algorithms that monitor the values of acceleration and compare them to predefined thresholds in order to determine if a fall event have occurred. (Wang, et al., 2008), proposed an algorithm that uses a triaxial accelerometer located on the head. The algorithm detects falls using two stages: First the algorithm computes the module of the acceleration vector of the three axis and checks if it's above 6g thus detecting a fall. If the sum is less than 6g, the algorithm computes the acceleration vector on the x and z axis, if it is larger than 2g, then it checks if the velocity is above 2m/s. A fall is recorded when these conditions are true. Positioning the sensor on the head offers some complications for some subjects since the head sways with some normal activities or simply certain walking patterns. As a result, the data fed to the algorithm might become faulty.

(Brouke, et al., 2008), designed an algorithm that detects falls using after impact body position. They fixed the sensor on the chest. The algorithm uses a previously set fall-impact threshold. After 0.5 s, if the body is still in the lying position then the algorithm recognizes a fall event; if the subject remained prone on the ground for 10 minutes, the algorithm launches a call to a medical assistance service. This method showed very good results when simulated tests were conducted which concluded to a 98.8% sensitivity and a 98.1% specificity, but these values dropped to 65.5% sensitivity and 75.7% specificity when real-time tests were conducted for impact detection and from 90.5% sensitivity to 41.2% and 99.4% specificity to 86% for event detection. The results show that in real-life scenarios, the efficiency has dropped due to higher false alarms.

2.2.2 Combined Accelerometry and Orientation Based Methods

Accuracy is key in fall detection, (Li, et al., 2009), composed an algorithm that detects falls using data captured from two combined inertial measurement units each having a triaxial accelerometer and a triaxial gyroscope. The algorithm runs through three stages. Within one second, it tests if the variation detected is below the thresholds which defines the variation as a static posture, otherwise, it is presumed as a dynamic transition. For static segments readings, they are used to construct a list of specific postures. A fall is detected when the algorithm, after a static segment is classified as lying down, reviews the last 5 seconds if the deduction is of an unintentional transition then it is a fall. Although the article states that the system has low computational time, the algorithm itself has to test and monitor four variables which are the concatenation of twelve parameters which may increase the response time as well as battery consumption.

3. PROPOSED METHOD

In this paper, we propose a fall detection algorithm taking into consideration the acceleration and the angular velocity along the axis of motion. This consideration is based on the hypothesis proved by Wu et al. from the University of Vermont-USA. In their paper (Wu, 2000), found that the vertical and the horizontal speeds are 3 times during a fall than for any other normal daily activity, and that both speeds are of the same amplitude at the time of the fall whereas, they are strongly dissimilar during "controlled" movements. Our method relies on the data collected from Inertial Measurement Unit (IMU) composed of an accelerometer and a gyroscope.

Our proposed detection scheme is composed of the rolling angular velocity and the acceleration on the axis of motion perpendicular to the frontal plane of the body as shown in figure 1. In this configuration, we reduce the number of monitored axis from 3 axis to a single axis for both the accelerometer and the gyroscope. In addition, the choice of this detection scheme was made possible because of the way the weight of some body parts is distributed. In fact, the human brain weights around 1.5 kg (McNamara, 2015) combined with the other components of the head, it averages between 3.8 and 4.5 kg. This assumption renders the head as the tipping point which affects the direction of falling. Given the rotational axis of the human neck and through our tests, we have concluded that the head will deviate the fall into a diagonal state giving the axis of motion the possibility to achieve the variation needed to detect a fall.

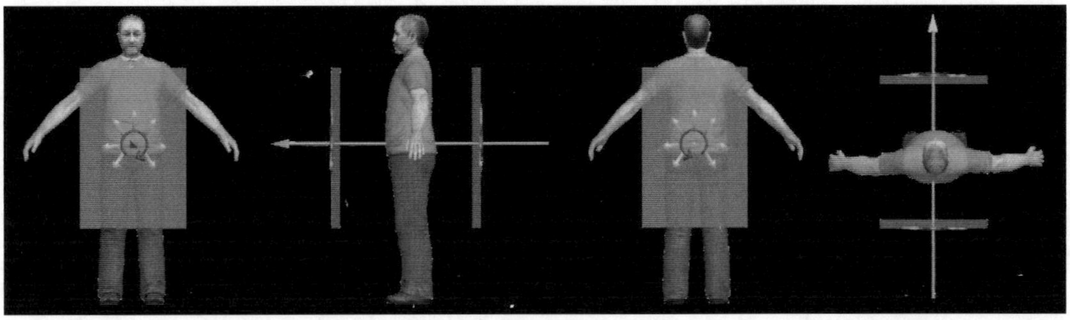

Figure 1. Representation of the detection scheme composed of the roll angular velocity and the acceleration of the x-axis

After all the test we have conducted, we determined that even with subjects who sway a little while walking; the difference in acceleration and angular velocity has a maximum of 25% between motion events (e.g. standing, sitting, between steps while walking, etc.). Adding to our finding the study conducted by (Wu, 2000), a fall will differ 3 times to the normal activity. Therefore, we defined our threshold for the acceleration and the angular velocity as a 30% difference along the axis of motion.

The algorithm will monitor variations on the x-axis for both acceleration and angular velocity. If the variation exceeds the set of defined thresholds, a fall event is detected in real-time. The algorithm will wait 5 minutes then send a SMS message to the appropriate care taker unless the elderly recovers and presses a button which will impede the algorithm from sending a message. The flowchart of the algorithm is represented in figure 2.

4. EXPERIMENTS AND RESULTS

4.1 Hardware Setup

As a first step, the algorithm was implemented on the Arduino UNO processing unit. Arduino UNO is a hardware development platform for prototyping and testing of control systems. It is based on the ATmega328P microcontroller running at a 16MHz crystal oscillator. Since the algorithm requires only one axis, the input data to the microcontroller running the algorithm are small, thus requiring less computation on the CPU and minimum power consumption providing an extended battery life to the wearable device. The MPU6050 triaxial iner-tial sensor was used to extract motion parameters (acceleration and angular velocity), however, one axis was selected. This sensor unit has the advantage of integrating both an accelerometer and a gyroscope onto the same chip. The M590 modem is used to send a SMS in case of a fall event.

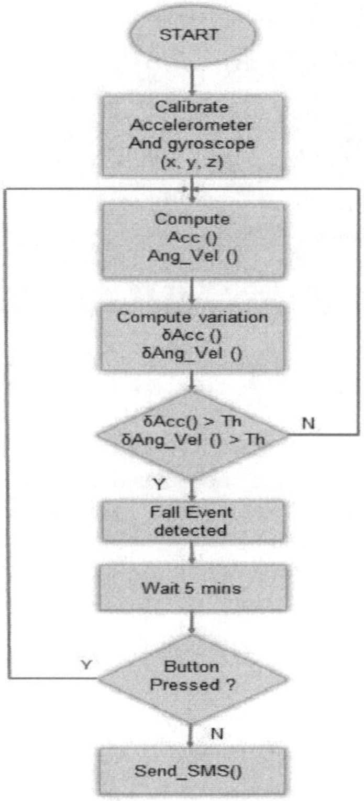

Figure 2. Fall detection algorithm flow diagram

4.2 Experimental Setup

To validate the performance of our fall detection algorithm, we conducted a series of experiments mimicking fall events and activities of daily living. We outlined a list of 12 tests divided into two groups: The first group simulated fall events whereas the second group is meant to test if the algorithm detects a fall when the user is doing daily activities. A group of 8 elders with ages equal or above 65 participated to the experiments. The elders were chosen such as 3 of them were healthy with full mobility, 4 subjects were able to walk and do daily activities but with some difficulties and 1 subject had an excess weight which makes some activities troublesome. Each of the 8 subjects carried out the 12 tests two times. The total number of registered records is 192. We needed to make the tests as genuine as possible without harming the elderly, therefore assistants were available to catch the elderly before they reach the ground in fall exercises without affecting the outcome of the test.

The first group of tests included fall scenarios. Falls were either to the front (fall on knees, end in lying down), back (end in sitting position, end in lying down) or diagonally. Through all fall scenarios the algorithm triggered an alarm. The second group of tests included activities of daily living such as sitting down on a chair, standing up from a chair, collapsing into a chair, bending forward, walking up the stairs and walking down the stairs; the tests registered 5 false positive situations. In fact, during the bending over tests, The 3 healthy subjects exceeded the threshold and therefore a fall was detected. Also, one of the healthy subjects stood up too quickly which caused the system to trigger an alarm. Finally, the subject with excess weight triggered an alarm while he collapsed into the chair. The efficiency of the system is determined by the sensitivity and the specificity which were measured as 99% and 94.8% respectively. The overall accuracy is computed as 97.8%.

Table 1. Statistical records of the fall scenarios

	TP	FN
Forward fall (fall on knees)	15	1
Forward fall (lie down)	16	
Backward fall (end in sitting position)	15	1
Backward fall (end in lying down)	16	
Fall diagonally (front right and front left)	16	
Fall diagonally (back right and back left)	16	

Table 2. Statistical analysis of the daily activities scenarios

	FP	TN
Sitting down in a chair	1	15
Standing up from a chair	1	15
Collapsing in to a chair		16
Bending forward	3	13
Walking up the stairs		16
Walking down the stairs		16

Table 3. Statistical analysis of the fall detection algorithm

	Sensitivity	Specificity	Accuracy
Fall events and activities of daily living	99%	94.8%	97.8%

5. CONCLUSION

This paper presents an optimized fall detection algorithm tak-ing into consideration the acceleration and the angular velocity across the axis of motion perpendicular to the frontal plane of the body. According to the algorithm, the detection of a fall event is typically based upon the variation of the acceleration and the angular velocity values along the axis of motion as described previously. The proof of concept of the proposed method has been validated during the experiments where the fall detection algorithm demonstrated its efficiency with a sensitivity of 99% and a specificity 94.8%. The registered accuracy is 97.5%. This study has shown that we could re-duce the number of variables required to detect a fall yet still obtaining very good results.

The alert part of the algorithm could be altered into a more systematic approach by introducing the ad hoc technology to the system instead of using a simple SMS module, thus allow-ing a large scale application of the algorithm. Future work could usher the inclusion of this algorithm in fall protection solutions to increase the speed of detection while decreasing the execution load, thus lessening the power consumption.

ACKNOWLEDGEMENT

The author would like to thank the supervisor for his helpful and objective comments on the article. A special thanks to the mayor of kawthariyet El Siyad for his help to prepare the volunteers who participated in the experiments.

REFERENCES

Alwan, M. et al., 2006. *A smart and passive floor-vibration based fall detector for elderly.* s.l., IEEE, pp. 1003-1007.

Brouke, A. K., ven, P. W. V. d., Chaya, p. A. & Nelson, J., 2008. *Design and test of a long-term fall detection system incorporated into a custom vest for the elderly.* s.l., IET, pp. 307-312.

Chaccour, K., Darazi, R., Hajjam, A. & Emmanuel, A., 2015. *Smart carpet using differential piezoresistive pressure sensors for elderly fall detection.* s.l., IEEE, pp. 225-229.

Chaccour, K., Darazi, R., Hajjam, A. & Emmanuel, A., 2016. From Fall Detection to Fall Prevention: A Generic Classification of Fall-Related Systems. *IEEE Sensors Journal,* 17(3), pp. 812 - 822.

Delahoz, Y. s. & Labrador, M. A., 2014. Survey on fall detection and fall prevention using wearable and external sensors. *Sensors,* 14(10), pp. 19806-19842.

Evitt, Quigley, C. P. a. & A, P., 2004. Fear of falling in older adults: a guide to its prevalence, risk factors, and consequences. *Rehabilitation Nursing,* 29(6), p. 207.

Fuke, S., Suzuki, T. & Doi, M., 2012. *Estimation of falling risk based on acceleration signals during initial gait.* s.l., IEEE, pp. 286-291.

Fu, Z., Delbruck, T., Lichtsteiner, P. & Culurciello, E., 2008. *An address-event fall detector for assisted living applications.* s.l., IEEE.

Greiffenhagen, M., Dorin, C., Heinrich, N. & Visvanathan, R., 2001. Design, analysis, and engineering of video monitoring systems: an approach and a case study. *Proceedings of the IEEE,* 89(10), pp. 1498--1517.

Li, Q. et al., 2009. *Accurate, fast fall detection using gyroscopes and accelerometer-derived posture information.* s.l., IEEE, pp. 138-143.

Litvak, D., Gannot, I. & Zigel, Y., 2008. *Detection of falls at home using floor vibrations and sound.* s.l., IEEE, pp. 514-518.

McNamara, A., 2015. *Science Focus.* [Online] Available at: http://www.sciencefocus.com/qa/top-10-what-are-heaviest-organs-human-body [Accessed 27 January 2017].

Miaou, S.-G., Pei-Hsu & Huang, C.-y., 2006. *A customized human fall detection system using omni-camera images and personal information.* s.l., IEEE, pp. 39-42.

Nait-Charif, McKenna, H. a. & J, S., 2004. *Activity summarisation and fall detection in a supportive home environment.* s.l., IEEE, pp. 323-326.

Penninx, B. W. a. G. et al., 1998. Depressive symptoms and physical decline in community-dwelling older persons. *Jama,* 279(21), pp. 1720--1726.

Popescu, M., Li, Y., Skubic, M. & Rantz, M., 2008. *An acoustic fall detector system that uses sound height information to reduce the false alarm rate.* s.l., IEEE, pp. 4628--4631.

Tamura, T. et al., 2009. A wearable airbag to prevent fall injuries. *IEEE Transactions on Information Technology in Biomedicine,* 13(6), pp. 910--914.

Unit, Organization, W. H. & Course, A. a. L., 2008. *WHO global report on falls prevention in older age.* s.l.:World Health Organization.

Wang, C.-c.et al., 2008. *Development of a fall detecting system for the elderly residents.* s.l., IEEE, pp. 1359-1362.

Werner, F. & Diermaier, J., 2011. *Fall detection with distributed floor-mounted accelerometers: An overview of the development and evaluation of a fall detection system within the project eHome.* s.l., IEEE, pp. 354--361.

Wong, W. K., Lim, H. L., Loo, C. K. & Lim, W. S., 2010. *Home alone faint detection surveillance system using thermal camera.* s.l., IEEE, pp. 747-751.

Wu, G., 2000. *Distinguishing fall activities from normal activities by velocity characteristics.* s.l., Elsevier, pp. 1497-1500.

IMPLEMENTATION OF ICT BASED INNOVATIONS AS ELECTRONIC MEDICAL RECORD IN SUB-SAHARA AFRICA: ISSUES OF RELEVANCE FOR FUTURE IMPLEMENTATIONS

Gabriel Nzarama Mugabe[1], Vivian Vimarlund[2] and Sofie Wass[3]
[1]*Assistant Lecturer in Business Information Technology, University of Rwanda, College of Business and Economics, Rwanda*
[2]*Professor in Informatics, Jonkoping University, Sweden*
[3]*PhD Candidate in Informatics, Jonkoping University, Sweden*

ABSTRACT

Electronic medical records (EMR) have been implemented in developed countries since 1972 when the first computer-stored medical record at Wishard Memorial Hospital was designed. However, less seem to be known about EMRs in an African context. The purpose of this paper is therefore to review studies on EMRs implemented in sub-Saharan Africa and to identify benefits and challenges met. Articles available in PubMed, PMC, Scopus, JAMIA and Google were searched through JIBS online library using the search string "EMR systems in Sub-Saharan Africa". In most the papers, EMRs have been implemented in HIV/AIDS settings allowing better monitoring of patients under antiretroviral therapy (ART). EMR systems have also succeeded to increase the number of patients under ART. Moreover, EMRs have improved work processes as they have reduced patients waiting time and enhanced monitoring of medical appointments. However, EMRs have suffered lack of electricity, poor Internet connectivity and computer illiteracy. Today, HIV/AIDS care providers have benefited on the implementation of EMRs and there is a possibility to extend the implementation to other healthcare departments.

KEYWORDS

EMR implementation, EMR Challenges and benefits, ICT in Health, eHealth in Sub-Sahara Africa

1. INTRODUCTION

Today, we live in an information age whereby most of sectors are leveraged by IT solutions. The healthcare sector has embraced the pace and many functions and services have been computerized. Today, using informatics, patients can provide their clinicians with critical information and share with relatives their health information. It is also possible for clinicians to use Information systems like Electronic Medical Records to coordinate care and share information with other clinicians (Snyder, 2011). The developed countries in Europe for instance, are far advanced in adopting technology in health sector and have reached the stage where the investments are used for providing new innovative ways of health care delivery and efficient methods of access and exchange of health information (WHO, 2016). African countries are following the trend and start to implement computerized patients records or electronic medical records systems to ensure a timely and accurate exchange of information to better utilize scarce healthcare resources (Rahimi & Vimarlund, 2007) but also to improve quality of services and to be able to offer more effective and personalized health and social care in the near future (Greiver et al., 2012). Through partnerships with western universities and donors, some healthcare facilities in Africa have succeeded to implement EMRs. Moreover, as other health computerized systems, these facilities are targeting the efficiency and safety in their services (Bahlol, Vivian, & Toomas, 2009) while implementing EMRs.

Studies about the impact of EMRs in Africa have shown that they contribute to improved quality of healthcare (Oluoch et al., 2012) and to more effective control of drug distribution and monitoring, avoiding stock-outs and rational drug forecasting. (Douglas et al., 2010). Currently they are a series of on-going implementation projects in Sub-Saharan Africa. It is therefore, of crucial importance to learn from the past, to overcome previous challenges and mistakes and to benchmark those which have been successful. The aim of this paper is to explore benefits and challenges that need to be considered when implementing EMR in sub-Saharan Africa. We expect that the outcomes will be of importance for decision makers, but also to end-users (practitioners, health personnel and patients).

2. METHODS

We performed a literature review for published articles on the implementation of EMR in Sub-Saharan Africa. Searches for publications were conducted in the Library database of Jönköping International Business School Library with the key words: "EMR systems in Sub-Saharan Africa". The search resulted in 44 articles found in PubMed, PMC (Pub Med Central), Scopus, JAMIA and Google. The abstracts were then read in-depth to confirm that the articles focused on EMR in the region of Sub-Saharan Africa. After reading the abstracts, 29 articles were excluded as they did not focus on EMR. Rather they focused on mobile health, telemedicine, ethics, and e-health or studied EMR implemented in regions outside Sub-Saharan Africa. The retained papers (n=15) were analysed and classified by the first author by identifying the domain of the study, study design, time of evaluation of the EMR and findings of the individual papers.

3. RESULTS

An overview of the included papers is given in Table 1.

Table 1. Summary of the papers included in the review

Authors	Domain	Study Design	Time of Evaluation	Aim of the study	Findings
Laing et al., 2015	Hospital	Survey	After implementation	Development of hybrid electronic medical record (HEMR) system for the accurate collection and integration of data into a structured morbidity and mortality (M&M)	6,217 patients were admitted within the tertiary surgical service of Greys Hospital. 1,314 (21.1 %) adverse events and 315 (5.1 %) deaths were recorded. The adverse events were divided into 875 ''pathology-related'' morbidities and 439 ''error-related'' morbidities.
Biruk et al., 2014	Hospital	Survey	Before implementation	To assess health professionals' readiness and to identify factors that affect the acceptance and use of electronic medical recording system in the pre-implementation phase at hospitals of North Gondar Zone, Ethiopia.	Out of 606 study participants (54.1%) were found ready to use the EMR. The majority of the study participants, 432 (71.3%) and 331(54.6%) had good knowledge and attitude for EMR system, respectively.
Oluoch et al., 2014	Clinic	Time series	Before and after EMR implementation	To assess the effect of transitioning from paper-based to an EMR-based system on appropriate placement on ART among eligible patients.	7298 patients were eligible for ART; 54.8% (n=3998) were enrolled in HIV care using a paper-based system while 45.2% (n=3300) were enrolled after the Implementation of the EMR. EMR was independently associated with a 22% increase in the odds of initiating ART among eligible patients. The proportion of ART-eligible patients not receiving ART was 20.3% and 15.1% for paper and EMR. Median time from ART eligibility to ART initiation was 29.1 days for paper compared to 27 days for EMR.

Tierney et al., 2002	Health center	Survey	After implementation	Description of the implementation and use of the first documented electronic medical record system in ambulatory care in sub-Saharan Africa.	After one year, the system has captured data for more than 13,000 patients making more than 26,000 visits.
Siikaa et al., 2005	Hospital and clinics	Survey	Before implementation	design EMR to support comprehensive outpatient HIV/AIDS care in referral hospital and rural health centers.	To date, the EMR contains more than 30,000 visit records for more than 4000 patients, almost half taking antiretroviral drugs.
Oluoch et al., 2015	Clinic	Survey	After implementation	Investigate the association of an electronic medical record system (EMR) with adherence to pre- ART guidelines in rural HIV clinics in Kenya.	A total of 18 523 patients were receiving pre-ART care, of whom 38.8% in the paper group had had at least one CD4 test compared to 3.4% in the EMR group ($p < 0.001$). The adjusted odds of performing a CD4 test in clinics using an EMR was 1.59. The median time from enrolment into HIV care to first CD4 test was 1.40 months for paper vs. 0.93 months for EMR. The median time from baseline to first CD4 follow-up was 7.5 months (IQR 5.97–10.73) for paper and 6.53 months (IQR 5.57–7.87) for EMR.
Hannan et al., 2000	Primary care	Software development	Before implementation	To improve the quality of health data collection and, subsequently, patient care.	Design of a core electronic medical record system within the Mosoriot Health Center.
Driessen et al., 2013	Hospital	Survey	Before and after implementation	To model the financial effects of implementing a hospital-wide electronic medical record (EMR) system in tertiary facility in Malawi.	Estimated cost savings in length of stay, transcription time, and laboratory use total of US $284 395 annually. With EMR system, there is a net financial. Over 5 years the estimated net benefit was US$613 681.
Douglas et al., 2010	Hospital	Survey	After implementation	Providing a point-of- care (POC) electronic medical record (EMR) system that combines healthcare delivery and data collection processes into one activity, with the added bonus of providing enhanced decision support to clinicians during the patient encounter.	In 2007, ten users at QECH were interviewed with a 25-question instrument to measure their impressions of the pilot EMR. Seven (70%) of the users expressed a preference for the touch screen over the paper system; two more (20%) had no preference.
Shah et al., 2013	Hospital	Survey	After implementation	development and evaluation of DataPall, an open-source electronic medical records system that can be used to track patients, manage data, and generate reports for palliative care providers in these settings.	In a study of health professionals in a Malawian hospital, DataPall enabled palliative care providers to find patients' appointments, on average, in less than half the time required to locate the same record in current paper records.
Chaplin et al., 2015	Hospital	Survey	After implementation	We describe the development of an electronic medical records system (EMRS) put in place at the beginning of a large HIV/AIDS care and treatment program in Nigeria.	The EMRS was used in 33 hospitals across the country, with 4,947,433 adult, paediatric and PMTCT records that had been created and continued to be available for use in patient care.

Castelnuov et al., 2012	Hospital	Statistical Analyses	After and before implementation	To compare the rate of errors in the database before and after the introduction of the provider based EMR.	The introduction of provider-based EMR improved the quality of data collected with a significant reduction in missing and incorrect information.
Were et al., 2010	Hospital	Time-motion and Survey	After implementation	To provide patient- specific Electronic Medical Record (EMR)-based clinical summaries for providers taking care of HIV-positive adult patients in the resource-limited setting of Mbarara, Uganda.	Providers spent more time in direct care of patients (2.9 vs 2.3 minutes, $p<0.001$), and the length of patient visits was reduced by 11.5 minutes. Clinical summaries improved care, reduced mistakes, and were generally accurate.
Alamo et al., 2002	Hospital	Statistical Analyses and Tests	Before and after implementation	To implement Electronic Medical Records (EMR) and same day patient tracing to minimize missed appointments in a community-based HIV clinic in Kampala.	The missed appointments reduced from 21 pre-EMR to 8 post-EMR. The main reason for missed appointments was forgetting (37%) but reduced significantly by 30% post-EMR. Loss to follow up (LTFU) also significantly decreased from 10.9 to 4.8% The median waiting time to see providers significantly decreased from 291 to 94 min.
Badei, et al., 2016	Clinic	Database search	After implementation	to discover the types of inquiry and range of objectives and outcomes addressed in studies of the impacts of Electronic Medical Record (EMR) implementations in limited resource settings in sub-Saharan Africa.	Three major themes: systems, software, and social considerations emerged from content analysis, with sustainability concerns prevailing. Although participants reported many systems (power, network, Internet, hardware, interoperability) and software (data integrity, confidentiality, function) challenges, social factors (identity management, training, use incentives) appeared the most important impediments to sustainability.

Out of the 15 papers analysed, nine papers focused on hospital settings, three were conducted in clinics, one in primary care settings, one in a health centre and the remaining study combined a hospital and a clinic. The majority of the publications captured effects after the implementation of the systems (Badei et al.,2016; Chaplin et al., 2015; Douglas et al., 2010; Laing et al., 2015; Oluoch et al., 2015; Shah et al., 2013; Tierney et al., 2002; Were et al.,2010). Three articles used data sampled before the implementation (Biruk et al., 2014; Hannan, et al., 2000; Siika, et al., 2005) and four articles used data captured both before and after the implementation of the EMR (Alamo et al.,2002; Castelnuovet al., 2012; Driessen et al., 2013; Oluoch et al., 2014). Tackling the study design, nine papers used a qualitative approach (survey), four used quantitative method as statistical tests and time series were used. The two remaining papers applied a software development approach and the last used a database search.

Concerning the focus of the publications, they discuss or argument in general about the expected or factual benefits of EMR implementation. When analysing the papers, we identified four main categories. The first category focuses on the development of EMR as software and specific features aligning with the needs in healthcare facilities (accurate collection and integration of data, providing enhanced decision support to clinicians). These studies were conducted at Greys Hospital in South Africa (Laing et al., 2015), rural health centres in Kenya (Tierney et al., 2002; Siikaa et al., 2005; Hannan et al., 2000) and hospitals in Nigeria (Chaplin et al., 2015).

The second category focus on papers that emphasised the benefits of EMR after implementation, for instance improved work process and data accuracy. The studies included health facilities across Kenya, Uganda and Malawi (Oluoch et al., 2014; Oluoch et al., 2015; Driessen et al., 2013; Shah et al., 2013; Castelnuovet al., 2012; Were et al., 2010; Alamo et al., 2002). One study focused on quality and accuracy issues and showed that the EMR improves the quality of data and information collected for specific groups of patients (HIV patients) (Castelnuovet et al., 2012). Another study indicated that the use of EMRs allowed the care providers to spend more time with patients and that the length of the patient visits was reduced (Were et al., 2010). Similar patterns were found in other papers, the EMR helped healthcare providers to reduce the number of missed appointments in a community based HIV clinic (Alamo et al., 2002). Shah et al (2013) found that the introduction of an EMR reduced the time needed to locate patient appointments. EMRs have also shown to improve the monitoring of patients under ART-treatment (Oluoch et al., 2014; Oluoch et al., 2015). One of the studies reported a financial return of investment 5 years after the implementation of the system. Even if this result is of importance for future investments in similar systems, it is interesting to note that there is no information about how the costs and benefits were taken or which methodological approach were used to evaluate the outcomes of the implemented system or if the outcomes could be validated in any manner (Driessen et al., 2013).

The third category include two papers that discussed attitudes and challenges of EMR. One study focuses for instance on the readiness and attitudes for EMR of healthcare agents and how it influences the acceptance of the EMR in a hospital in Ethiopia (Biruk et al., 2014). The second paper identifies challenges related to use of EMR in a hospital in Malawi (Douglas et al., 2010). The study shows that incomplete data or errors in the paper-based system influence the accuracy of the EMR (Douglas et al., 2010). The last category includes one paper which is a review (Badei, et al., 2016) that identified challenges raised by other papers like power failures, lack of data integrity, lack of incentives as major barriers to EMR systems sustainability.

4. DISCUSSION

An analysis of the reviewed articles shows that the studies have focused on different phases in the implementation. It is interesting to note that none of the studies were performed as comparative studies or clearly reported differences between data sampled before and after the implementation. A majority of the papers used qualitative methods to collect data and that only some few used statistical analyses and time series. Future studies should therefore include both comparative and quantitative measures. All included papers aim to capture some benefits or positive outputs of the EMRs implementation and most papers have tried to capture the financial gain or the level of patients' satisfaction. However, there is no paper that captures negative outputs or challenges that need to be considered and prevented for a successful implementation of EMRs in the future.

Even if the included studies aim to show the benefits that EMRs can bring to the organisation, personnel and patients, there is no generic output that can be used to analyse the value of the benefits or compare outputs from different contexts, clinic, hospitals etc. Despite similarities between countries such as Kenya, Uganda and Nigeria, it is rational to assume that some differences like cultural, economic, social, IT maturity etc. should exist. If these are issues of relevance for a successful implementation and use of EMR, it is not possible to elucidate in this paper. Hence, there is a need to further investigate how the challenges of EMR implementation can be managed and if there exist some cultural differences between the countries belonging to Sub-Sahara area. Some of the studies included in our sample show that EMR are of high benefits for diseases such as HIV/AIDS that affect a high number of the population in Sub-Saharan Africa. It is necessary to learn from the past and implement EMR in other areas that can benefit other patient groups.

The analysed studies show a lack of consensus about the strategies, standards and technologies that EMR implementation should be based on. None of the articles discuss the importance of the architecture of the system, the terminology used or organisational issues. Decision makers should therefore, develop clear policies about:

a) How resource management and governance of the system will be followed-up
b) How perceived value, communication patterns and demand of ICT-maturity should be communicated and developed to avoid negative impacts at the organizational level
c) How assignments, reimbursements and responsibilities of the leaders should be managed during the implementation process
d) How workload will be distributed or in some cases re-distribute to avoid unexpected effects that influence the quality of the services or the use of the EMR

Finally, because of the economic constrains that some countries have, and considering the huge investment required by the adoption and implementation of EMR, this could explain the low number of countries in Sub-sahara adopting the EMR as health IT.

5. CONCLUSIONS

The purpose of this paper was to perform a literature review to learn more about the effects of the implementation and use of EMRs in sub-Saharan Africa. The results show that there is no specific pattern about how to implement this kind of applications. The analysis show that different methodologies have been used to capture and present the outcomes of the studies. Both qualitative and quantitative methodologies are used. Most of the studies focus on the importance of EMR for some specific diseases i.e., antiretroviral therapy to HIV/AIDS patients either in urban settings or rural settings. Any new implementation of EMR or other kind of technological innovations should consider cultural, managerial, economic and IT-maturity based issues and develop clear strategies to avoid inefficiencies.

Further studies on how technological innovations or which kind or innovations should be implemented need policies and strategies. Since the Sub-Sahara countries need to do re-allocation of resources to implement technological innovations it is of much relevance that decision makers and stakeholders consider the suggestions presented in this paper to diminish errors, inefficiencies and economic failures. Finally, this study show that several studies focused on HIV patients. In the future, it will be necessary to include other areas with potential positive impacts for the society and consider how EMR can support and improve the delivery of health care services to for instance children and women.

The literature on EMR lacks publications that discuss the implementation processes in a Sub-Sahara African context and there is a need for further studies. Even if we did not identify many studies, the publications selected give an initial overview of issues related to implementation of EMRs in this region.

REFERENCES

Alamo, S. T., Wagner, G. J., Sunday, P., Wanyenze, R. K., Ouma, J., Kamya, M., et al. (2002). Electronic Medical Records and Same Day Patient Tracing Improves Clinic Efficiency and Adherence to Appointments in a Community Based HIV/AIDS Care Program, in Uganda. *AIDS Behav , 16* (2), 1-12.

Badei, J., Dave, L., Louane, K., David, Z., & Robert, H. (2016). Benefits and challenges of EMR implementations in low resource settings: a state-of-the-art review. *BMC Medical Informatics and Decison Making* , 1-12.

Badei, J., Louanne, K., David, Z., Dave, L., Abraham, I., Abdullah, S., et al. (2016). Barriers and facilitators to Electronic Medical Record(EMR) use in an urban slum. *International Journal of Medical Informatics* , 246-254.

Bahlol, R., Vivian, V., & Toomas, T. (2009). Health Information Systems Implementation: A Qualitative Meta data Analysis. *J Med Syst , 33*, 359-368.

Biruk, S., Yilma, T., M. A., & Tilahun, B. (2014). Health Professionals readiness to implement electronic medical record system at three hospitals in Ethiopia: a cross sectional study. *Medical Informatics and Decision Making* , 1-8.

Castelnuovo, B., Kiragga, A., Afayo, V., Ncube, M., Orama, R., Magero, S., ... & Kambugu, A. (2012). Implementation of provider-based electronic medical records and improvement of the quality of data in a large HIV program in Sub-Saharan Africa. PloS one, 7(12), e51631.

Chaplin, B., Melonia, S., Eisena, G., Jolayemib, T., Banigbeb, B., Adeolab, J., et al. (2015). Scale-up of networked HIV treatment in Nigeria: Creation of an integrated electronic medical records system. *International Journal of Medical Informatics , 84*, 58-68.

Douglas, G. P., Gadabu, O. J., Joukes, S., Mumba, S., McKay, M. V., Ben-Smith, A., et al. (2010). Using Touchscreen Electronic Medical Record Systems to Support and Monitor National Scale-Up of Antiretroviral Therapy in Malawi. *PLoS Medecine*, *7* (8), 1-12.

Driessen, J., Cioffi, M., Alide, N., Landis-Lewis, Z., Gamadzi, G., Gadabu, O. J., et al. (2013). Modeling return on investment for an electronic medical record system in Lilongwe, Malawi. *J Am Med Inform Assoc*, *20*, 743-748.

Greiver, M., Barnsley, J., Glazier, R. H., Moineddin, R., & Bart, J. H. (2012). Measuring data reliability for preventive services in electronic medical records. *BMC Health Services Research*, *12* (116), 2-9.

Hannan, T. J., Rotich, J. K., Odero, W. W., Menya, D., Esamai, F., Einterz, R. M., et al. (2000). The Mosoriot medical record system: design and initial implementation of an outpatient electronic record system in rural Kenya. *International Journal of Medical Informatics*, *60*, 21-28.

Laing, G., Bruce, J., Skinner, D., Allorto, N., Aldous, C., Thomson, S., et al. (2015). Using a Hybrid Electronic Medical Record System for the Surveillance of Adverse Surgical Events and Human Error in A Developing World Surgical Service. *World Journal of Surgery*, *39*, 70-79.

Oluoch, T., Katana, A., Ssempijja, V., Kwaro, D., & Langat, P. (2014). Electronic medical record systems are associated with appropriate placement of HIV patients on antiretroviral therapy in rural health facilities in Kenya: a retrospective pre-post study. *J Am Med Inform Assoc*, *21*, 1009-1014.

Oluoch, T., Kwaro, D., Ssempijja, V., Katana, A., Langat, P., Okeyo, N., et al. (2015). Better adherence to pre-antiretroviral therapy guidelines after implementing an electronic medical record system in rural Kenyan HIV clinics: a multicenter pre–post study. *International Journal of Infectious Diseases*, *33*, 109-113.

Oluoch, T., Santas, X., Kwaroc, D., d, M. W., & Biondichd, P. (2012). The effect of electronic medical record-based clinical decision support on HIV care in resource-constrained settings: A systematic review. *International Journal of Medical Informatics*, *81*, 83-82.

Rahimi, B., & Vimarlund, V. (2007). Methods to Evaluate Health Information Systems in Healthcare Settings: A Literature Review. *J Med Syst*, *31*, 397-43.

Shah, K. G., Slough, T. L., Yeh, P. T., Gombwa, S., Kiromera, A., Oden, Z. M., et al. (2013). Novel open-source electronic medical records system for palliative care in low-resource settings. *BMC Palliative Care*, *12* (31), 1-10.

Siikaa, A. M., Rotich, J. K., Simiyu, C. J., Kigotho, E. M., Smith, F. E., Sidle, J. E., et al. (2005). An electronic medical record system for ambulatory care of HIV-infected patients in Kenya. *International Journal for Medical Informatics*, *74*, 345-355.

Snyder, C.F.,Wu,A.W.,Miller,R.S.,Jensen,R.E.,Bantug,E.T.,& Wolff,A.C.(2011).The Role of Informatics in Promoting Patient-Centered Care. *Cancer Journal*. 17(4), 211-218

Tierney, W. M., Rotich, J. K., Smith, F. E., Bii, J., Einterz, R. M., & Hannan, T. J. (2002). Crossing the "Digital Divide:" Implementing an Electronic Medical Record System in a Rural Kenyan Health Center to Support Clinical Care and Research. *AMIA Annual Symposium Proceeding.*

Were, M. C., Shen, C., Bwana, M., Emenyonu, N., Musinguzi, N., Nkuyahaga, F., et al. (2010). Creation and Evaluation of EMR-based Paper Clinical Summaries to Support HIV-Care in Uganda, Africa. *International Journal for Medical Informatics*, *79* (2), 1-13.

WHO Europe (2016). From Innovation to Implementation. eHealth in the WHO European Region

ABBREVIATION AND ACRONYM IDENTIFICATION AND EXPANSION WITHIN MEDICAL HEALTH RECORDS

Duncan Wallace and Tahar Kechadi
University College Dublin, Belfield, Dublin, Ireland

ABSTRACT

Recent years have seen the rapid increase in digitised medical information. In particular, the massive expansion of Electronic Health Records (EHRs), which are designed to document all information that is clinically relevant in a patient's use of a healthcare facility, has introduced unprecedented volumes of relatively unstructured data. This paper intends to determine the extent to which knowledge discovery in relation to both abbreviations and acronyms within heterogeneous data can be achieved. Heterogeneous data such as the narrative-based free-text notes found within patients' EHRs may use inconsistent ways to indicate contractions within the text and may use non-standard definitions for both abbreviations and acronyms. We approached this task through the retrieval and classification of contractions as well as using a novel method of combining multiple publicly available repositories. In order to provide better coverage of abbreviations, and also to address the issue of neologisms in general, word embeddings were applied to find semantically similar lexemes.

KEYWORDS

Bio-Informatics, Text-Mining, Natural-Language-Processing, Feature-Selection

1. INTRODUCTION

Continuity of care in medical industries has necessitated the increased adoption of digital recording of medical records. Much of this information, particularly in diagnostic contexts, is recorded in narrative based free-text. The free-text medication data in Electronic Health Records (EHRs) is predominantly unsanitised, and its unstructured nature makes it inaccessible to other computer applications that rely on coded data in healthcare settings (e.g, electronic medication reconciliation systems), as well as clinical research that uses structured medication data (Kushima, 2012). Despite providing a means of reducing paper-based inaccuracy, Electronic Medical Record Management systems are still subject to human error (Koppel, 2009).

Feature extraction is among one of the more challenging and important Natural Language Processing (NLP) tasks when considering the treatment of free-text medical records. Two particular complications in performing such extraction are the ambiguity of feature identification, and the plurality of forms similar features may present themselves (Huaug, 2009). Ambiguity frequently occurs because high value words or phrases may be hard to recognise in the relatively unstructured form that most clinical narratives take. A particular challenge emerges however in that many terms and phrases are contracted to abbreviations or acronyms, thereby significantly increasing the challenge posed in both retrieving these terms and identifying their meaning. Yet, this obfuscation of meaning is not the only contributing factor to the plurality of forms that similar features may exhibit. Synonymous terms may be recorded as morphologically unique contractions.

A perennial issue in relation to contractions is the ambiguity inherent in potential reading, when canonical definitions are not provided in the text. Unlike scientific journals, medical free-texts typically do not provide glossaries or in-line explanations of contraction, and even where an organisation may provide guidelines concerning the use of acronyms and abbreviations; these may not necessarily be followed by individual users.

Note that, for the purposes of simplicity, this paper is conflating both true acronyms which are pronounceable (such as AIDS), and letter sequences, (such as COPD). (Jurafsky, 2014).

Although a number of contractions have common usage throughout the medical domain, users unfamiliar with the stylistic habits of a particular organisation may have difficulty in correctly interpreting short-hand particular to that body. Contractions may also be subject to neologisms as non-standard, emergent forms, become spontaneously popular among individuals. It is therefore no surprise that NLP applications may struggle in correctly distinguishing contractions and their potential meaning within unstructured text. Furthermore, features which are in practical terms synonymous may easily be treated as distinct in NLP applications. As most potential features within free-text notes, with the exception of pharmaceutical entities, are recorded in some type of contracted form, these issues consequently have significant negative consequences on classifier performance, and upon knowledge discovery as a whole, within the context of clinical text.

2. PROPOSED SOLUTION

In this paper we describe the means we have employed to identify contractions and subsequently resolve them to their full-length forms. To this end we have developed a text analysis system which collects candidate contractions and extracts features relating to such, based upon lexical structure and sparse contextual details. We subsequently developed a supervised classifier to distinguish true positive acronym and abbreviation candidates from spelling errors and outlier lexemes.

In the second part of our paper we describe how we attempted to derive the long forms for contractions classified as true positives through two separate methods. The first method for correctly attributing contractions to their long forms was broached by vectorising true-positive contractions. These vectors were then compared with their semantic neighbours for syntactic similarity, with substitution taking place in the event of a successful match.

We also developed a database of long forms by analysing three separate repositories of contraction definitions. This was achieved by having a majority vote between the three repositories where conflicts arose, and by automatically parsing long forms for similarity. No long forms where chosen where consensus between the three repositories could not be reached.

While the first method's approach of substituting semantic matches would only be able to find the correct long form for abbreviations, as opposed to acronyms, this method was nonetheless given precedence over potential repository forms in order to avoid false-positive attribution of acronym definitions. It was furthermore hoped that, where a long form could not be derived, that synonymous terms may be successfully combined.

This research is using a corpus of 211000 cases treated in 2014 in an Out-of-Hours (OOH) general practitioner cooperative in Ireland. Electronic Health Records used in the operation of OOH coops are composed of both normalised and free-text clinical notes. The EHR software used by the co-op and the majority of OOH medical providers within Ireland and Great Britain is Ad Astra™. We discuss the extent to which this approach was successful, what limitations are present, and the future applications that this approach can promise.

The proposed solution was to build a system to provide text normalisation by taking high value terms and, through recourse to publicly available online repositories; reduce ambiguity, remove peculiarities of the local dataset, and rationalise the consequent extracted features. This system was to include an information retrieval and supervised learning classification of contractions, and comparison of both contractions and pharmaceuticals (two of the most important constituents to clinical free-text) with freely available third party data repositories. The ultimate aim of this was to transform features recorded in the vernacular to more generic forms. This transformation would include the expansion of contractions to their full length forms, and feature reduction in the case of pharmaceuticals. A successful combination of these techniques would increase the value of medical text for use in NLP applications.

3. RELATED RESEARCH

The value of the consolidation of clinical data to standard classifications has long been understood in terms of the integrity and analysis of biomedical text. As stated by Mate et al., due to the freedom accorded to users in entering data, unstructured free-text in EHRs are consequently both the most comprehensive data source, and the most susceptible to noise and local variation (Mate, 2015).

The value of abbreviation and acronym unrolling has long been appreciated within biomedical literature. However, the quality of biomedical literature treated to the end of contraction expansion varies significantly. Much of the extant research concerning the identification of contractions and their full length forms are based upon corpori where contractions are defined at some point in the text. For instance, Singh et al. look at identifying abbreviations exclusively within the context of Medline, a database of high quality journal publications in biomedical sciences, where contraction definitions are written into the publication in tandem with the contraction's usage (Singh, 2013). This type of contraction is defined as a "local abbreviation" and is outside the scope of this paper, with our research instead focused upon "global abbreviations" (Collard, 2015). Moreover, the clinical note-taking discussed in this paper is recorded by OOH phone operators who consistently discard verbs and other standard parts-of-speech for the purposes of speed, thereby making contextual analysis in this context more challenging than other types of biomedical corpora.

Like many other authors, Nautial et al. look exclusively at identifying acronyms and their respective long forms (Nautial, 2014). Although unlike the related research quoted by Nautial et al, whereby definitions are provided in close proximity to the acronym's usage (e.g. (Taghva, 2011)), Nautial et al. are nonetheless dependent upon the entire string relating to the full-length form be present somewhere in the text. Unfortunately, this approach may be unsuitable for lower quality textual environments where legibility is sacrificed for transcription speed. For instance, in our corpus the common acronym “copd” is written 5320 times, but its long form “chronic obstructive pulmonary disease” is not written once within the corpus. However, the long forms of abbreviations, which are considerably faster and easier to write than that of acronyms, are much more likely to appear within the corpus.

Notwithstanding the lack of application that such methodologies would have in the context of our corpus, this paper intends using existing research relating to the generation of acronym long forms through recourse to Medline abstracts. This research has helped automatically generate disambiguated forms of acronyms which can be combined with publically available, manually recorded definitions, such as that available on Wikipedia.

4. METHODOLOGY

In initial exploration it was discovered that contractions had a number of distinguishing characteristics within free-text. Other than the fact that contractions, by their nature, tended to have short length, they could be written as letters separated by symbols, in block capitals, or potentially followed by periods. Although a number of these identifiers may exist simultaneously, at times none of these characteristics may be present as writing styles vary greatly from one author to the next. A lexeme exhibiting any of these characteristics in isolation by no means indicates it being a contraction. For instance, some authors may use block capitals to indicate the use of a contraction, while others may habitually use block capitals for emphasis or the purposes of legibility.

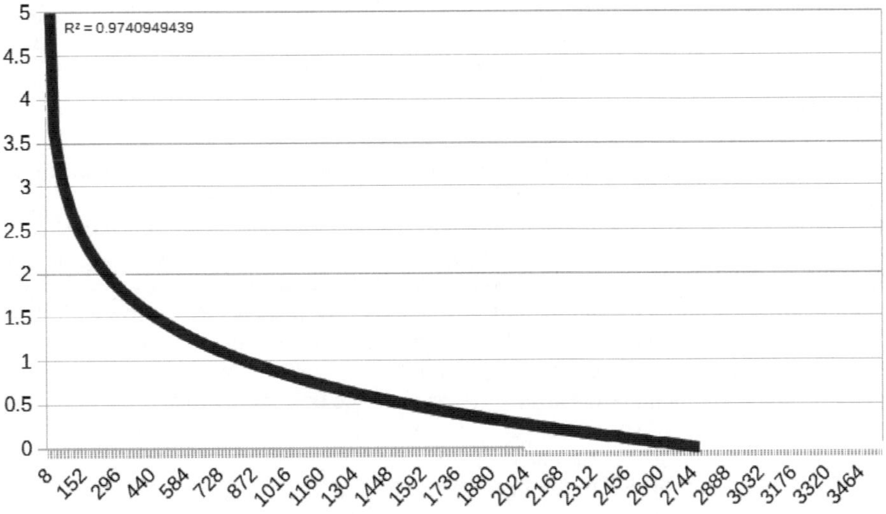

Figure 1. Exponential Curve of Contraction Candidates

Contractions were predominantly non-standard English words. A truncated version of SCOWL (Spell Checker Oriented Word Lists), totalling some 50000 words was used for reference. By using regular expressions to find characters separated by repeating symbols, and retrieving lexemes that were non English words, the frequency of all non-dictionary lexemes less than six characters in length were recorded. Contractions that appeared in different forms (e.g. a+e and A&E) were counted together. As anticipated, contraction candidate frequencies followed an exponential distribution as seen in **Figure 1** (y axis scale is $\log_{10}$). As expected also, the vast majority of unique lexemes collected were, in fact, unintentional spelling errors.

While this underpinned the value that the identification of true positive contractions would have on the process of removing textual errors, it also indicated that frequency was a key feature of true positive contractions.

4.1 Classification

While we made efforts to look at potential semantic structures of lexemes which represented true positive contractions, in terms of both the occurrence of vowels and consonants, and potential phonetic structures which could be derived, no consistency between true positives could be determined using such a methodology. Unfortunately, using an N-gram-Over-Context model (NOC) similarly provided little better than random results in testing, as contextual features varied wildly for different types of contractions.

Instead, features of candidate contractions were extracted based upon syntactic characteristics, with the value determined by frequency. As contraction frequency distribution was exponential, with a long tail of potential candidates, frequency values were consequently discretised into quartiles. Syntactic features were related to use of case (where the context was dissimilar), composition using symbols, and symbol suffixes. The absence of all the above characteristics was also derived as a feature. Originally, candidate length was also used as a feature, but this was later discarded due to it having a mildly negative impact on classification accuracy.

250 candidates were randomly extracted for training purposes. These candidates were next classed as either true or false positives by domain experts. Taking a two-third training and one-third testing split, candidate contractions were examined by three separate classifiers.

Decision Trees achieved an F1-score of 0.88
Naïve Bayes achieved an F1-score of 0.91
Support Vector Machine achieved an F1-score of 0.72

As Naïve Bayes had performed well, and features were logically independent of one another, this classifier was chosen to identify true-positives within the corpus.

4.2 Repository Voting

To the end of developing a system to inflate contractions to their full length forms, we approached a number of domain specific repositories with the aim of both achieving a comprehensive list of full length descriptions and the provision of disambiguation. The repositories used were the structured list of medical abbreviations on Wikipedia, the official list of abbreviations produced by the Irish Health Service Executive, and Acromine's RESTful API populated from Medline (Okazaki, 2006). Both Wikipedia and Acromine provide disambiguated results, while both the HSE and Wikipedia consist of manually written entries.

In the event of a particular contraction being provided multiple definitions by one of the repositories, these definitions would be compared with any definitions that may be provided by the other repositories. If a non-disambiguated match could be made, this definition would be chosen; otherwise a majority vote between repositories would be performed, with the most frequent entry within Acromine taken as the definition from that repository. In the event of disagreement between any two repositories a similar voting procedure would take place. If a consensus could not be reached between the repositories, no definition was chosen.

In order to achieve this mechanic some cleaning of all repository entries had to be performed (Wikipedia had any text occurring within a final set of parentheses deleted, as these were typically notes describing etymology or term usage). Exact matches were not required in the voting mechanic, and in the event of string similarity the longer candidate was chosen to as the definition for the contraction.

After entries with conflicting definitions in more than two of the repositories were deleted, the following list of definitions was generated. The process described as "No contention" refers to the scenarios where the definitions present have no conflicting definitions within other repositories.

Table 1. Definition List

Source	Process	Results
Wikipedia	**No contention**	1339
	+ Acromine	31
	+ HSE	325
HSE	**No contention**	722
	+ Acromine	42
Acromine	**No contention**	4020
Total		6484

4.3 Word Embeddings

A distinction arose between acronyms and abbreviations when finding full length forms. Abbreviations tend to be more colloquial and are more susceptible to neologisms. The exhaustive nature of the long version deduction, combined with the specificity of the resources used, initially produced flawed results with some common abbreviations. For instance "ok" was correctly classified as a contraction, but resolved to Opposum Kidney instead of "okay" due to a high occurrence of this acronym within Medline. Similarly, the abbreviation "pt" was interpreted as the acronym for "prothrombin time" rather than the intended meaning of "patient".

In order to mitigate against incorrect long form matches, a neural network, in the form of a Word2Vec model, was used to find semantically similar lexemes to the contractions classified as true-positives. In the case that syntactic similarity between a candidate and its vectors was identified, that vector was chosen as the long form of the candidate. These vectors included both English words and other contractions.

Many of the long forms derived from word embeddings represented forms which were not necessarily correct, but were closer to their correct form than initially presented. For instance the abbreviations symps and sympt were expanded to the form "sympotms", while pres was expanded to "prescreption". These misspellings represent very small edit distances from the correctly identified long form, making their correction in post-processing a relatively trivial task. This process also included the clustering of different contractions, such as phx and pmhx, which both represent "past medical history". Unfortunately "pmhx" was itself too morphologically dissimilar from its long form "history" to successfully provide a derivation ("history" had a cosin distance of 0.54 from pmhx). 32.43% of contractions which were substituted by a semantic neighbour were changed to a better lexicological form in this manner.

Of other semantic substitutions, 37.29% represented an exact match with their long form (or synonymous lexeme), while 19.45% were expanded to incorrect long forms. Incorrect long form substitution included "lrti" to "laryngitis", where "lrti" is an acronym meaning "lower respiratory tract infection" and laryngitis is a specific respiratory tract infection (which is often in the upper respiratory tract). Similarly "opd", an acronym meaning "out-patient department" was incorrectly associated with "orthopaedic". A further 10.27% of substitutions provided no substantial improvement (such as the clustering of om and som, which relate to slightly different conditions (otitis media versus serous otitis media respectively)). Also it must be noted that typographical errors could be incorrectly associated with a long form in this process, particularly in the case of shorter abbreviations. For instance, "f" was associated with the abbreviation fallw (which itself stands for "follow"). However in almost 7% of cases, "f" is actually an incorrectly written version of the word "of".

5. RESULTS

Testing in relation to the contractions was performed in relation to 150 randomly selected cases, totalling some 7251 words. Manual analysis of each of these cases was performed, providing the results in Table 2 below.

Items classed as contractions but for whom no long form was found were marked up in the results as contractions. Long forms were found for 97.4% of candidates classified as contractions, of which 82.76% were correct. The program achieved a recall of 0.90. The program, from start to finish (from contraction detection to long form generation), achieved an f1-score of 0.86.

Table 2. Abbreviations and Acronyms Identification within Test Data

Type	Description	Number	Precision
Short	**No inflation**	31	
Long	**Inflation**	1120	
	from repositories	557	0.87
	from embeddings	563	0.78
Undiscovered		88	
Total		1239	

Results over the entire corpus can be seen below in Table 3

Table 3. Long Form Sources

Expansion source	Total number	Percentage of whole
Repository	727056	**38.18**
Repository voting	240196	**12.61**
Word embedding	936848	**49.20**
No long form	30944	**1.6**

6. CONCLUSIONS AND FUTURE WORK

This paper details a suitable means to address poor quality medical text where the use of abbreviations and acronyms may be habitual, but may have poor identifying features. Moreover, where definitions for contractions are not provided in the text under examination, this paper outlines a successful approach to automatically choose the most likely suitable long form. The ability to provide the expansion of abbreviations promises greater potential interoperability between different systems, or comparisons between corpora. While identifying true positive contractions can be useful to prevent accidental deletion in potential automated spelling correction processes, the primary value lies in consolidation of features to more generic forms.

Word embeddings, though nominally achieving lower precision than repository derived longforms, provided a valuable alternative source of data. This was particularly important in relation to a small number of prevalent abbreviations which had no long forms provided within repositories, partially due to their ubiquity within medical notes. As human readers would be unlikely to be confused about the meaning of these abbreviations, users who manually populate written repositories would likely place little value in recording these definitions.

However, while the classifier described above accurately detects contractions, it does not distinguish between abbreviations and acronyms. This can have negative consequences when attempting to correctly attribute long forms to their respective contractions. While there is unlikely to be any method that will be able to perfectly distinguish between the two, morphological characteristics can potentially be used to gain a confidence measure in the decision process. Similarly, Soundex could potentially be used to obtain more accurate association of abbreviations to their long forms, though this again is unlikely to provide a catchall solution.

A more significant consideration is that while the methodology outlined in this paper takes a context-sensitive approach when considering contraction candidates and their potential meaning as a whole, it does not consider context in relation to individual contractions in the task of textual substitution. Where spelling errors and overloaded use of contractions can occasionally occur, providing a means to exclude false positives could improve final results.

ACKNOWLEDGEMENT

This publication has emanated from research conducted with the financial support of Science Foundation Ireland (SFI) under Grant Number SFI/12/RC/2289, in collaboration with Carlow Emergency Doctors On Call – CAREDOC.

REFERENCES

Collard, B. and Royal, A., 2015. The use of abbreviations in surgical note keeping. *Annals of Medicine and Surgery*, *4*(2), pp.100-102.

Huang, Bing, Y. Zhang, and M. Kechadi. "Preprocessing techniques for online handwriting recognition." *Intelligent text categorization and clustering* (2009): 25-45.

Jurafsky, D. and James, H., 2014. Speech and language processing an introduction to natural language processing, computational linguistics, and speech. Volume 3

Koppel, R., 2009. EMR entry error: not so benign. AHRQ mortality & morbidity rounds on the web.

Kushima, M., Araki, K., Suzuki, M., Araki, S. and Nikama, T., 2012. Text data mining of the electronic medical record of the chronic hepatitis patient. *Hong Kong: IMECS.*

Mate, S., Köpcke, F., Toddenroth, D., Martin, M., Prokosch, H.U., Bürkle, T. and Ganslandt, T., 2015. Ontology-based data integration between clinical and research systems. *PloS one*, *10*(1), p.e0116656.

Nautial, A., Sristy, N.B. and Somayajulu, D.V., 2014, October. Finding acronym expansion using semi-Markov conditional random fields. In *Proceedings of the 7th ACM India Computing Conference* (p. 16). ACM.

Okazaki, N. and Ananiadou, S., 2006. Building an abbreviation dictionary using a term recognition approach. *Bioinformatics*, *22*(24), pp.3089-3095.

Singh, S., Sharma, G., Nazeer, A.K. and Singh, S., 2013. Designing of an efficient algorithm for identifying Abbreviation definitions in biomedical Text. *International Journal of Computer Science & Information Technology*, *5*(3), p.143.

Taghva, K. and Vyas, L., 2011, August. Acronym expansion via Hidden Markov Models. In *Systems Engineering (ICSEng), 2011 21st International Conference on* (pp. 120-125). IEEE.

SEQUENCE PREDICTION ALGORITHM FOR HEART FAILURE PREDICTION

Carine Bou Rjeily[1], Georges Badr[2], Amir Hajjam El Hassani[1] and Emmanuel Andres[3]
[1] *Nanomedecine Lab, Imagery & Therapeutics, Université de Technologie de Belfort Montbéliard, France*
[2] *Ticket Lab, Antonine University, Hadat-Baabda, Lebanon*
[3] *Université de Strasbourg, Centre Hospitalier Universitaire, 67000 Strasbourg, France*

ABSTRACT

Cardiovascular diseases are the leading causes of death worldwide, from which heart attack and coronary artery disease are the most common ones. Both diseases are direct causes of Heart Failure, which affects the heart's pumping job, leading to an abnormal distribution of nutriments and oxygen to the body. Data mining techniques have been used to predict different heart diseases. This paper describes the application of a data mining technique, namely the sequence prediction algorithm, CPT+ or Compact Prediction Tree plus, to predict the absence and the presence of heart failure in patients. To evaluate the efficiency of adopted technique, we ran the algorithm in a dataset from the UCI Machine Learning Repository, containing a list of 14 attributes, including the attribute to be predicted. The evaluation showed promising results in term of predicting the absence and presence of heart disease leading to heart failure.

KEYWORDS

Data Mining, Prediction, CPT, Chronic disease, Cardiovascular, Heart Failure

1. INTRODUCTION

The increasing burden of chronic diseases such as cardiovascular diseases, diabetes and many others, has become the main concern of nowadays researchers in the health domain. Chronic diseases have an intense impact to the health of the patient, influencing their quality of life for the rest of their living. According to the World Health Organization (WHO), more than 15 million patients today suffer from such diseases and this number is expected to increase to 20 million by 2020.

Scientists and researchers have invested all their efforts in order to help heath care professionals in their challenges. One domain that has been exploited for this purpose is the knowledge discovery. Knowledge Discovery in Databases has been defined as the "non-trivial extraction of implicit, previously unknown and potentially useful information from data" (Bramer). Basically, it is the extraction of hidden information about data in a specific domain. Data Mining is the core step of this process. It involves using a variety of data analysis tools and algorithms, to explore the data, develop models, and discover previously unknown patterns and relationships that may be used to make valid predictions. Today's healthcare data mining is widely studied. Academics and researchers have been using several data mining techniques, including decision trees, neural networks, association rules, etc., to predict different diseases. Heart diseases are mostly taken into consideration, ranking first in deaths worldwide. All heart diseases affect, in a way or another, the heart's pumping action, which results a lack in delivery of the oxygen and nutrient-rich blood, needed for the cells. This is known as "Heart Failure".

In this paper, we are presenting the use of a data-mining algorithm to predict, the absence or presence of heart failure. We used a sequence prediction algorithm, namely the Compact Prediction Tree plus, CPT+, on a medical dataset. The rest of this paper is divided as follows. The next section defines the heart failure, its causes and symptoms. Then we present the related works and the adopted method. The conducted experiments and the results are presented afterwards, before ending with a conclusion and future works.

2. HEART FAILURE

2.1 Definition

The human body functions normally when all its cells are nourished properly. This is established by the heart's pumping action, which results in delivery of the oxygen and nutrient-rich blood, needed for the cells. When the heart fails in establishing properly this action, or cannot keep up with this workload, this is known as "Heart Failure". In definition, Heart Failure (HF) is a chronic, progressive condition in which the heart muscle is unable to pump enough blood through the heart to meet the body's needs for blood and oxygen. As a consequence, the blood supply to the heart muscle suddenly goes wrong, therefore lowering its oxygen supply and causing its death (Cannon). HF should not be mistaken with heart attack (HA) (known as Myocardial Infraction). HA happens when one of the heart's own blood vessels becomes blocked by a blood clot reducing the heart's power to squeeze out blood as it should. HA is one of the major causes of HF.

2.2 Causes and Symptoms

For heart diseases in general, smoking, high cholesterol levels, high blood pressure, physical inactivity, obesity, diabetes, age, gender, and heredity (including race) are major risk factors. (Mohan). The most common causes of heart failure are Coronary Artery Disease and Hypertension. The authors in (Aha) listed the conditions and risks that lead to HF: coronary artery disease, past heart attack, high blood pressure, abnormal heart valves, heart muscle disease, heart defect present at birth, severe lung disease, diabetes, obesity, sleep apnea, alcohol / drug abuse.

Heart failure symptoms can vary widely from person to person, depending on the type of his heart failure. Symptoms are unlikely to be noticed in the early stages, but with HF progress, they become more likely experienced. The main symptoms of heart failure are caused by fluid accumulation or congestion (shortness of breath, coughing or wheezing, weight gain, swollen ankles), and poor blood flow to the body (tiredness / fatigue, dizziness, rapid heartbeat, loss of appetite, the need to urine at night, confusion, impaired thinking). (Dickstein n.d.).

3. RELATED WORKS

Many researchers have implemented and compared different algorithms in order to predict different events related to heart diseases. Results have varied regarding the attributes used and the number of records selected. Below, we are trying to present the most important and recent related (later than 2012) works that used data mining techniques and especially frequent patterns and sequences to predict heart diseases.

In (Srinivas K. et al.), the authors used the Attribute Association to find the association among frequent, and infrequent attributes of a dataset. Their goal was to find the strength between the symptoms and their frequencies for the coronary vascular disease (CVD).

The authors in (Mai S. et al.) predicted heart disease using k-means clustering with the decision tree method. The experiments were conducted using the 13 attributes of the Cleveland Clinic Foundation Heart Disease dataset. Different combinations for the centroid were tested and the maximum prediction accuracy calculated was 83.9%.

An intelligent heart disease prediction system was proposed by (Dangare & Apte) using data mining classification techniques, based on a historical heart database. Two more important attributes were added to the 13 known attributes (obesity and smoking). Values were input to a 3-layers perceptron neural network in order to predict the heart disease.

In order to find the frequency of diseases affecting patients living in various geographical locations during different time periods, (Ilayaraja & Meyyappan), proposed in their work an association rule based Apriori data mining technique. The WEKA tool was used to apply this algorithm on data.

The research published in (Pandey A.K. et al.) uses the gain ration decision tree in order to predict the heart failure. This decision tree is based on the information gain method. This is done by calculating the difference between the original information and what is needed. Ranking is based on this metric. Top ranked features are selected as input for the decision tree.

(Nahar J. et al.) used the Apriori, Predictive Apriori, and Tertius algorithm, on the UCI Clevland dataset. They first extracted rules based on the gender (male or female) and then consider other attributes in order to classify and indicate sick and healthy conditions.

For effective heart disease prediction, (Aditya M. et al.) have used both Classification Modeling Techniques, and Association classification technique to predict the likelihood to have a heart failure. Medical profiles with 13 attributes were extracted from the Cleveland Dataset. They tested many algorithms like Decision Trees, Naïve Bayes and Neural Network. On the other hand, the Apriori algorithm, along with MAFIA algorithm, was used to find significant relations in heart diseases.

For predicting and analyzing the type of heart disease in patients, Decision Trees, Naïve Bayes, and Association Rules were also used in (Sudhakar & Manimekalai).

(Ilayaraja & Meyyappan) proposed a method to predict the heart disease risk using frequent itemsets. The frequent itemsets were produced using some symptoms and minimum support value. The proposed method showed efficient results in identifying risk level of heart disease using the frequent itemsets.

Another method that extracts hidden knowledge from the text documents, text mining, was used by (Subramanian S. et al.) to predict Coronary Heart Disease. The collected data was converted into a structured format. Perditions were made, based on the rules generated by the Apriori Algorithm. Results were efficient and accurate.

Many other researches were conducted in order to predict heart disease. These methods include Support Vector Machine (SVM), the C4.5 decision tree classifier, Fuzzy logic, CART algorithm, Genetic algorithm, feature subset selection, swarm optimization algorithm, etc.

4. HEART FAILURE PREDICTION USING SEQUENCE PREDICTION ALGORITHM

Before presenting the proposed method, it is important to define some basic terms used in sequential pattern mining in order to understand the mining process.

a. An item is an entity that can have multiple attributes: date, size, color, etc.
b. $I = \{i_1, \ldots, i_n\}$ is a non empty set of items. A k-item set is an item set with k items.
c. A sequence "α" is an ordered list of item sets.
d. A sequential Database (SDB) is a list of sequences with a sequence ID (SID).
e. A sequential rule, denoted $X \rightarrow Y$, is a relationship between two unordered item sets. This means that if items of X appear in a sequence, items of Y will also occur in the same sequence.
f. The support of a rule r in a sequence database SDB is defined as the number of sequences that contains $X \cup Y$ divided by the number of sequences in the database.
g. A rule r is a frequent sequential rule iff $supSDB(r) \geq minsup$, with $minsup \in [0, 1]$ is a threshold set by the user.
h. The confidence of a rule r in a sequence database SDB is defined as the number of sequences that contains $X \cup Y$, divided by the number of sequences that contains X.
i. A rule r is a valid sequential rule iff it is frequent and $confSDB(r) \geq minconf$, with $minconf \in [0, 1]$ is a threshold set by the user.
j. Sequence prediction is the fact of predicting the next element in given sequence. This prediction is preceded by a learning phase on a set of sequences, called training sequences.

4.1 CPT+

CPT (Compact Prediction Tree) is a sequence prediction model (Gueniche T. et al.) that is used to perform sequence prediction. CPT+ is an improved version of CPT and is up to 98 times more compact and 4.5 times faster than CPT (Gueniche T. et al.). Both algorithms take as input a sequence database that is used for training, in order to predict the next symbol in a given sequence.

CPT+ was chosen in our work because of its performance. It consumes less resources, responses are faster and with better accuracy. In fact, its main principal characteristics are: (1) It stores, in a compressed form, all the training sequences without loss or with a minimal loss of information. (2) It uses a measure of similarity to identify the sequences to be predicted to make a prediction. This measure is noise-tolerant, which allows CPT to predict future sub-sequence elements that have not been seen in the training sequences, while other approaches cannot make prediction in this case. The CPT model is defined by two processes: a training process and a prediction process.

4.1.1 Training

The training process takes sequences, one by one, from the training set given as input, to incrementally build its three structures: the Prediction Tree (PT), the Inverted Index (II), and the Lookup Table (LT).

Prediction Tree: It is a type of prefix tree composed of recursively-defined node with all training sequences. Each node has a pointer to its parent node and contains an item representing a list of children nodes. The sequence is defined by the path from a direct child of the root node to an inner node or leaf.

Inverted Index: It's a Hash Table, where each unique item is a key, leading to a set of bits. Value 1 represents the presence of an i-th element in the i-th sequence, 0 otherwise. The II will rapidly find the sequences in which an item appears, and will find all sequences with a set of items.

Lookup Table: The LT is an associative array. The LT points to the last node of the sequence in PT. This will help getting the sequences form the PT using their ID. LT is updated after each insertion in the PT. Note that, this mapping guarantees a lossless representation of the data.

Figure 1 illustrates the creation of the CPT structures by successive insertion of the sequences S1 = (A, B, C), s2 = (A, B), s3 = (A, B, D, C), where the alphabet Z = {A, B, C, D, E} is used.

4.1.2 Predicting

The prediction process uses the three structures described above. Making a prediction for a sequence S, consists of finding all the "sequences similar to S". In other words, this consists first in finding all sequences containing the last X items from S, in any order and in any position. X is an integer called "prefix length". Then, for each similar sequence, CPT considers its consequent. The consequence of a sequence Y is the subsequence beginning after the last element in common with X until the end of Y. Each element E in one of these consequents is then stored in hash table called Count Table (CT) with its number of occurrences. The element with the greatest number of occurrences is the element predicted by CPT. The II is used to find these sequences, by an intersection of the bit sets of the last x items from S. These sequences are accessed in the PT using the LT.

4.1.3 Optimization

CPT+ presents a Prediction with Improved Noise Reduction, PNR, which affects the algorithm's accuracy, by removing items considered noises, from subsequences. An item is listed as noise if it has a low frequency (support).
The algorithm takes in parameters two double attributes:

- noiseRatio: % of items in a sequence considered as noise
- minimumPredictionRatio: minimum number of updates

The algorithm removes item having low frequency from subsequences and updates the CT. When the minimum number of updates specified is reached, the prediction is made.

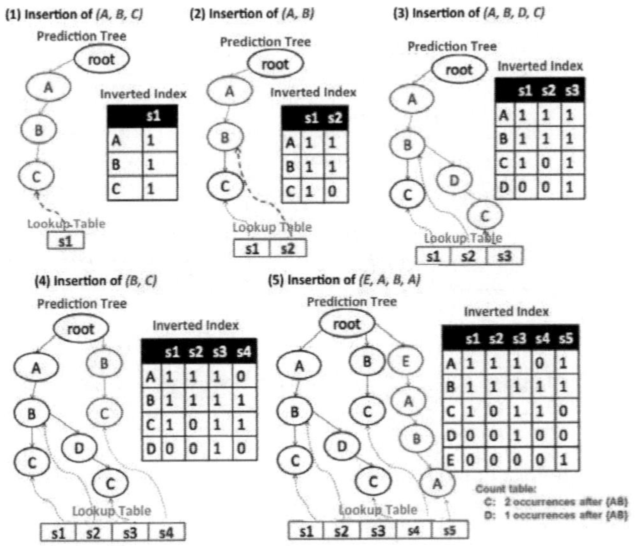

Figure 1. Example illustrating the structures used in CPT+

5. EXPERIMENTS AND RESULTS

Experiments have been conducted to prove if a sequence prediction algorithm can be useful to predict the presence or absence of a disease considering the vital signs of a user. In this section, we will list the used datasets and will present the obtained results, the discussions and interpretations.

5.1 Datasets

In the experiments, we used the dataset, from the UCI Machine Learning Repository. The Cleveland dataset has 270 rows without any missing value. It has a set of 13 attributes (cf. table 1 below), followed by the predicted one. The predicted attribute is Boolean, indicating the absence or presence of the disease. 80% of sequences in the datasets were used as training set, and the remaining 20% were used for testing and validation. 54 rows were tested, 30 rows showing the presence of Heart Failure, the remainder 24 rows do not.

Table 1. Attributes (vital signs) considered in heart failure prediction

Attributes	Type	Description
Age	Continuous	Age in years
Sex	Discrete	Gender (1: male, 0: female)
CP	Discrete	Chest pain (1: typical angina, 2: atypical angina, 3: non-anginal pain, 4: asymptomatic)
Chol	Continuous	Serum cholesterol in mg/dl
Trestbps	Continuous	Resting blood pressure in mm Hg
Fbs	Discrete	Fasting blood sugar > 120 mg/dl (1: true, 0: false)
Restecg	Discrete	Resting electrocardiography results (0: normal, 1: having ST-T wave abnormality, 2: left ventricular hypertrophy)
Thalach	Continuous	Maximum heart rate
Exang	Discrete	Exercise induced angina (1: yes, 0: no)
Oldpeak	Continuous	Depression induced by exercise relative to rest
Slope	Discrete	The slope of the peak exercise ST segment (1: up sloping, 2: flat, 3: down sloping)
Ca	Discrete	Number of major vessels colored by fluoroscopy (from 0 to 3)
Thal	Discrete	3: normal, 6: fixed defect, 7: reversible defect
Presence / Absence	Discrete	The predicted attributes (0: Absence, 1: Presence)

5.2 Results

The confusion matrix was used to calculate the results. True Positive (TP), and True Negative (TN), are both correct classifications for positive and negative outcomes respectively. False Positive (FP) and False Negative (FN), occur respectively when the outcome is incorrectly predicted as positive when it is actually negative, and incorrectly predicted as negative when it is actually positive. These can be arranged in a confusion table shown in Table 2.

Table 2. Confusion Matrix

	Predicted Positive	Predicted Negative	
Actual Positive	TP	FN	$\text{Sensitivity} = \frac{\text{TP}}{\text{TP+FN}}$
Actual Negative	FP	TN	$\text{Specificity} = \frac{\text{TN}}{\text{TN+FP}}$
$\text{Accuracy} = \frac{\text{TP+TN}}{\text{TP+TN+FP+FN}}$	$\text{Precision} = \frac{\text{TP}}{\text{TP + FP}}$	$\text{NPV} = \frac{\text{TN}}{\text{TN + FN}}$	

The calculated measurements are defined as follow:

- Accuracy: the total number of correct predictions
- Sensitivity or true positive rate (TPR): the number of positives that are correctly predicted
- Specificity, or true negative rate (TNR): the number of negatives that are correctly predicted
- Precision, or positive prediction value (PPV): proportions of positive results that are true positive
- Negative Prediction Value (NPV): proportions of negative results that are true negative

For this dataset, the highest result was achieved five times with:

- minPredictionRatio >= 0.5
- noiseRatio = 1.0

The corresponding confusion matrix is shown in table 3.

Table 3. Confusion Matrix from the dataset.

	Predicted Positive	Predicted Negative	
Actual Positive	TP = 19	FN = 5	Sensitivity = 79.16%
Actual Negative	FP = 2	TN = 28	Specificity = 93.33%
Accuracy = 87.03%	Precision = 90.47%	NPV=84.84%	

5.3 Comparison with Other Algorithms

The results obtained using the CPT+ are compared with those of other algorithms used to predict heart failure. The table below lists the three articles having as objective "Heart Failure Prediction". For each article, the algorithm used is stated, followed by the obtained accuracy, sensitivity and specificity.

Table 4. Comparison with results of some others prediction algorithms.

Algorithm used	**Accuracy**	**Sensitivity**	**Specificity**
CPT+	**87.03%**	79.16%	93.33%
C4.5 decision tree classifier (Aljaaf A. et al.)	86.5%	86.5%	95.5%
Classification and Regression Tree (Melilo et al.)	85.4%	93.3%	63.6%
Alternating Decision Tree (Bohacik J. et al.)	77.65%	37.30%	91.53%
Naive Bayes (Aditya M. et al.)	86.53%		
ANN 85.53 (Aditya M. et al.)	85.53%		
CARD Decision Tree (Chaurasia & Pal)	83.49%		
Decision tree (Pandey A.K. et al.)	75.73%		
K-means Clustering and Decision Tree (Mai S. et al.)	83.9%		

As shown in Table 4, the method that we adopted has achieved the highest accuracy, with a value of 87.03%. Therefore, values in the table show that a sequence prediction algorithm (CPT/CPT+) is promising in predicting heart failure and heart disease.

6. CONCLUSION

Data mining techniques are widely used nowadays, especially in the medical fields, where heart diseases are considered of the leading causes of mortality worldwide.

This paper presents the implementation and the experimentation of a sequence prediction algorithm in order to predict heart failure. We used the CPT+, a sequence prediction algorithm, which predicts the next symbol or element from a sequence. In other words, this consists in finding all sequences containing items from a defined sequence, in any order and in any position. We presented the algorithms and its structures.

To validate the ability of CPT+ in predicting heart failure, experiments were performed on the Cleveland dataset containing vital signs of patients. There were 14 attributes. 13 among them correspond to patient data, and the last one represents the absence or presence of heart failure, which is the attribute to be predicted.

Results showed an accuracy of 87.03%, a sensitivity of 79.16% and a specificity of 93.33%. In comparison of some other algorithm with same objective, the adopted method revealed promising results.

As for future works, a test of this algorithm on real data and histories collected from hospitals will be done, in order to detect the sequence patterns contributing in heart failure, and predicting the attributes leading to the compensation of patients with heart failure

REFERENCES

Aditya M. et al., 2014, Early Heart Disease Prediction Using Data Mining Techniques, *Computer Science & Information Technology (CS & IT),© CS & IT-CSCP.*, pp. 53 - 59.

Aha, 2016, *Causes Of Heart Failure*, viewed 21 June 2016, <http://www.heart.org/HEARTORG/Conditions/HeartFailure/CausesAndRisksForHeartFailure/Causes-of-Heart-Failure_UCM_477643_Article.jsp#.V2kq2ut97IU>.

Aljaaf A. et al., 2015, Predicting the Likelihood of Heart Failure with a Multi Level Risk Assessment Using Decision Tree, *Proceedings of The Third International Conference on Technological Advances in Electrical, Electronics and Computer Engineering*, Beirut.

Bohacik J. et al., 2013, Alternating decision tree applied to risk assessment of heart failure patients, *Journal of Information Technologies*, vol 6, no. 2, pp. 25-33.

Bramer M., 2007, *Principles of Data Mining*, Springer-Verlag, London.

Cannon, DE, 2009, *What's the difference between heart attack and heart failure?*, viewed 13 August 2016, <http://www.dailymail.co.uk/health/article-1199492/Whats-difference-heart-attack-heart-failure.html>.

Chaurasia, V. & Pal, S., 2013, Early prediction of heart diseases using data mining techniques, *Caribbean Journal of Science and Technology*, vol 1, pp. 208 - 217.

Dangare, C. & Apte, S., 2012, Improved Study of Heart Disease Prediction System using Data Mining Classification Techniques, *International Journal of Computer Applications*, vol 47, no. 10, pp. 875 - 888.

Dickstein, K., *Symptoms Of Heart Failure*, viewed 29 June 2016, <http://www.heartfailurematters.org/en_GB/Understanding-heart-failure/Symptoms-of-heart-failure>.

Gueniche T. et al., 2013, Compact prediction tree: A lossless model for accurate sequence prediction, *International Conference on Advanced Data Mining and Applications*, Springer, Berlin Heidelberg.

Gueniche T. et al. 2015, CPT+: Decreasing the time/space complexity of the Compact Prediction Tree, in *Pacific-Asia Conference on Knowledge Discovery and Data Mining*, Springer International Publishing.

Ilayaraja, M. & Meyyappan., T, 2013, Mining Medical Data to Identify Frequent Diseases using Apriori Algorithm, *Proceedings of the 2013 International Conference on Pattern Recognition, Informatics and Mobile Engineering*.

Ilayaraja, M. & Meyyappan, T., 2015, Efficient Data Mining Method to Predict the Risk of Heart Diseases through Frequent Itemsets, *4th International Conference on Eco-friendly Computing and Communication Systems, ICECCS*.

Nahar J. et al., 2013, Association rule mining to detect factors which contribute to heart disease in males and females, *Expert Systems with Applications*, vol 40, no. 4, pp. 1086-1093.

Mai S. et al., 2012, Integrating Decision Tree and K-Means Clustering with Different Initial Centroid Selection Methods in the Diagnosis of Heart Disease Patients, *International Conference on Data Mining*.

Melilo et al., P, 2015, Automatic prediction of cardiovascular and cerebrovascular events using heart rate variability analysis, *PloS one*.

Mohan, F., 2016, , viewed 12 July 2016, <http://www.mohanfoundation.org/organ-failure.asp>.

Pandey A.K. et al., 2013, A Heart Disease Prediction Model using Decision Tree, *Journal of Computer Engineering (IOSR-JCE)*, vol 12, no. 6, pp. 83 - 86.

Subramanian S. et al., 2016, Prediction of Outbreak of heart disease using Text Mining, *Discovery*, vol 52, no. 245, pp. 1070-1077.

Sudhakar, K. & Manimekalai, M., 2014, Study of Heart Disease Prediction using Data Mining, *International Journal of Advanced Research in Computer Science and Software Engineering*, vol 4, no. 1, pp. 1157 - 1160.

Srinivas K. et al., 2012, Analysis of Attribute Association in Heart Disease Using Data Mining Techniques, *International Journal or Engineering Research and Applications (IJERA)*, vol 2, pp. 1680 - 1683.

A SYSTEMATIC REVIEW ON THE EFFECT OF ICT ON SOCIAL SUPPORT MEASURES IN HEALTHCARE

Uchenna Nnabuko and Stuart Anderson
School of Informatics, University of Edinburgh, United Kingdom

ABSTRACT

Background: With increased popularity in the use of ICT in healthcare to provide support to individuals, it is imperative to investigate the impact of ICT on social support measures in health and social care.
Objective: This study aims to review literature on the effectiveness of ICT-based tools and intervention on social support measures with reference to health and illness.
Methods: Relevant databases (PubMed\MEDLINE, clinicaltrials.gov and Cochrane Library) were systematically searched using a combination of key search terms. To be included in the review, studies had to be published in English language, be published between 2000 and 2017, apply ICT intervention on a health-related condition and report the effect of ICT on social support measures.
Results: The database search produced 4,226 articles. After screening, 30 eligible papers were selected for the review. The studies were quite heterogeneous in terms of study design, age of participants, reported outcome, outcome measuring tool and health condition of participants. 20% of included studies were rated as low-quality evidence, with a high risk of research bias. Over 75% of reviewed studies reported a positive impact of ICT on social support measures. The results show that ICT interventions have a statistically significant positive impact on social support measures. Social network was found to have the most impact on social support measures.
Conclusion: There is need for more high-quality research on the effect of ICT on social support measures. The results of this systematic review suggest that ICT could effectively provide social support to individuals, although the degree of its effect could depend on the nature of ICT tool used and the well-being status of individuals. Further work in the use of ICT to provide social support for preventive healthcare is recommended. Also, more research investigating the effect of Smartphone-based instant messaging applications (such as WhatsApp and Snapchat) and virtual reality technology on social support is encouraged.

KEYWORDS

Social Support, ICT Intervention, Health, Impact, Social Network, Internet

1. INTRODUCTION

The computerization of healthcare has changed the expectations of people concerning service delivery and the way health is delivered, and it appears those expectations exceed the changes already realized in health. This computerization is achieved through the use of Information and Communication Technology (ICT) tools such as the Internet and services it facilitates like social media, online games and the like. With the present shift of health from a focus on treatment to wellness, a greater proportion of these services are targeted towards wellness management. In 2015, consumer health apps for wellness management accounted for about two-thirds of the mHealth apps in Apple iOS and Google app platforms [1]. Particularly, the Internet has the potential to provide a more effective medium of communication between the parties involved in healthcare - patients, healthcare professionals and other caregivers [3].

More recently, ICT has been identified as technology capable of creating transformative ways of providing healthcare services that would better meet the needs of the society [15]. The stakeholders of healthcare have somewhat different needs to be met. Patients need faster service, better availability and high quality of healthcare services, the doctors need high quality equipment and services, conducive work environment and perhaps an opportunity for research, and healthcare providers are interested in procuring more affordable budget, acceptable quality and limiting unfavourable media coverage. With the fast changing needs of the population for efficient health care services, healthcare providers are growing more interested in finding ways to support more physically or mentally ill people, who might have difficulties meeting their everyday personal and social needs, at home and this has increased the popularity of ICT devices in health and social care over the years [37]. Hence the question - do individuals actually experience social support when using ICT in the context of healthcare and social care?

Social support is a multifaceted concept; hence it can mean different things to various people. It is defined as the feeling of being accepted or cared for experienced by an individual or tangible support received by an individual from other individual(s) within a group [50]. It is also highly intercorrelated with loneliness as they are both considered lower-order endpoints of a higher-order construct of general social attachment [39]. According to [9], the four functional dimensions of social support are emotional, informational, instrumental and validation.

Searching literature identified four existing reviews that investigate the effect of ICT on general health and social care outcomes [2, 15, 31] and the impact of social support on health outcomes [50]. It has been reported that ICT can improve coordination of care and exchange of knowledge [15], enhance the relationship between the patient and healthcare professional [2] and manage eating disorders [31]. Higher levels of social support have been reported to improve clinical outcomes and help individuals adopt healthy lifestyle activities [50]. However, little is known on the impact ICT has on social support measures in healthcare. To our knowledge, the only existing review with similar focus is that of Chen and Schulz [10] that investigated the effect of ICT interventions on social isolation in the elderly. They reported that ICT has a positive effect on social support, although this effect seemed to be short-lived and failed to last more than six months after the ICT intervention was administered.

The objective of this systematic review is to present evidence on the impact of ICT interventions on social support measures in health and social care context, irrespective of age, methodology or setting.

2. METHODS

To conduct this systematic review, the fundamental steps outlined in [22] were followed.

2.1 Definition of Review Question

The aim of this systematic review is to answer the question *Does ICT have an impact on social support measures in healthcare?* Although some evidence exists on the impact of social support on health outcomes, few evidence-based reviews on the impact of ICT on social support have been conducted. Answering this question is important because it could help inform cost-effective policies on the use of ICT to provide social support to improve health outcomes. It could also inform policies on the coproduction of healthcare, which enhances collaboration between individuals and healthcare providers towards the creation of healthcare services, via the use of eHealth apps.

2.2 Literature Search Strategy, Inclusion Criteria and Study Selection

A search on the PubMed\MEDLINE, clinicaltrials.gov, and Cochrane Library databases was conducted from March 2016 to January 2017, using a combination of these keywords: social support, ICT, social media, social network, telemedicine, telecare, telehealth, tele* and online games. These keywords were chosen in order to capture as many forms of ICT intervention as possible.

This search produced 4,209 citations. The references of reviews returned in the search results were also assessed for relevant studies and 17 citations were identified as relevant. This yielded 4,226 citations in total.

Studies were first sifted using the pre-screening method which involved deciding which studies to retrieve for further attention based on their titles (and abstracts when titles do not provide sufficient information). The second sifting process involved selecting retrieved studies to be included in the review by reading the full text. Eligible studies were selected based on the inclusion criteria which are:

- published in 2000 - January 2017, to ensure the review is current and relevant
- published in English language, in consideration of the language limitations of the authors
- non-qualitative study

- apply ICT intervention on a health- and care-related condition
- interventions/programs administered on more than one participant, to ensure the study is not based on a single person's opinion
- social support measured as an independent variable

After the first sift, 4020 articles were excluded and 206 articles were retrieved for further assessment. The second sift further excluded 167 articles. During the data extraction process, 9 articles were also excluded because they (i) were a sub-paper of another included paper (n = 3); (ii) did not measure social support with a research tool (n = 4) and; (iii) were a secondary data analysis study (n = 2). A total of 30 articles, which met the inclusion criteria, were included in this review. An overview of the study search and selection process is outlined in Figure 1.

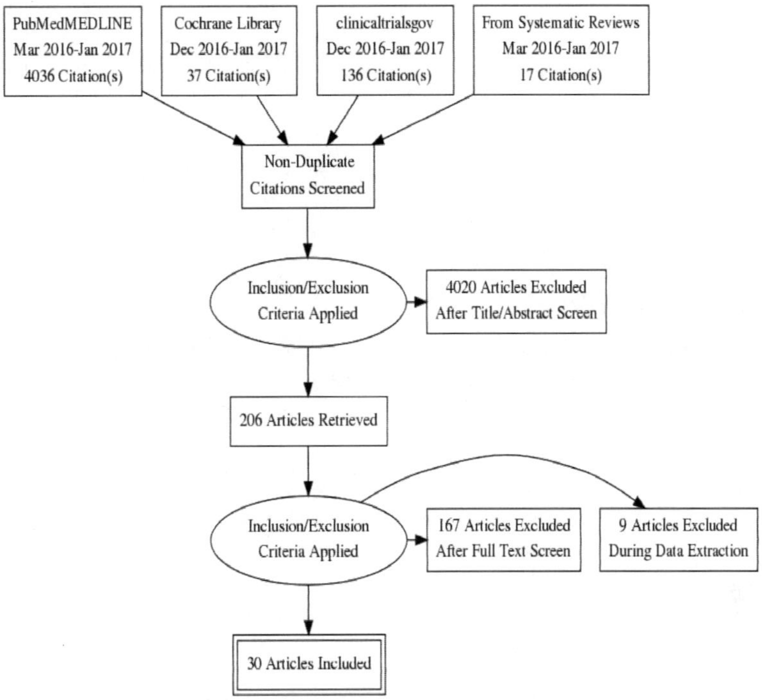

Figure 1. Study Selection flowchart

2.3 Study Quality Assessment

A revised version of MacLehose *et al.*'s instrument outlined in [36] was used to assess the methodological quality of studies. This instrument was chosen because it permits quality assessment across different study designs. The instrument asked questions concerning reporting, external validity (EV), internal validity (bias [IVB] and confounding [IVC]) of a study. Scores from these questions were summed to give an overall quality score for each study, with higher scores indicating higher study quality.

The assessment yielded 3 articles (all randomized controlled trials [RCTs]) as high quality evidence, 6 as low quality evidence and the remaining 21 as fair quality. A summary of the quality assessment for each study is available on request. The result of this assessment is similar to the findings in [36] as RCTs were discovered to have better quality than non-randomised studies (NRSs), although not statistically significant ($P = .09$), and RCTs also had a significantly higher IVC score than NRSs ($P = .02$). The combined quality of all studies is rated as fair quality evidence. To receive a rating of high quality, the score had to be greater or equal to the 80% mark of the maximum score; a rating of fair required a score greater or equal to the 50% mark while low quality was assigned if otherwise.

2.4 Data Analysis

Data on study setting (research location, sample and participant characteristics), study design, type of ICT intervention, and study outcomes were extracted from each study. A summary of studies included in this review is available on request. The included studies were heterogeneous in their design, outcome measuring tool, and ICT intervention; however, a forest plot helps present a clear picture of the overall result of this review. The tool used for building the forest plot is Cochrane's Review Manager 5.3 (http://community.cochrane.org/tools/review-production-tools/revman-5/about).

3. RESULTS

3.1 Study Setting

3.1.1 Location and Date of Publication

All included studies were published between 2000 and 2017, with 11 published before 2010 and 19 published in or after 2010. The studies were conducted in 11 countries (Australia, Canada, Germany, Italy, Netherlands, Norway, South Korea, Sweden, Taiwan, United Kingdom, and United States of America) with the highest number of studies from the United States of America (n = 19).

3.1.2 Sample Characteristics

All but 4 studies were fully conducted at the participants' homes or regular living environments. Three had the study conducted at home and senior center [30], hospital [32], clinic or community center [23] (where participants went for follow-up interview), and nursing homes [52]. The sample size of included studies ranged from 15 to 1,503 participants. Excluding studies which did not describe the number of participants lost to follow-up [14, 27, 32, 33, 38] and an exploratory study [34], the overall participant attrition (or drop-out) rate of included studies is 26.85%. The length of studies ranged from 1 month to 18 months, with majority of the studies lasting for 6 months (n = 9). See figure 2 for a distribution of the study lengths.

3.1.3 Participant Characteristics

Participants in the included studies had mean age ranging from 8-83 years. Twenty-two studies were designed for male and female participants, seven for female participants alone and one [26] for male participants alone. Although [41] was designed for both genders, only male participants were recruited for the study. Previous research has reported that women are more likely to easily exchange social support than men [5], this could account for the significant difference observed in the number of female- and male-specific studies.

In terms of participants' health characteristics, nine studies targeted participants with a chronic illness [14, 20, 23, 27, 28, 30, 33, 40, 41], ten studies targeted caregivers [4, 7, 16, 18, 19, 32, 35, 38, 49, 51], two studies targeted participants with cancer [24, 44], four studies on participants working on improving their physical activity and weight maintenance [8, 21, 29, 43], three studies were interested in improving participants' psychological well-being [26, 34, 52] and two studies had an interest in improving participants' overall well-being [12, 48].

3.2 Study Design

The study design of included studies include nineteen (63%) randomized controlled trials (RCTs) [7, 8, 12, 18–21, 23, 24, 27–29, 33, 40, 41, 43, 44, 48, 49], five (17%) quasi-experimental studies [14, 30, 32, 38, 52], two (7%) pre- and post- trials [4, 35], two (7%) pilot studies [26, 51], one (3%) feasibility trial [16] and one (3%) exploratory online survey [34]. Only nine RCTs reported using an adequate method of randomization [7, 20, 21, 23, 29, 40, 43, 44, 49]. Given the nature of the intervention, it was impossible to blind study participants to intervention group assignment. However, only seven studies made an attempt to blind the outcome assessors from participants' group assignment [7, 12, 16, 19, 20, 40, 49].

3.3 Type of ICT Intervention

There are ten different types of ICT intervention administered in the included studies. Fifteen studies (50%) administered a web-based application; all but two of them had a dedicated social network incorporated in the application. One of the two studies without a dedicated social network [8] used Facebook to facilitate social interaction between participants. Four studies (14%) administered a computer-telephone integrated (CTI) technology, which permits the interactions on a computer and telephone to be integrated in such a way that the computer can initiate and manage telephone calls. Two studies (8%) used telehealth technology, which provides services for remote exchange of data and information between a patient and clinician via electronic technology such as Skype or telephone. Three studies (10%) administered video technology which consisted of video-conference technology, video telehealth and videophone. Telephone, Internet, Online game, Social media (Facebook) were all used by one study (3%) each. One study (3%) administered a PC-based application with social network and one study (3%) used social network and videophone. See figure 3 for a distribution of the types of ICT intervention used. Some studies administered more than one ICT intervention; in this case, the main ICT intervention in the study has been used to make reporting uniform.

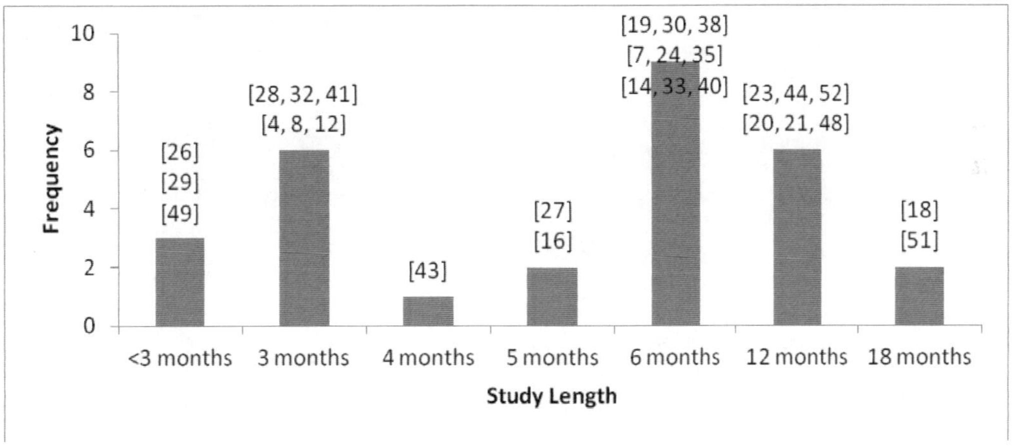

Figure 2. Distribution of Study Length

3.4 Study Outcomes

Social support is the outcome of interest for this review. Of the included thirty studies, twenty-three (77%) reported a positive impact of ICT intervention on social support measures while seven (23%) reported no impact of ICT intervention on social support [4, 8, 14, 43, 44, 48, 49]. A positive impact was either significant or insignificant (in which case, the improvement in social support measures could not confidently be attributed to the ICT intervention). Sixteen studies (54%) reported a significant positive impact [7, 16, 19, 20, 23, 24, 26, 28–30, 32, 33, 34, 38, 41, 51] while seven studies (23%) reported an insignificant positive impact of ICT intervention on social support [12, 18, 21, 27, 35, 40, 52]. Hence, the study outcomes are grouped into three categories: significant positive impact, insignificant positive impact and no impact of ICT on social support measures. The last category is tagged "no impact" instead of "negative impact" because there isn't enough evidence to conclude that ICT had a negative impact on social support in those studies. See figure 4 for the distribution of the study outcomes. The studies that reported a difference in social support measures by follow-up which favoured the control group or pre-intervention condition were placed in the "no impact" category, in addition to studies which found no between-group differences in social support measures [43, 44, 48].

Since there are no known widespread devices or medical instruments for measuring social support, different instruments (in the form of questionnaires) are used to measure social support. The instruments used in included studies are Medical Outcomes Study Social Support Survey (MOS-SSS) [47], The Personal Resource Questionnaire (PRQ) [54], Social Support Behaviours Scale [53], Inventory of Socially Supportive

Behaviors [6], Multidimensional Scale of Perceived Social Support (MSPSS) [55], Interpersonal Support Evaluation List (ISEL) [13], Social Influence on Physical Activity Scale [11], Revised University of California, Los Angeles (UCLA) Loneliness Scale [42], Social Support for Exercise [45], de Jong-Gierveld Loneliness Scale [17], questionnaires designed by study authors themselves, and unnamed scales used in existing literature. Two studies [26, 33] did not report the instrument used to measure social support. MOS-SSS is the most used instrument in the included studies (n = 8, 27%). MOS-SSS, MSPSS, and De Jong Gierveld Loneliness Scale were identified by [46] as three of the leading instruments for the assessment of social functioning/isolation. However, no significant effect of instrument used on social support outcome was found (P = .71).

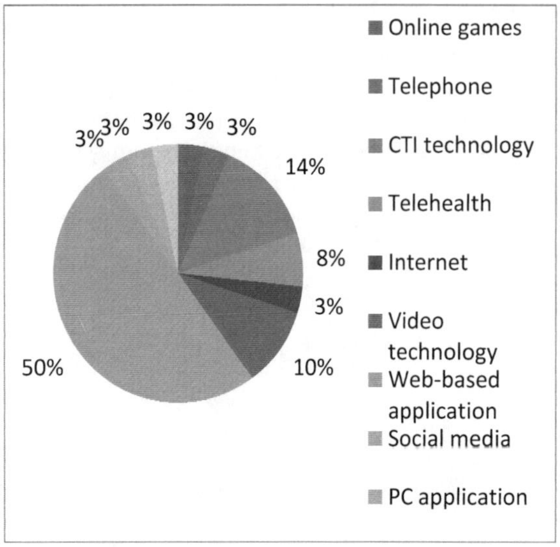

Figure 3. Type of ICT intervention (n = 10)

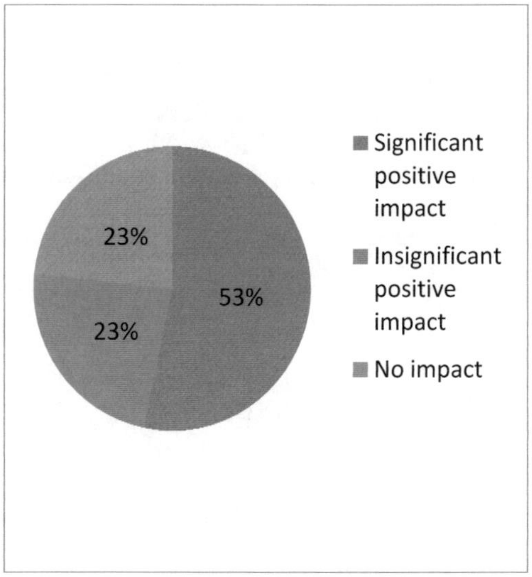

Figure 4. Distribution of study outcomes

Significant positive impact: Of the 16 studies in this category, majority of the studies (n = 10, 63%) are RCTs. The most commonly-used type of intervention is Web-based application with social network features (n = 6, 38%). The mean sample size is 141.25 (median = 99.5) and the modal study length is 6 months (n = 6, 38%). Excluding studies without a description of participant drop-out or attrition [32, 34, 38], collective participant attrition in this category is 12.79%.

Insignificant positive impact: Of the 7 studies in this category, 5 studies (71%) were RCTs, one study was a quasi-experimental study and another was a pre-/post- trial. The most commonly-used type of intervention is Web-based application with social network features (n = 3, 43%). The mean sample size is 384.57 (median = 225). The collective participant attrition in this category is 41.14%, excluding studies with no description of participant drop-out or attrition [27]. The modal study length is 6 and 12 months (n = 2 each, 29%).

No impact: Of the 7 studies in this category, five studies (71%) were RCTs, one study was a quasi-experimental study and another was a pre-/post- trial. The most used type of intervention is Web-based application (n = 6, 86%), which includes the two applications without social network features. The mean sample size is 194.14 (median = 179). Excluding studies without a description of participant drop-out/attrition [14], the collective participant attrition is 18.39% in this category.

3.5 Data Synthesis

A forest plot combines these results to obtain a single estimate of the relationship between ICT intervention and social support (see figure 5). Social support estimates (21 studies with 3001 participants) were heterogeneous (I^2 = 53%, P = .003), with an average effect size of 0.17 (CI, 0.05 to 0.29). This method of analysis has been used with the intention of presenting an estimate of social support measures across studies with varying design, target population, and settings. Nine studies were not included in the forest plot because they did not report mean and/or SD/SE measures at follow-up/post-intervention stage [12, 19, 23, 24, 32, 43, 44], were an exploratory study without follow-up measures [34] or the social support instrument used varied from the rest in that the higher the score, the lower the social support received [48]. The forest plot consists of RCTs and NRSs; in the case of a study without a control group, the pre- and post-intervention measures were used instead.

4. DISCUSSION

This systematic review aimed to describe evidence from quantitative studies of the impact of ICT intervention on social support measures in health- and care-related conditions. To our knowledge, this is the first review to address this question without any age, cultural or health-related restrictions. More than 70% of the included studies report a positive impact of ICT intervention on social support measures.

4.1 Social Network as the Most Effective ICT Intervention

For the purpose of this analysis, the web-based applications and PC application with features for social network, and social media are grouped as social network interventions. Of the 16 studies that administered this kind of intervention, all but 4 studies report a positive impact of ICT on social support. Thus, we can suggest that social network is the most effective ICT intervention used in this review. The sense of social support is better increased by the provision of real-time interaction in the form of regular interaction with another person interested in the participants' well-being [41]; which is not readily obtainable from programs which do not provide individually tailored content or feedback (such as Internet programs). Particularly, Internet programs when used alone are arguably a poor medium for improving social support because they offer more informational and network support [33]. However, when used in conjunction with an ICT intervention that provides real-time interaction, it tends to be more effective as was the case in [51].

	With ICT intervention			Without ICT intervention				Std. Mean Difference
Study or Subgroup	**Mean**	**SD**	**Total**	**Mean**	**SD**	**Total**	**Weight**	**IV, Random, 95% CI**
Barbabella 2016	58.7	14.2	94	60.7	14.2	94	6.4%	-0.14 [-0.43, 0.15]
Belle 2006	38	43.8	323	28	32.7	319	8.8%	0.26 [0.10, 0.41]
Cavallo 2012	2.2	0.93	67	2.22	0.91	67	5.5%	-0.02 [-0.36, 0.32]
Cobb 2014	0	0	0	0	0	0		Not estimable
Czaja 2013	9	3.2	38	8.2	3.5	72	4.7%	0.23 [-0.16, 0.63]
Côté 2015	60.77	20.03	99	70.23	21.61	80	6.2%	-0.45 [-0.75, -0.16]
Eisdorfer 2003	24.32	10.15	77	24.26	7	148	6.6%	0.01 [-0.27, 0.28]
Finkel 2007	0	0	0	0	0	0		Not estimable
Gellis 2012	56.3	31.9	57	46.7	32.3	58	5.1%	0.30 [-0.07, 0.66]
Gerber 2013	8.73	3.73	45	8.15	3.48	43	4.4%	0.16 [-0.26, 0.58]
Gustafson 2001	0	0	0	0	0	0		Not estimable
Gustafson 2012	0	0	0	0	0	0		Not estimable
Hightow 2015	77.4	16	15	69.7	17.3	15	2.1%	0.45 [-0.28, 1.18]
Hill 2004	135.1	17.56	75	132	23.81	167	6.6%	0.14 [-0.13, 0.41]
Hill 2006	83.46	12.42	61	78.96	17.15	59	5.2%	0.30 [-0.06, 0.66]
Joseph 2015	25.43	7.98	14	19.98	10.44	15	2.0%	0.57 [-0.18, 1.31]
Jung 2015	55.9	16.1	33	43.8	17.4	35	3.6%	0.71 [0.22, 1.20]
Kim 2012	0	0	0	0	0	0		Not estimable
Lindsay 2008	16.94	4.85	54	13.77	6.84	54	4.9%	0.53 [0.15, 0.91]
Longman 2009	0	0	0	0	0	0		Not estimable
Lykens 2014	19.41	5.47	152	19.09	6.09	152	7.5%	0.06 [-0.17, 0.28]
Marziali 2011	39.44	6.2	91	37.44	8.66	91	6.3%	0.26 [-0.03, 0.56]
Nguyen 2008	45.6	8.8	26	44.35	11.1	24	3.1%	0.12 [-0.43, 0.68]
Nield 2012	68.9	21.89	11	49.9	23.88	11	1.5%	0.80 [-0.08, 1.67]
Richardson 2010	0	0	0	0	0	0		Not estimable
Ruland 2013	0	0	0	0	0	0		Not estimable
Slegers 2008	0	0	0	0	0	0		Not estimable
Smith 2012	38.4	5.72	19	39.9	5.77	19	2.5%	-0.26 [-0.89, 0.38]
Torp 2008	60.7	6.31	18	57.3	6.16	19	2.4%	0.53 [-0.12, 1.19]
Tsai 2011	138.08	19.36	40	134.08	12.74	50	4.5%	0.25 [-0.17, 0.67]
Total (95% CI)			**1409**			**1592**	**100.0%**	**0.17 [0.05, 0.29]**

Heterogeneity: $Tau^2 = 0.03$; $Chi^2 = 42.15$, df = 20 (P = 0.003); $I^2 = 53\%$

Test for overall effect: Z = 2.86 (P = 0.004)

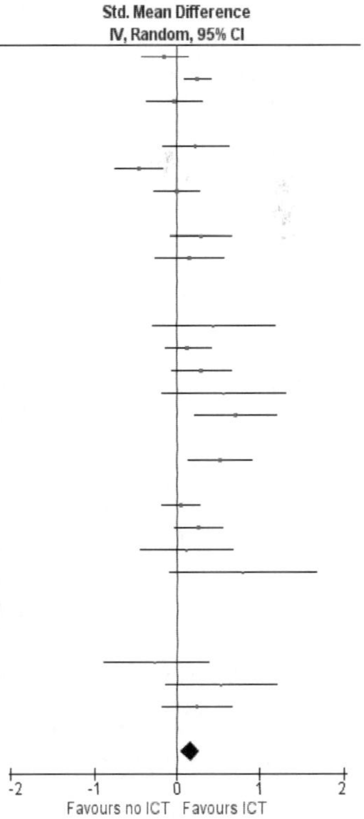

Figure 5. Forest Plot of Included Studies

4.2 Impact of ICT on Social Support

The findings from figure 5 suggest that ICT intervention has a statistically significant, positive impact on social support measures ($P = .004$). However, this result should be interpreted carefully as 53% of observed between-studies variance could be due to real differences in the effect size, rather than random error.

4.2.1 Lack of ICT Impact on Social Support

It would be helpful to discuss plausible explanations as to why seven studies reported no impact of ICT on social support measures. It appears the highest occurring limiting factor is the lack of proper control in order to limit the effect of intervention use in the study control group. All the studies in this review were investigating the effect of a certain ICT intervention on social support measures; however, some studies still administered some form of ICT intervention to participants in the control group. This was the case in [49] and [8] where both study groups had access to the website intervention, although the control group could only access educational features and were not invited to join the study's Facebook group (applies to [8]). In the same vein, [44] gave participants in its control group access to publicly-available, cancer-relevant Internet sites; even though the ICT intervention administered to experimental group participants was a Web-based application with social support features. Giving the control group access to any form of the intervention under consideration could have unexpected effects on outcome measures.

The social support instrument used in [43] was a single-item unvalidated survey question designed to provide data to a message-tailoring algorithm and not to precisely measure social support. Social support is a multifaceted concept which, arguably, cannot be sufficiently captured with a single question. An absence of randomization and presence of deep selection bias in [14] led to the formation of highly heterogeneous groups in terms of affective and cognitive variables, as the participants in the intervention group reported less perceived social support than those in the control group at baseline. Unsurprisingly, this between-group difference was also observed at follow-up.

The authors' suggestion for the slight decrease in social support by post-intervention in [4] is that being exposed to the intervention could have caused the caregivers to recognize the lack of adequate support received from family and significant others due to the website's provisions for information and support. This, in turn, could have stimulated a new appraisal of the caregiving situation which could have caused participants to rate social support received much lower than baseline measures. As this study had no control group, it is difficult to ascertain the validity of this assumption.

The participants in [48] were fit older adults (between 64-75 years old) who were not yet limited in their physical, mental and social capabilities (as observed in many of the outcome variables). The authors intentionally chose elderly participants with the assumption that people at that age are usually retired from work and hence, would have enough time to participate in the study. This assumption could be wrong, given that participants had no functional limitations. Additionally, the ICT intervention administered was the Internet. The use of Internet alone for health promotion may be more valuable to people with a chronic illness or susceptible to poor health [33]. The participants in this study had no chronic illness and the eligibility criteria ensured they were not susceptible to poor health at the time of joining the study. These factors could account for the non-positive impact reported in this study, even though the study was properly controlled.

4.2.2 Insignificant Impact of ICT on Social Support

The reasons for insignificant impact of ICT on social support in some studies include lack of proper control for intervention effect [18, 27], insignificant intervention utilization [21, 40], limitations in outcome measure tool [12, 52], and high attrition rate [35]. Interestingly, the collective participant attrition rate for studies in this category is 41.14%, which is substantially higher than the collective rate for studies in the other two categories. The occurrence of drop-out or attrition in studies can deteriorate generalizability of study results and affect study outcomes. However, there are cases where attrition is not necessarily viewed as a negative occurrence. For instance, if an application is designed to help the user achieve a change in health behaviour(s), attrition is considered a positive occurrence if users drop out when they become less dependent on the application to achieve behavioural change.

The ICT technology administered by [21] was not utilized as planned; 47% of the participants in the intervention group did not engage in DVR (video telehealth) viewing. Participants did not also utilize the opportunity to communicate with an instructor and other members of the intervention group via email. In [40], numerous significant technical difficulties and usability challenges were encountered with the Web and PDA tools used in the study which decreased participant engagement with the intervention. If participants did not engage properly with the intervention, it is clear to see how their social support measures might not significantly increase by follow-up.

Participants in the control group of [18] and [27] received support via a form of ICT intervention (telephone) different from that administered to participants of experimental group. Receiving such support could have influenced the outcome measures. Post-intervention measures for participants who dropped out in [35] were not available; this is particularly important because participant attrition for this study is 64.17%.

In addition to having a high attrition rate of 39%, the social support measure used in [52] computed total social support value as a summation of values for emotional, instrumental, informational, and appraisal support collected via the questionnaire. This could have affected the total social support value as only emotional and appraisal support increased by post-intervention since family members could be limited in providing proper instrumental and informational support. The social support measure used in [12] is an abridged version of the original tool which captured questions that refer to accessibility of physically local support which might not be very useful in capturing social support received via the ICT intervention.

Most of the studies in this category are longitudinal studies which lasted for 6 months or more. Longitudinal studies are considered important in public health; but unfortunately the longer the follow-up period, the higher the tendency of participants to drop out [25]. Hence there is a possibility that the longer an ICT intervention is used, the less effect it could reportedly have on social support measures. Further research into this phenomenon is encouraged.

4.3 Further Work

With the current shift of healthcare from treatment to wellness, it is becoming increasingly relevant for individuals to learn how to prevent illness and diseases by practising preventive healthcare. And with the focus of healthcare in developed countries shifting to "well" individuals, it is more important now than before to understand how ICT can provide support needed to help individuals adopt healthy lifestyles - as healthy individuals might have less motivation to use health-related applications. Hence, we recommend that more research is conducted to present more evidence on the role ICT plays in providing social support to individuals, irrespective of their susceptibility to poor health.

Also given that different cultural groups have preference for different sources of social support; it would be helpful to gain more knowledge on why these preferences exist and conduct research to test if these preferences could be fairly generalizable across the groups. For instance, [50] reports that individuals in minority groups exhibited greater preference for social support from family and friends as opposed to Caucasians who tended to rely more on support from media and health professionals than from family and friends.

With the rising popularity of instant messaging platforms such as WhatsApp and Snapchat, investigations could be conducted to ascertain how these platforms provide social support (informational and emotional) for individuals and staff in health and social care institutions. Also with the rapid development of ICT, it would be interesting to investigate how virtual reality technology/headset influences social support and health outcomes.

4.4 Limitations

This study presents results from randomized and non-randomized studies which can be interpreted as either a strength or a limitation. Its strength lies in its integration of various designs and methodologies to produce a single conclusive result. However, this makes it mandatory for the reader to carefully interpret the results as difference in study methodologies could have unprecedented effect on outcomes.

The limited number of electronic databases searched could be a limitation as some high-quality relevant studies may have failed to be included in this review. Generalizability of the results could also be limited by the heterogeneous nature of the included studies. However, the choice of varied study types was intentional in order to give an overview of how ICT influences social support.

5. CONCLUSION

In this review paper, we have explored the impact of ICT on social support measures with reference to health and illness. It was discovered that the most effective ICT intervention on social support measures is social network while the use of Internet alone only seems to work with individuals who are susceptible to poor health. There is need for more literature on the effect of ICT on social support measures in health and social care. The sparse quantity of existing research papers could be a limitation in this study. However, this paper has added to the knowledge in the field by reviewing the available literature to present a conclusive result - there is promising evidence that ICT has a positive effect on social support measures. However, the degree of impact could depend on the nature of ICT intervention used and the physical well-being of the users.

REFERENCES

[1] Aitken M, Lyle J (2015). Patient Adoption of mHealth: Use, Evidence and remaining Barriers to Mainstream Acceptance. *Parsippany, NJ: IMS Institute for Healthcare Informatics.*

[2] Åkesson KM, Saveman BI, Nilsson G (2007). Health Care Consumers' Experiences of Information Communication Technology – A Summary of Literature. *International Journal of Medical Informatics*, 76(9):633–645.

[3] Ambinder EP (2005). A History of the Shift toward Full Computerization of Medicine. *Journal of Oncology Practice*, 1(2):54–56.

[4] Barbabella F, Poli A, Andréasson F, Salzmann B, Papa R, Hanson E, Efthymiou A, Döhner H, Lancioni C, Civerchia P, Lamura G (2016). A Web-Based Psychosocial Intervention for Family Caregivers of Older People: Results from a Mixed-Methods Study in Three European Countries. *JMIR Research Protocols*, 5(4).

[5] Barbee AP, Cunningham MR, Winstead BA, Derlega VJ, Gulley MR, Yankeelov PA, Druen PB (1993). Effects of Gender Role Expectations on the Social Support Process. *Journal of Social Issues*, 49(3):175–190.

[6] Barrera M, Sandler IN, Ramsay TB (1981). Preliminary Development of a Scale of Social Support: Studies on College Students. *American Journal of Community Psychology*, 9(4):435–447.

[7] Belle SH, Burgio L, Burns R, Coon D, Czaja SJ, Gallagher-Thompson D, Gitlin LN, Klinger J, Koepke KM, Lee CC, Martindale-Adams J (2006). Enhancing the Quality of Life of Dementia Caregivers from Different Ethnic or Racial Groups: A Randomized, Controlled Trial. *Annals of internal medicine*, 145(10):727–738.

[8] Cavallo DN, Tate DF, Ries AV, Brown JD, DeVellis RF, Ammerman AS (2012). A Social Media–Based Physical Activity Intervention: A Randomized Controlled Trial. *American journal of preventive medicine*, 43(5):527–532.

[9] Chaparro-Díaz L (2013). ICT as a Social Support Mechanism for Family Caregivers of People with Chronic Illness: A Case Study. *Aquichan*, 13(1):27–40.

[10]Chen YRR, Schulz PJ (2016). The Effect of Information Communication Technology Interventions on Reducing Social Isolation in the Elderly: A Systematic Review. *Journal of medical Internet research*, 18(1).

[11]Chogahara M (1999). A Multidimensional Scale for Assessing Positive and Negative Social Influences on Physical Activity in Older Adults. *The Journals of Gerontology Series B: Psychological Sciences and Social Sciences*, 54(6):S356–S367.

[12]Cobb NK, Poirier J (2014). Effectiveness of a Multimodal Online Well-being Intervention: A Randomized Controlled Trial. *American journal of preventive medicine*, 46(1):41–48.

[13]Cohen S, Mermelstein R, Kamarck T, Hoberman HM (1985). Measuring the functional components of social support. In *Social support: Theory, research and applications*, pages 73–94. Springer.

[14]Côté J, Godin G, Ramirez-Garcia P, Rouleau G, Bourbonnais A, Guéhéneuc YG, Tremblay C, Otis J (2015). Virtual Intervention to Support Self-Management of Antiretroviral Therapy among People Living with HIV. *Journal of medical Internet research*, 17(1).

[15]Craig SL, Calleja Lorenzo MV (2014). Can Information and Communication Technologies Support Patient Engagement? A Review of Opportunities and Challenges in Health Social Work. *Social work in health care*, 53(9):845–864.

[16]Czaja SJ, Loewenstein D, Schulz R, Nair SN, Perdomo D (2013). A Videophone Psychosocial Intervention for Dementia Caregivers. *The American Journal of Geriatric Psychiatry*, 21(11):1071–1081.

[17]de Jong-Gierveld J, Kamphuls F (1985). The Development of a Rasch-type Loneliness Scale. *Applied psychological measurement*, 9(3):289–299.

[18]Eisdorfer C, Czaja SJ, Loewenstein DA, Rubert MP, Argüelles S, Mitrani VB, Szapocznik J (2003). The Effect of a Family Therapy and Technology-based Intervention on Caregiver Depression. *The Gerontologist*, 43(4):521–531.

[19]Finkel S, Czaja SJ, Martinovich Z, Harris C, Pezzuto D, Schulz R (2007). E-care: A Telecommunications Technology Intervention for Family Caregivers of Dementia Patients. *The American journal of geriatric psychiatry*, 15(5):443–448.

[20]Gellis ZD, Kenaley B, McGinty J, Bardelli E, Davitt J, Ten Have T (2012). Outcomes of a Telehealth Intervention for Homebound Older Adults with Heart or Chronic Respiratory Failure: A Randomized Controlled Trial. *The Gerontologist*, 52(4):541–552.

[21]Gerber BS, Schiffer L, Brown AA, Berbaum ML, Rimmer JH, Braunschweig CL, Fitzgibbon ML (2013). Video Telehealth for Weight Maintenance of African-American Women. *Journal of telemedicine and telecare*, 19(5): 266–272.

[22]Gopalakrishnan S, Ganeshkumar P (2013). Systematic Reviews and Meta-analysis: Understanding the Best Evidence in Primary Healthcare. *Journal of family medicine and primary care*, 2(1):9.

[23]Gustafson D, Wise M, Bhattacharya A, Pulvermacher A, Shanovich K, Phillips B, Lehman E, Chinchilli, V, Hawkins R, Kim JS (2012). The Effects of Combining Web-based eHealth with Telephone Nurse Case Management for Pediatric Asthma Control: A Randomized Controlled Trial. *Journal of medical Internet research*, 14(4):e101.

[24]Gustafson DH, Hawkins R, Pingree S, McTavish F, Arora NK, Mendenhall J, Cella DF, Serlin RC, Apantaku FM, Stewart J, Salner A (2001). Effect of Computer Support on Younger Women with Breast Cancer. Journal of general internal medicine, 16(7):435–445.

[25]Gustavson K, von Soest T, Karevold E, Røysamb E (2012). Attrition and Generalizability in Longitudinal Studies: Findings from a 15-year Population-Based Study and a Monte Carlo Simulation Study. *BMC Public Health*, 12(1):1.

[26]Hightow-Weidman LB, Muessig KE, Pike EC, LeGrand S, Baltierra N, Rucker AJ, Wilson P (2015). HealthMpowerment.org Building Community Through a Mobile-Optimized, Online Health Promotion Intervention. *Health Education & Behavior*, 42(4):493–499.

[27]Hill W, Schillo L, Weinert C (2004). Effect of a Computer-Based Intervention on Social Support for Chronically Ill Rural Women. *Rehabilitation Nursing*, 29(5):169–173.

[28]Hill W, Weinert C, Cudney S (2006). Influence of a Computer Intervention on the Psychological Status of Chronically Ill Rural Women: Preliminary Results. *Nursing research*, 55(1):34.

[29]Joseph RP, Keller C, Adams MA, Ainsworth BE (2015). Print versus a Culturally-Relevant Facebook and Text Message Delivered Intervention to Promote Physical Activity in African American Women: A Randomized Pilot Trial. *BMC women's health*, 15(1):1.

[30]Jung H, Lee JE (2015). The Impact of Community-based eHealth Self-management Intervention among Elderly Living Alone with Hypertension. *Journal of telemedicine and telecare*, page 1357633X15621467.

[31]Kendal S, Kirk S, Elvey R, Catchpole R, Pryjmachuk S (2016). How a Moderated Online Discussion Forum Facilitates Support for Young People with Eating Disorders. *Health Expectations*.

[32]Kim S, Kim E, Cheon J, Chung S, Moon S, Moon K (2012). The Effectiveness of Home-based Individual Tele-care Intervention for Stroke Caregivers in South Korea. *International nursing review*, 59(3):369–375.

[33]Lindsay S, Bellaby P, Smith S, Baker R (2008). Enabling Healthy Choices: Is ICT the Highway to Health Improvement? *Health*, 12(3):313–331.

[34]Longman H, O'Connor E, Obst P (2009). The Effect of Social Support Derived from World of Warcraft on Negative Psychological Symptoms. *Cyber Psychology & Behavior*, 12(5):563–566.

[35]Lykens K, Moayad N, Biswas S, Reyes-Ortiz C, Singh KP (2014). Impact of a Community Based Implementation of REACH II Program for Caregivers of Alzheimer's Patients. *PLoS One*, 9(2):e89290.

[36]MacLehose R, Reeves B, Harvey I, Sheldon T, Russell I, Black A (1999). A Systematic Review of Comparisons of Effect Sizes Derived from Randomised and Non-randomised Studies. *Health technology assessment (Winchester, England)*, 4(34):1–154.

[37]Martin S, Kelly G, Kernohan WG, McCreight B, Nugent C (2008). Smart Home Technologies for Health and Social Care Support. *Cochrane Database Syst Rev*, 4.

[38]Marziali E, Garcia LJ (2011). Dementia Caregivers' Responses to 2 Internet-based Intervention Programs. *American Journal of Alzheimer's Disease & Other Dementias®*, 26(1):36–43.

[39]Newcomb MD, Bentler PM (1986). Loneliness and Social Support: A Confirmatory Hierarchical Analysis. *Personality and social psychology bulletin*, 12(4):520–535.

[40]Nguyen HQ, Donesky-Cuenco D, Wolpin S, Reinke LF, Benditt JO, Paul SM, Carrieri-Kohlman V (2008). Randomized Controlled Trial of an Internet-Based versus Face-to-Face Dyspnea Self-Management Program for Patients with Chronic Obstructive Pulmonary Disease: Pilot Study. *J Med Internet Res*, 10(2):e9.

[41]Nield M, Hoo GWS (2012). Real-Time Telehealth for COPD Self-Management using Skype™. *COPD: Journal of Chronic Obstructive Pulmonary Disease*, 9(6):611–619.

[42]Peplau LA, Cutrona CE (1980). The Revised UCLA Loneliness Scale: Concurrent and Discriminant Validity Evidence. *Journal of personality and social psychology*, 39(3):472–80.

[43]Richardson CR, Buis LR, Janney AW, Goodrich DE, Sen A, Hess ML, Mehari KS, Fortlage LA, Resnick PJ, Zikmund-Fisher BJ, Strecher VJ (2010). An Online Community improves Adherence in an Internet–Mediated Walking Program. Part 1: Results of a Randomized Controlled Trial. *Journal of medical Internet research*, 12(4):e71.

[44]Ruland CM, Andersen T, Jeneson A, Moore S, Grimsbø GH, Børøsund E, Ellison MC (2013). Effects of an Internet Support System to Assist Cancer Patients in Reducing Symptom Distress: A Randomized Controlled Trial. *Cancer Nursing*, 36(1):6–17.

[45]Sallis JF, Grossman RM, Pinski RB, Patterson TL, Nader PR (1987). The Development of Scales to Measure Social Support for Diet and Exercise Behaviors. *Preventive medicine*, 16(6):825–836.

[46]Sansoni J, Marosszeky N, Sansoni E, Fleming G (2010). Final Report: Effective Assessment of Social Isolation.

[47]Sherbourne CD, Stewart AL (1991). The MOS Social Support Survey. *Social science & medicine*, 32(6):705–714.

[48]Slegers K, Van Boxtel MP, Jolles J (2008). Effects of Computer Training and Internet Usage on the Well-Being and Quality of Life of Older Adults: A Randomized, Controlled Study. *The journals of gerontology series B: Psychological sciences and social sciences*, 63(3):P176–P184.

[49]Smith GC, Egbert N, Dellman-Jenkins M, Nanna K, Palmieri, PA (2012). Reducing Depression in Stroke Survivors and their Informal Caregivers: A Randomized Clinical Trial of a Web-based Intervention. *Rehabilitation psychology*, 57(3):196.

[50]Strom JL, Egede LE (2012). The Impact of Social Support on Outcomes in Adult Patients with Type 2 Diabetes: A Systematic Review. *Current diabetes reports*, 12(6):769–781.

[51]Torp S, Hanson E, Hauge S, Ulstein I, Magnusson L (2008). A Pilot Study of how Information and Communication Technology may Contribute to Health Promotion among Elderly Spousal Carers in Norway. *Health & social care in the community*, 16(1):75–85.

[52]Tsai HH, Tsai YF (2011). Changes in Depressive Symptoms, Social Support, and Loneliness over 1 Year After a Minimum 3-month Videoconference Program for Older Nursing Home Residents. *Journal of medical Internet research*, 13(4):e93.

[53]Vaux A, Riedel S, Stewart D (1987). Modes of Social Support: The Social Support Behaviors (SS-B) Scale. *American Journal of Community Psychology*, 15(2):209–232.

[54]Weinert C, Brandt PA (1987). Measuring Social Support with the Personal Resource Questionnaire. *Western Journal of Nursing Research*, 9(4):589–602.

[55]Zimet GD, Powell SS, Farley GK, Werkman S, Berkoff KA (1990). Psychometric Characteristics of the Multidimensional Scale of Perceived Social Support. *Journal of personality assessment*, 55(3-4):610–617.

Short Papers

A MOBILE APP TO MANAGE CHILDREN DENTAL ANXIETY: CONTEXT AND APPROACH

María del Carmen Romero-Ternero, Rocío García-Robles, Daniel Cagigas-Muñíz and Octavio Rivera-Romero
Universidad de Sevilla, ETSI Informática, Avda. Reina Mercedes s/n 41012 Sevilla, Spain

ABSTRACT

Anxiety and fear related to dentistry interventions have been identified as problems affecting children. This reduces their quality of life and may have a negative impact on aspects such as sleep, self –esteem, mood, social relationships, and other psychological issues.The ARCADE project aims to design and develop a technological solution to manage children dental anxiety. This solution consists on a mobile system co-designed with children. An ecological momentary intervention is proposed using this solution before, during and after dentistry treatments. This paper presents a methodological approach to develop the project.

KEYWORDS

e-Health, Mobile Devices, Children Dental Anxiety, Usability

1. INTRODUCTION

Anxiety related to dental interventions is a common problem in children (*Colares et al. 2013)*. There is evidence reporting the dentist role as a scary person (*Majstorovic and Veerkamp et al. 2004*). Colares et al. (2013) found a prevalence of dental anxiety of 14.4% in a study involving 970 children aged 5-12 years. Nicolas et al. (2010) assessed 1303 children aged 5 to 12 years and observed a slightly lower prevalence of 7.6%. Raja et al. 2015 conducted a study in Islamabad aimed to estimate the prevalence of dental anxiety in children aged 5 to 10 years. Their results showed that 38% of the 252 participants had moderate or severe anxiety. Bezabih et al. 2013 reported a prevalence of 74.1% of dental anxiety between moderate and severe in a study involving 240 children.

Children and teenage anxiety and fear have a meaningful impact on their dental health, as well as on their cooperative attitude when visiting dentist (*Klingberg and Broberg 2007, Porritt et al. 2012*). Those problems may even be the reason to avoid or discard some dentistry treatments, especially in the case of children. Therefore, they suppose a great challenge in children treatments, becoming a barrier for dental health professionals (*Cohen et al. 2000*). Managing those patients is stressful for those professionals, demanding longer treatments and more resources. The resulting experienceis also less pleasant for both, patient and dentist (*Moore and Brødsgaard 2001, Brahm et al. 2012*).

Anxiety and fear produce emotional, physical, cognitive and behaviour interferences in individuals (*Cohen et al. 2000*). Scientific literature evidence suggests that children suffering anxiety and fear are likely to avoid dental health. That resultsin a higher incidence of untreated deteriorations and cavities compared to children with less anxiety and more cooperative attitude (*Freeman 2007, Nicolas et al. 2010, Rantavuori et al. 2004, Townend et al. 2000, Versloot et al. 2004*). Dental health and quality of life are connected, and therefore, dental anxiety may have a negative impact on children and teenagers mood and social relationships. Besides, it may cause sleep disorders, low self-esteem, as well as psychological problems (*Armfield et al. 2006, Carvalho et al. 2012*). On the other hand, it has been proved the existence of a narrow correlation between anxiety, pain stimuli and pain perception. In this sense, anxious patients feel higher and longer painful, increasing pain memory (*Weisenberg et al. 1984, Al Absi and Rokke 1991*).

2. DENTAL ANXIETY INTERVENTIONS

Dentistry interventions cause common anxiety and fear problems in some children resulting in a decrease of their quality of life. Thereforeit is crucial to form evidence-based therapiesto reduce or avoid those problems. Some therapies have been currently suggested which can be classified in three main different categories: psychotherapeutic, pharmacological,or a combination of both. Pharmacological therapies have showed a lower patients acceptance, being only effective in short-timetreatments (*Forbes et al. 2012*). Appukuttan (2016) conducted a literature review on management strategies for dental anxiety and phobia patients. He identified psychological strategies such as: iatrosedative technique, behaviour management techniques, relaxation techniques, guided imagery, biofeedback, hypnotherapy, acupuncture, distraction, increased control, systematic desensitization or exposure therapy, positive reinforcement, cognitive therapy and cognitive behavioural therapy.

The current project aims to study the feasibility of designing and developing a technological solution to reduce dental anxiety problems amongchildren 6-12 years of age. Some of the aforementioned techniques will be further implemented.

3. OBJETIVES AND APPROACH

3.1 Objectives

The main goal of ARCADE (App for Reducing Children's Anxiety in Dentistry Environment) project is to design and develop a technological solution to reduce anxiety that children suffer around dentistry interventions. This paper describes a methodology for:

1) Gathering and analysing children data about:
   - Dental anxiety.
   - Possible factors affecting anxiety.
   - Possible adoption barriers of technological solution to prevent or manage dental anxiety.
   - Preferences about games and possible distractor elements.
2) Gathering and analysing opinion from health professional and relatives about:
   - Barriers and facilitators to adopt technological solutions to prevent or manage dental anxiety.
   - Possible functionalities to include in technological solutions that can be useful to the patients.
   - Identifying possible challenges in the UCD (User-Centered Design) development process for the target collective.
   - Studying qualitatively and determining key functionalities for the app.
   - Establishing a typology of potential end users based on qualitative or quantitative variables to customize the solution.
   - Analysing different strategies of participatory design with the target collective.
   - Studying emotional modelling techniques as support to the intervention.
   - Assessing usability of the proposed solution, as well as satisfaction gradeof all its users.
3) Doing co-design with children.

3.2 Approach

The protocol proposed in ARCADE project has three stages:

1) The first one consists in a user research study aimed to understand needs, preferences and capacities using a mobile digital assistive system of children suffering from dental anxiety. In this sense, three target groups are involved in the study: patient children (between 8 and 15 children), their relatives and health professionals (at least 2) who treat them. First, standardized questionnaires are used to assess children's dental anxiety. Then, children participate in an interviewadapted to their ages. On the other hand, semi-structured interviews to relatives are carried out to complete data and identify possible

factors affecting to children dental anxiety. Finally, stakeholder interviews to health professionals are accomplished to identify relevant aspects for design and development of the mobile solution.

2) During the second stage, co-creation experiences are done by involving children (not necessarily patients) in design and develop tasks for the proposed technological solution.
3) During the third stage, an expert review is done with the abstract prototype, participating Information Technology professionals. Finally, prototype usability tests are accomplished with a group of children who are different to those participated in the previous stage.

3.2.1 Recruitment

Children are recruited from two dental clinics which have collaboration agreements with the University of Seville. Potential participants are identified initially by health professionals during interventions. Then, relatives are informed about ARCADE project and they are invited to participate in it. During the design and development phases(where the experiences of co-creation are performed), 10 children with ages between 6 and 12 years will participate.These children will not be patients.In all cases, it will be mandatory to obtain the informed consent of participants or their legal guardians.

3.2.2 Qualitative User Research

Semi-structured interviews are conductedin working sessions with children. Visual and/or graphic resources (pictograms and photographs) are used when convenient.Pictograms with faces representing the extracted scale of the SFP-R (Smiling Faces Program - Revised)(Buchanan, 2010) are used in not opened orYes/No questions.

Similar techniques are followed in sessions with family members orhealth professionals. These sessions are conducted by an interviewer and participants communicate to him/her their assessments without interfering with his/her cultural beliefs, particularities, prejudices or opinions. The script of interviews are defined presenting first general purposed questions and then more specific ones.

The information collected during these interviews serve as a requirement for the design and functionality of the solution to be developed in ARCADE project.

3.2.3 Co-design

There are many articles in the scientific literature about co-creation (participatory design or co-design) with children and/orteenagers.In these processes children make the user interface design along with the collaboration and guidance of expert designers and using techniques adapted to their ages. In this project and during this experience no children data collection is made.

These participatory methods allow designers to identify design problems from the children's point of view.In addition, problems related tothechildren's lack of maturity when expressing themselves or even problems of shyness may be overcome (Baek, 2008). As a result, better and more usable designs are obtained.

Examples of co-creation techniques can be found in (Chung, 2010), (Clark, 2011), (Walsh, 2010) or more recently in (Dodero, 2014). Here gamification methods are proposed for making more attractive and productive the co-creation process.

4. CONCLUSIONS AND FURTHER WORK

Children dental anxiety is a health problem impacting on their quality of life. A literature review has been conducted to identify the context. Moreover, a methodological approach to design a technological solution for children with dental anxiety has been presented.

ARCADE project results will serve to expand knowledge about the use of technological solutions to reduce dental anxiety in children between 6 and 12 years. They will allow a better understanding of the possible facilitating factors and potential barriers of this type of solutions. The knowledge acquired in this study will allow the development of technological solutions adapted to this target group. The effectiveness of these solutions will be investigated in future projects.

ACKNOWLEDGEMENT

The work described in this paper has been partially funded by Cátedra Telefónica "Inteligencia en la Red".

REFERENCES

Al Absi, M., Rokke, P. D., 1991.Can anxiety help us tolerate pain? *In Pain*. 1991; 46(1):43–51

Appukuttan, D.P., 2016. Strategies to manage patients with dental anxiety and dental phobia: literature review. *In Clinical, Cosmetic and Investigational Dentistry*, 8, 35–50. http://doi.org/10.2147/CCIDE.S63626.

Armfield, J.M. et al., 2006. Dental fear in Australia: who's afraid of the dentist? *In Australian Dental Joruna*l,51:78-85

Baek, J.-S. & Lee, K.-P., 2008. A participatory design approach to information architecture design for children. *In CoDesign*, 4, 173-191.

Bezabih, S. et al., 2013. Dental anxiety: prevalence and associated factors, among children who visited Jimma University Specialized Hospital Dental Clinic. *In Ethiopian Medical Journal*, 51(2), 115–21.

Brahm, C.O. et al., 2012. Dentists' views on fearful patients. Problems and promises. *In Swedish Dental Journal*, 36(2):79–89

Buchanan, H., 2010. Assessing dental anxiety in children: the Revised Smiley Faces Program. *In Child: Care, Health and Development*, 36: 534–538.

Carvalho, R.W.F. et al., 2012. Anxiety regarding dental treatment: prevalence and predictors among Brazilians. *In Ciência&SaúdeColetiva*, 17:1915-22, http://dx.doi.org/10.1590/S1413-81232012000700031

Chung, H. & Gerber, E., 2010. Emotional-Storyboarding : A Participatory Method for Emotional Designing for Children. *In Proceedings from the 7th International Conference on Design & Emotion*, 1-7.

Clark, A., 2011. Breaking methodological boundaries? Exploring visual, participatory methods with adults and young children. In European Early Childhood Education Research Journal, 19, 321-330.

Cohen, S.M. et al., 2000. The impact of dental anxiety on daily living. *In British Dental Journal*, 189:385-90

Colares, V. et al., 2013. Dental anxiety and dental pain in 5- to 12-year-old children in Recife, Brazil.*InEuropean Archives of Paediatric Dentistry*, 14:15-9, http://dx.doi.org/ 10.1007/s40368-012-0001-8

Dodero, G. et al. (2014). Towards tangible gamified co-design at school: two studies in primary schools. *In Proceedings of the extended abstracts of the 32nd annual ACM conference on Human factors in computing systems - CHI EA '14*, 707-718.

Forbes, M.D. et al., 2012.Acceptability of behaviour therapy for dental phobia. *In Community Dentistry and Oral Epidemiology*, 40(1):1–7.

Freeman RA., 2007. Fearful child attends: a psychoanalytic explanation of children's responses to dental treatment. *In International Journal of Paediatric Dentistry,* 17:407-18.

Klingberg, G., Broberg, A.G., 2007. Dental fear/anxiety and dental behaviour management problems in children and adolescents: a review of prevalence and concomitant psychological factors. *In International Journal of Paediatric Dentistry*, 17:391-406.

Majstorovic, M., Veerkamp, J.S.J., 2004. Relationship between needle phobia and dental anxiety. *In Journalof Dentistry for Children (Chic),* 71:201-5.

Moore, R., Brødsgaard, I., 2001. Dentists' perceived stress and its relation to perceptions about anxious patients. *In Community Dentistry Oral Epidemiology*, 29(1):73–80.

Nicolas, E. et al., 2010. Factors affecting dental fear in French children aged 5–12 years. *In International Journal of Paediatric Dentistry,* 20:366-73.

Porritt, J. et al., 2012. Understanding children's dental anxiety and psychological approaches to its reduction. *In International Journal of Paediatric Dentistry,* 22:397-405.

Raja, G.H. et al., 2015. Dental anxiety among children of age between 5 to 10 years visiting a teaching dental hospital in Islamabad, Pakistan. *In Journal ofAyub Medical College: Abbottabad*, 27(3):587-90.

Rantavuori, K. et al., 2004. Dental fear and oral health and family characteristics of Finnish children. *In ActaOdontologicaScandinavica*, 62:207-13.

Townend, E. et al., 2000. A clinical study of child dental anxiety. *In Behaviour Research and Therapy*, 38:31-46.

Versloot, J. et al., 2004. Children's coping with pain during dental care. *In Community Dentistry Oral Epidemiology*, 32:456-61

Walsh, G. et al., 2010. Layered elaboration: a new technique for co-design with children. *In Conference on Human Factors in Computing Systems*, 1237-1240.

Weisenberg, M. et al., 1984. Relevant and irrelevant anxiety in the reaction to pain. *In Pain,* 20(4):371–383.

INSPIRERS: AN APP TO MEASURE AND IMPROVE ADHERENCE TO INHALED TREATMENT

Cristina Jácome [1], Rute Almeida [1,2], João Pedro Teixeira [3], Pedro Vieira-Marques [1], Rita Vilaça [4], José Manuel Fernandes [4], Ana Ferreira [1] and João Almeida Fonseca[1,5,6]

[1] CINTESIS - Center for Health Technology and Services Research, Faculty of Medicine, University of Porto Rua Dr. Plácido da Costa 4200-450 Porto, Portugal

[2] CMUP - Centre of Mathematics of the University of Porto - Rua do Campo Alegre, 687; 4169-007 Porto, Portugal

[3] INESC TEC - Campus da FEUP - Rua Dr. Roberto Frias, 4200 - 465 Porto, Portugal

[4] BloomIdea - Rua Quinta de Cabanas, 110, 6°, 4700-003 Braga, Portugal

[5] MEDCIDS - Department of Community Medicine, Information and Health Decision Sciences, Faculty of Medicine, University of Porto, Rua Dr. Plácido da Costa 4200-450 Porto, Portugal

[6] Imunoalergologia, CUF Porto Instituto & Hospital, Estrada da Circunvalação 14341, 4100-180 Porto, Portugal

ABSTRACT

Inhaled controller medications are the cornerstone of asthma treatment and adherence is of critical importance to achieve good clinical results. However, suboptimum adherence has been the rule rather than the exception in patients with asthma. Two of the key challenges to change this scenario are: 1) development of easy-to-disseminate objective measures of inhaled drugs adherence, and 2) the promotion of behavior changes within the patients' routine daily-life. The knowledge that gaining and maintaining a person's attention is the first step in promoting behavior change and that smartphones and virtual community gaming can have a relevant role in enhancing motivation led to the concept of a mobile app. Inspirers is an attempt to transform the process of adherence to treatment into a positive experience through gamification and social interaction, while allowing for ubiquitous verified monitoring of treatment adherence. The main purpose of this work is to present the Inspirers features, development phases and forthcoming developments. We first describe the current version of Inspirers focusing on two major features: innovative inhaler usage detection based on imaging processing and the gamification approach based on social/peer support. Then we present the highly iterative development process implemented, which incorporated input/feedback from patients and physicians throughout. Finally, we discuss the forthcoming developments, mainly the integration of a feature related to symptoms monitoring; the generalization of the inhaler usage detection tool, now working with one type of inhaler, to other inhalers and oral treatments; and the implementation of feasibility and validation studies.

KEYWORDS

mHealth, app, medication adherence, asthma, gamification, image processing

1. INTRODUCTION

According to the World Health Organization (WHO), it is estimated that 235 million people suffer from asthma worldwide (WHO, 2013). Asthma is characterized by wheeze, shortness of breath, chest tightness and coughing and is punctuated by exacerbations, a major cause of morbidity and hospitalizations (Global Initiative for Asthma [GINA], 2017). As a lifelong disease that is not curable, the goals of asthma management are to achieve good symptom control and minimize future risk of exacerbations (GINA, 2017).

Inhaled controller medications, particularly inhaled corticosteroid, are the cornerstone of effective asthma treatment (WHO, 2013, GINA, 2017). This group of medications has well established effects in decreasing the frequency of symptoms and exacerbations (Pauwels et al., 2003). However, to achieve these benefits, adherence to daily medication is of critical importance. Suboptimum adherence to maintenance medication has been associated with poor asthma control, exacerbations, emergency department visits and hospitalizations, resulting in unnecessarily high health costs (Doz et al., 2013). Yet suboptimal adherence has been the rule rather than the exception, with adherence rates among patients with asthma ranging from 19% to 64%, and remaining unchanged in the last 3 decades (Bender, 2016).

With the recognition that nonadherence is a major problem and that patient self-reports of high adherence rates are unreliable, attempts have been made to objectively measure and improve adherence. Electronic monitoring devices to record adherence rates by logging the exact date and time an inhaler is actuated and to provide detailed information about patterns of treatment use have been developed (Chan et al., 2015). Two recent randomized control trials in children with asthma demonstrated benefits on adherence rates (70%), but a decrease over time is observed (Morton et al., 2017). Implementation of strategies capable of cost-effectively measuring, improving and maintaining adherence in the long run, impacting large numbers of patients and being easily disseminated are still needed to explore.

Smartphones are now very common in most parts of the world, together with the advantages of being personal, portable, connected, increasingly low cost and computationally powerful. In addition, adolescents and young adults are demographic groups most comfortable with the use of smartphones. Mobile Health applications may have the potential to measure and improve adherence, by being easily integrated in adolescents and adults everyday lives, anytime/anywhere, and by delivering adherence tools based on smartphone's embedded sensors (Marcano Belisario et al., 2013). However, there are no current solutions dedicated to this. In addition, mobile applications allow the combination of computation, interactive communication, and display ability of a smartphone with gamification elements and peer-support as potential means to shape user behavior change (Deterding et al., 2011, Haase et al., 2017). Gaining and maintaining a person's awareness and attention is the first step in promoting behavior change and virtual community gaming, through the addition of elements of fun and peer support, can have a role in enhancing motivation and behavior change, namely on adherence to inhalers (Baranowski et al., 2008).

Inspirers app was conceived as an attempt to transform the process of adherence to treatment into a positive experience through gamification and social interaction, while allowing for ubiquitous verified monitoring of treatment adherence. The main purpose of this work is to present the Inspirers features, development phases and forthcoming developments.

2. INSPIRERS APP

2.1 Features

Inspirers' essence is focused on supporting patients' medication management, by providing consistent monitoring of inhaled medication intakes and promoting adherence to treatment.

The app includes the registration of current medications (name, dose, medication bar code, treatment duration, treatment dosage and schedule) and the record of performed inhalations. The physician involvement is also considered by providing the user with the possibility of sharing data. The medication management is supported by a timeline that reflects the registered medication plan and provides a quick reference when a medication is due (Figure 1). This timeline provides also a quick shortcut for registering the medication intake. It allows to register not only the planned medication but also the registration of relief medication intake.

Inspirers, by combining features of inhaler usage detection and a gamification approach based on peer support, is an innovative way to measure and improve the adherence to inhalers.

2.1.1 Inhaler Usage Detection

The most innovative technology of the Inspirers app is the inhaler usage detection tool based on advanced image processing, validating the inhaler use through dose tracking. The tool can thus be used as a pervasive low-cost means of collecting data on patients' adherence to inhalers, using only the smartphone built-in camera. This functionality is triggered from the timeline when a new inhalation is registered.

The developed detection tool is based on computer vision methods and key visual features which are common on dose trackable devices: i) a contour or outer shape; ii) a specific written label/canisters; and iii) a dose counter indicating the remaining doses. It consists of several processing steps. First, the mobile device camera displays a centered capture mask, so that the user can align the inhaler to the camera (Figure 1), guaranteeing a minimum resolution on the dose counter for posterior automatic character recognition. An 8-bit RGB image is acquired and the height is reduced to 640 pixels, keeping the aspect ratio. The image is pre-processed by mild thresholding in the HSV space (invalidating high saturation pixels), using a morphological closing operation and converting to greyscale. Then, the grey image is lightly smoothed with a mean filter, a Canny edge detector (Canny, 1986) is employed and a moving edge weighted average (3 frames) is calculated. At the center of the algorithm, is a double edge-template matching. Two templates of the inhaler are created based on previously rendered edge maps. A larger template focuses on detecting the outer contours and a smaller one focuses on the dose counter, its placement and validation of the object size. The correlation between the averaged edge map and each template is calculated and each matching result is smoothed with a Gaussian filter to obtain more stable maximums. Finally, the inhaler is confirmed when both correlation maximum values appear within a small pixel range and if the contour match is also within that range of the centered capture mask. The detection of each dose in the dose counter uses numerical dose OCR (optical character recognition) standard techniques together with character positioning in addition to object (foreground) and dial (background) color, when available, for partial number correction. The detection tool is at a proof-of-concept stage, currently working with one type of inhaler.

2.1.2 Gamification

In order to promote user engagement, a gamification approach was developed for wrapping the base functionalities and the process of medication detection and registration into a motivating experience. Inspirers driving story and gameplay derives from promoting users' social engagement in a quest for other users' asthma adherence increase. The main objective is to increase the sphere of influence by coaching an expanding network of users that are designated as *Warriors*.

Users start by assuming the role of a *Warrior* (beginner player), whose aim is to become an *Inspirer* in order to be able to socially influence other players. The *Inspirer* gives support to his/her *Warriors* promoting actively their evolution in medication adherence through social interaction.

A points system support users' progress throughout levels making gradually available new game interaction features and user capabilities. Points are earned when users take certain actions, such as register their medication intake at the right time, update medications, or get a positive assessment from other players in their network (*Inspirer* or *Warrior*). In addition, *Inspirers* may earn points from actions that promote their *Warriors* to earn points themselves (e.g., alerting that they should take their medication at the right time). This may be accomplished by exchanging messages and sending medication reminders (buzz). These features enable *Inspirers* to stimulate *Warriors* that are not compliant with the therapeutic plan, allowing for a more valuable network of influence.

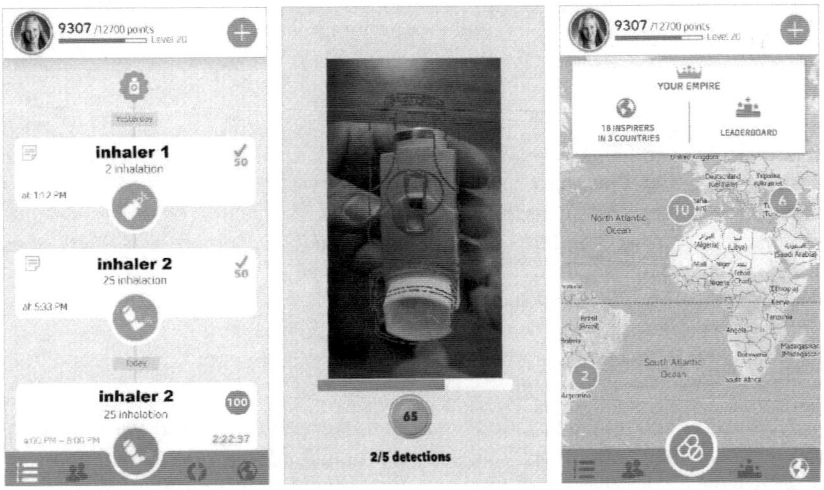

Figure 1. Inspirers app screenshots: timeline, video detection of inhaler usage, network of *Inspirers* and *Warriors*

Another encouragement for user's interaction are virtual badges used to reward individuals with high app engagement. Whenever the user reaches a certain goal or does something special, him/her will get rewarded and get a virtual badge for that. As an example, when an *Inspirer* becomes linked with his first *Warrior*, the user will get a badge "Role Model".

Users are able to see their impact in the world by visualizing the region/country of each element of his/her network of *Inspirers* and *Warriors* (Figure 1) and position on the leaderboard. They can also share and demonstrate their points/badges through social networks achieving additional social recognition.

2.2 Development

Inspirers is the product of a highly iterative development process, incorporating input/feedback from patients and physicians throughout. The development phases are described in Figure 2.

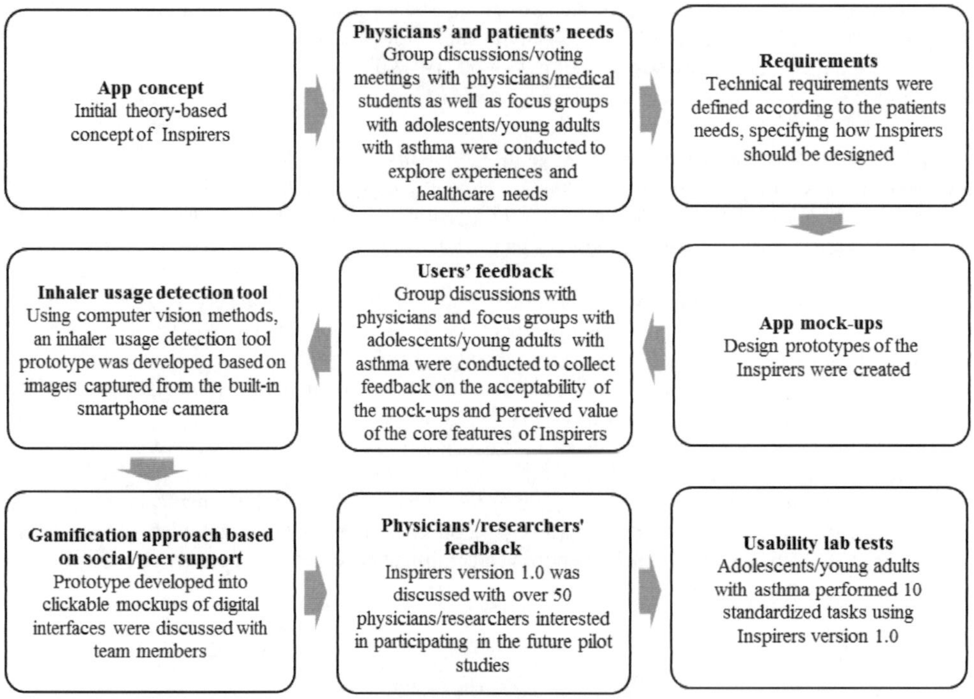

Figure 2. Inspirers app development phases

This app was developed in native Swift language for iOS. The Android version is under development and will be available in the 3rd trimester of 2017. The web services were designed based on Representational State Transfer architecture and, in order to allow the synchronization of users' data, a communication architecture among web services and iOS was developed through Alamofire, a swift-based HTTP networking library. In the web component, Drupal 7 was used as content management system and data is stored in a MySQL database. Inspirers use CoreData as Open Source, file-based database engine.

2.3 Forthcoming Developments

From the feedback obtained from physicians/researchers, we are further developing Inspirers to incorporate a feature related to symptoms monitoring. This feature will allow patients to daily record their asthma-related symptoms using visual analogue scales; to check their asthma control every 4 weeks using the Control of Allergic Rhinitis and Asthma Test (CARAT) (Fonseca et al., 2010); and to report any asthma exacerbations.

The Inhaler usage detection tool currently works with one type of inhaler and provides a confirmation of the inhaler presented to the camera. Although there are different models and shapes of inhaler devices in the market, the key visual features used allow to consistently enlarge the inhaler database for numerical dose OCR. We devised a template-base format for each inhaler and we are now defining the templates for the other inhaler devices available on the market. The next step will be to develop image processing methods to detect adherence to oral medications.

The previous interactions with users give us confidence that Inspirers can be a successful app, but we do not have yet any data on sustaining awareness and ongoing use. Therefore, acceptability and usefulness of Inspirers will be assessed in real-world studies to inform app further development. Prospective observational feasibility and validation studies among adolescents and young adults with asthma followed at secondary care in Portugal are being designed and are anticipated to start in the 3rd trimester of 2017.

3. CONCLUSION

Inspirers, by combining features of inhaler usage detection and a gamification approach based on social/peer support, is an innovative way to measure and improve the adherence to inhalers in adolescents and young adults with asthma. The proposed application can be used as a reliable and ubiquitous means of collecting data on patients' adherence to treatment, using only smartphone embedded sensors. Moreover, the proposed inhaler usage detection tool based on imaging processing technologies offers enormous potential to be integrated in other self-management apps. The inclusion of oral medication adherence detection will allow the generalization not only to several respiratory diseases but also to other chronic diseases, such as hypertension and diabetes.

ACKNOWLEDGEMENT

We would like to acknowledge Mariana In-uba and Magna Correia for organizing the focus groups/meetings and recruiting participants, and Andreia Barbas for conducting and analyzing the focus groups. We would also like to acknowledge Mundipharma-Portugal, particularly to Margarida Mateus, Salvador López Orland and Lígia Nunes, for funding the dissemination of the app and for organizing the meeting with physicians/researchers. This work was partially supported by FEDER through the operation POCI-01-0145-FEDER-007746 funded by the Programa Operacional Competitividade e Internacionalização – COMPETE2020 and by National Funds through FCT - Fundação para a Ciência e a Tecnologia within CINTESIS, R&D Unit (reference UID/IC/4255/2013). Rute Almeida is financed by the Project NORTE-01-0145-FEDER-000016 (NanoSTIMA), financed by the North Portugal Regional Operational Programme (NORTE 2020), under the PORTUGAL 2020 Partnership Agreement, and through the European Regional Development Fund (ERDF).

REFERENCES

Baranowski, T. et al, 2008. Playing for Real: Video Games and Stories for Health-Related Behavior Change. *American journal of preventive medicine,* Vol. 34, pp 74-82.e10.

Bender, B. G, 2016. Nonadherence to Asthma Treatment: Getting Unstuck. *The Journal of Allergy and Clinical Immunology: In Practice,* Vol. 4, pp 849-851.

Canny, J. (1986). A Computational Approach to Edge Detection. *IEEE Transactions on Pattern Analysis and Machine Intelligence,* PAMI-8, pp 679-698.

Chan, A. H. Y. et al, 2015. Using Electronic Monitoring Devices to Measure Inhaler Adherence: A Practical Guide for Clinicians. *The Journal of Allergy and Clinical Immunology: In Practice,* Vol. 3, pp 335-349.e5.

Deterding, S., et al. 2011. Gamification. using game-design elements in non-gaming contexts. *CHI '11 Extended Abstracts on Human Factors in Computing Systems.* Vancouver, BC, Canada: ACM.

Doz, M., et al, 2013. The association between asthma control, health care costs, and quality of life in France and Spain. *BMC Pulmonary Medicine,* Vol. 13, No. 15, pp1-10.

Fonseca, J.A. et al, 2010. Validation of a questionnaire (CARAT10) to assess rhinitis and asthma in patients with asthma. *Allergy,* Vol. 65, No. 8, pp 1042-1048.

GINA 2017. Global Strategy for Asthma Management and Prevention, 2017. Available from: www.ginasthma.org.

Haase, J., et al, 2017. Mobile Applications to Improve Medication Adherence. *Telemed J E Health,* Vol. 23, pp 75-79.

Marcano Belisario, J. S. et al, 2013. Smartphone and tablet self management apps for asthma. *The Cochrane database of systematic reviews*, CD010013.

Morton, R. W. et al, 2017. STAAR: a randomised controlled trial of electronic adherence monitoring with reminder alarms and feedback to improve clinical outcomes for children with asthma. *Thorax,* Vol. 72, pp 347-354.

Pauwels, R. A. et al, 2003. Early intervention with budesonide in mild persistent asthma: a randomised, double-blind trial. *Lancet,* Vol. 361, No. 9363, pp 1071-6.

WHO 2013. Asthma, 2013. Available from: http://www.who.int/mediacentre/factsheets/fs307/en/.

SERVICE ARCHITECTURE FOR GASTRIC CANCER SCREENING

Jaakko Lähteenmäki, Juha Leppänen, Janne Pajukanta, Juha M. Kortelainen and Raimo Launonen
VTT Technical Research Centre of Finland, Tietotie 3, FI-02650 Espoo, Finland

ABSTRACT

General purpose mobile phones and modern web technologies enable the development of cost-effective solutions for screening and monitoring of diseases. Such solutions may be used independently by individuals at home or at the clinic under the supervision of healthcare professionals. In this paper we present a service architecture for a gastric cancer screening system, including the related software components and their interfaces. The architecture has been designed to support the whole screening process involving both patients and clinicians. In the operational phase the screening system needs to exchange information with Electronic Health Records (EHRs) and Personal Health Records (PHR) in order to facilitate proper documentation of care, and access to the monitoring and screening data by all care process participants. We estimate the new HL7/FHIR draft standard to be well-suited for achieving the required interoperability. A proof-of-concept of the screening system including three components (sensor firmware, mobile application and server) is being implemented in the context of the SNIFFPHONE project.

KEYWORDS

Mobile health, Health monitoring, Healthcare interoperability, eHealth architecture

1. INTRODUCTION

Prevention and early diagnosis of diseases are essential when pursuing reduction in healthcare costs and increased quality of life. New methods have emerged for screening and monitoring of diseases, enabling fast and easy measurement and analysis of biomarkers either at clinic or at home. A cost-effective and user-friendly measurement device can be constructed by combining a general-purpose mobile device with the appropriate sensor system. Such measurement devices are typically connected to back-end cloud services enabling the measurement results to be saved and be accessible to care process participants.

This paper describes the service architecture being set-up for gastric cancer screening. Recent research (Amal, 2016) shows that early phases of gastric cancer can be detected based on volatile organic compounds (VOC's) present in the exhaled breath. The measurement of the VOC's can be done by nanomaterial-based sensor arrays (Broza & Haick, 2013). The SNIFFPHONE project is setting up a proof-of-concept system for supporting the measurement of the breath sample, analysing the sample and sharing the result in the appropriate form for use in the care process.

This paper focuses on the service architecture of the SNIFFPHONE screening system. Although such systems do not currently exist, similar service architectures are used in health monitoring systems (Franz et al., 2016; Urbauer et al., 2015). The SNIFFPHONE project has specifically targeted at a modular architecture enabling data exchange also with external information systems. Note, that gastric cancer screening may be applied either for healthy individuals or patients with precancerous conditions. In this paper, the individual taking the screening test is referred always as "patient".

2. SERVICE ARCHITECTURE

The top-level SNIFFPHONE service architecture is depicted in Figure 1. The patient uses a mobile phone equipped with a sensor module for providing the breath sample. The mobile application guides the user through the sample-collection process. During the process, the application transmits the sensor outputs and any related contextual information over the SP-IF interface to the Data Analysis Server (DAS) for analysis. At the server, a Linear Discriminant Analysis (LDA) model is used for classification of the sample based on a training set comprised of previously recorded and analysed breath samples. The DAS provides a direct response indicating if there is a need for the patient to contact with a healthcare professional. Additionally, a more detailed offline analysis is carried out at the server. This involves the Disease State Index algorithm (DSI) (Mattila et al., 2012), which exploits a heterogeneous set of clinical background data (e.g. earlier diagnoses) and contextual data (e.g. whether the test was made indoors or outdoors) registered at the time when the sample was taken. The architecture includes a web-based user interface enabling healthcare professionals to follow-up the pre-screening results.

In operational use, the pre-screening system needs to be interoperable with Electronic Health Records (EHR) and Personal Health Records (PHR) (Jones et al., 2010) as indicated in Figure 1. The EHR system captures all relevant documentation related to the patient, and therefore it is important that the screening results can be transferred from the screening system to the EHR system via an open interface (HIS-IF). The interface should also allow clinical background data to be retrieved from the EHR to the screening system. The PHR system takes care of maintaining health data for the needs of the patient. It may be a stand-alone system or connected with the EHR (Archer et al., 2011). In a typical scenario, the patient may like to have the screening results transferred to the PHR system to be synchronized with other personal health data (White et al., 2016).

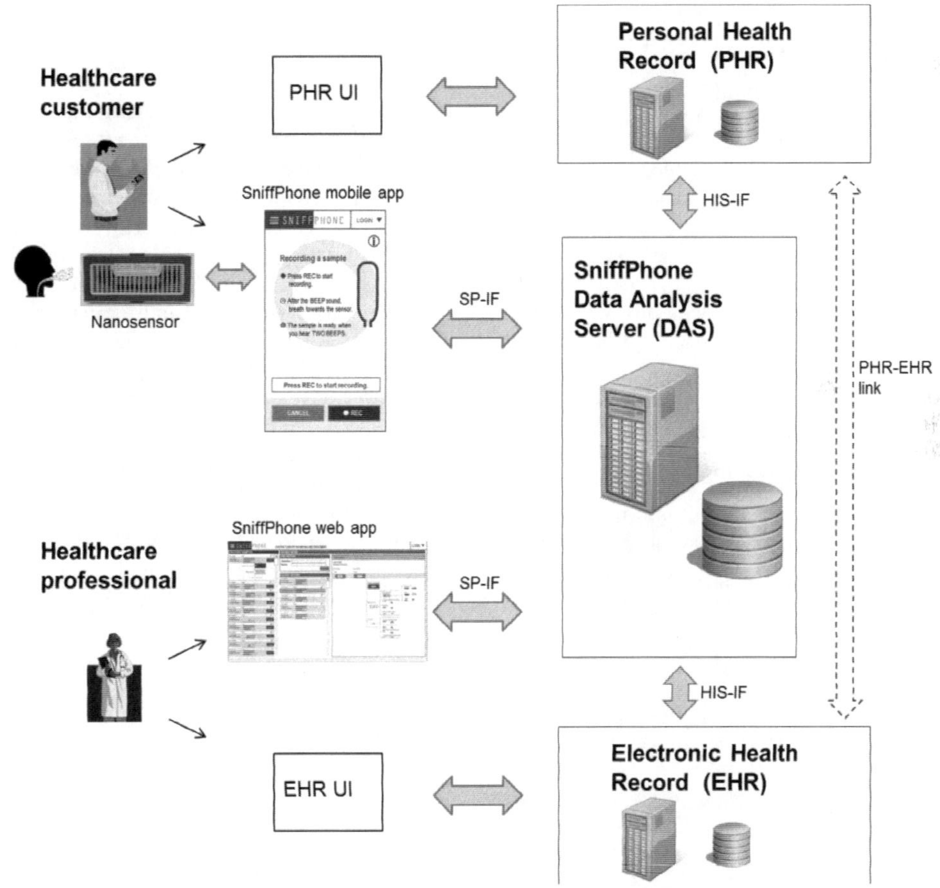

Figure 1. The SNIFFPHONE Service Architecture

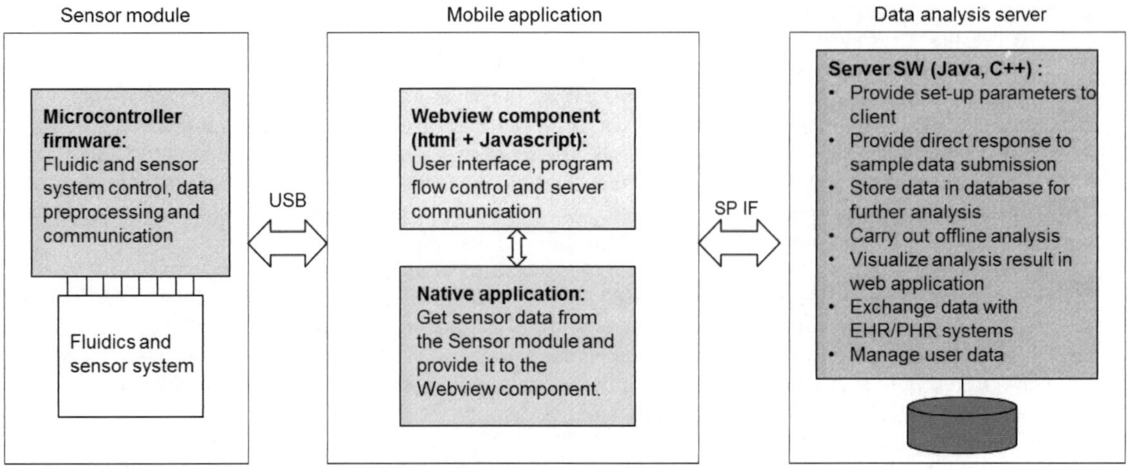

Figure 2. SNIFFPHONE Software Components

3. INTEROPERABILITY

Data exchange with health record systems is important in order to deploy SNIFFPHONE in the healthcare process. Modern EHR and PHR systems are increasingly equipped with flexible interfaces, enabling data exchange with other information systems and health applications. This way ecosystems of connected services and applications are being formed. Most recently, several large EHR providers have published interfaces[1,2] based on the draft HL7 standard FHIR (Fast Healthcare Interoperability Resources) (Benson, 2016) to complement the existing interfaces largely based on HL7 v2 messaging and CDA content structures. Also centralized, national EHR systems based on FHIR are being deployed[3]. FHIR provides a "developer-friendly" interoperability approach based on widely known protocols and formats such as REST and JSON (JavaScript Object Notation) (Sundvall et al. 2013). It builds on a base set of resources (data structure definitions) which, either by themselves or combined, satisfy most needs of clinical information systems and health applications. Additionally, custom profiles for specialized applications may be created.

A high-level analysis of the needs of SNIFFPHONE and the availability of corresponding FHIR resources is presented in Table **1**. There is a need to exchange data in two directions. First, patient's clinical background data is needed by the pre-screening algorithm and should be retrieved from the EHR. Second, the screening result and related information need to be stored in the EHR system for later need. The pre-screening outcome is described by using the observation resource. It is important to note, that the observation resource is generic by nature and applicable for various types of health measurements and subjective observations. Profiling is well supported by FHIR and will be needed to adapt the observation resource for this specific use-case.

[1] https://open.epic.com/Interface/FHIR
[2] http://fhir.cerner.com/
[3] http://www.kanta.fi/en

Table 1. Needs to exchange data between the SNIFFPHONE system and EHR (or PHR) systems

Data direction	Need	Relevant FHIR resources (Benson, 2016)
EHR→ SP	The basic demographic data and clinical health record data needed as input to the analysis algorithm	Patient, Condition, Observation, MedicationStatement, MedicationRequest FamilyMemberHistory, RiskAssessment
SP → EHR (or PHR)	Saving the outcome of the screening test needs to be possible for healthcare process participants	Observation, Patient
EHR→ SP & SP → EHR	Process data needed to integrate the screening system with the clinical care process (including the needed patient's consent)	Encounter, Appointment, DeviceUseRequest, DeviceUseStatement, Contract

Since the SNIFFPHONE system manages and transfers personal health data, it is essential to address the related privacy and security issues. The patient access needs to be protected by authentication which enables the pre-screening result to be stored in the server with user identification information. Additionally, an authorization mechanism is needed for enabling data exchange between the SNIFFPHONE system and external EHR and PHR systems. Such functionality can be implemented e.g. by the OAuth2 protocol (Kamran et al., 2013).

In addition to EHR and PHR interoperability, it is relevant to consider possible standards for the complete system coverage of the SNIFFPHONE client-server interface (SP-IF), and the sensor USB-interface. Such a system is defined by the end-to-end reference architecture of the Continua Design Guidelines (CDG)[1]. The reference architecture employs HL7 v2 messages and the IEEE 11073 protocols (x73). This approach could not be adopted for SNIFFPHONE, since the screening method is new and the associated data model is not covered by the x73 protocol stack. Instead, a dedicated JSON structure has been defined for carrying the sensor outputs and contextual information over the SP-IF interface.

4. CONCLUSIONS

General purpose mobile phones and modern web technologies enable the development of cost-effective solutions for high throughput screening and monitoring of diseases. Such solutions may be used independently by patients at home or at the clinic under supervision of a healthcare professional. The SNIFFPHONE project is setting up a system for gastric cancer screening. In this paper we have described the architecture of the screening system including the main software components currently under development. We have also presented an approach of connecting the pre-screening system with external EHR and PHR systems. This kind of connectivity is commonly needed in screening and self-care systems. We estimate the new HL7/FHIR draft standard to be well-suited for achieving the required interoperability.

ACKNOWLEDGEMENT

This work was supported by funding from the European Union's Horizon 2020 Programme for research, technological development and demonstration under grant agreement No 644031 (SNIFFPHONE). The authors wish to acknowledge the contribution of the project partners, especially Technion, JLM Innovation and Cellix in developing the sensor module and related software components.

[1] http://www.pchalliance.org/resources

REFERENCES

Amal, H., 2016. Detection of precancerous gastric lesions and gastric Q1 cancer through exhaled breath. *Gut*. Vol. 65, No. 3, 400-407.

Archer, N., et al., 2011. Personal health records: a scoping review. *J Am Med Inform Assoc*, Vol. 18, No. 4, 515-522.

Benson, T., 2016. *Principles of Health Interoperability*. Springer, Switzerland.

Broza, Y. and Haick H., 2013. Nanomaterial-based sensors for detection of disease by volatile organic compounds. *Nanomedicine*, Vol. 8, No. 5, 785-806.

Franz, B., et al, 2015. Applying FHIR in an Integrated Health Monitoring System, *EJBI*, Vol. 11, No. 2, 53-56.

Jones, D. A., et al., 2010. Characteristics of personal health records: Findings of the medical library Association/National library of medicine joint electronic personal health record task force. *Journal of the Medical Library Association: JMLA*, Vol. 98, No. 3, 243–249.

Kamran S., et al., 2013. An infrastructure for secure sharing of medical images between PACS and EHR systems. *In Proceedings of the 2013 Conference of the Center for Advanced Studies on Collaborative Research (CASCON '13)*, IBM Corp., NJ, USA, 245-259.

Mattila, J. et al., 2012. Design and Application of a Generic Clinical Decision Support System for Multiscale Data. *IEEE-TBME*, Vol. 59, No. 1, 234-240.

Sundvall, E. et al, 2013. Applying representational state transfer (REST) architecture to archetype-based electronic health record systems. *BMC Medical Informatics and Decision Making*, Vol. 13, No. 57.

Urbauer, P., et al., 2015. Applicability of IHE/Continua components for PHR systems: Learning from experiences. *Computers in Biology and Medicine*, Vol. 59, 1 April 2015, 186-193.

White, H. et al., 2016. Requirements and access needs of patients with chronic disease to their hospital electronic health record: results of a cross-sectional questionnaire survey. *BMJ Open,* Vol. 6, No. 10.

INVOLVING END-USERS IN THE DEVELOPMENT AND IMPLEMENTATION OF A WEB-BASED, PHYSICAL ACTIVITY PLATFORM FOR ELDERLY

Inge van Bruinessen[1], Jan-Willem van 't Klooster[2], April Boessen[3], Loek van der Heide[3], Miriam Vollenbroek-Hutten[4] and Sandra van Dulmen[5]

[1]*Netherlands Institute for Health Services Research, Utrecht, The Netherlands*
[2]*Roessingh Research & Development, Enschede, The Netherlands*
[3]*Zuyd University of Applied Sciences; Maastricht University, Maastricht, The Netherlands*
[4]*Ziekenhuisgroep Twente, Enschede, The Netherlands*
[5]*Netherlands Institute for Health Services Research; Radboudumc; University College of Southeast Norway Utrecht, The Netherlands; Nijmegen, The Netherlands; Drammen, Norway*

ABSTRACT

Physical activity is an important health behavior when it comes to preventing or slowing down disablement caused by ageing and chronic diseases. With the LIFE project we aspired to support pre-frail older adults to deploy and maintain a physical active lifestyle by integrating existing on- and offline services via a web-based self-management platform. Contrary to the often applied top-down 'waterfall' methods used to develop such web-based interventions, we applied a bottom up inspired procedure. Targeted end users (elderly and (health) professionals) were involved from the early beginnings. In this way their knowledge, preferences and needs could influence the design, functionality and implementation of the platform. The applied process, inspired on Design Thinking, comprised seven rounds. These rounds were not all planned in detail at the start of the project; outcomes of the first sessions guided the goals and structure of the successive steps. We experienced that it was relatively easy to get elderly and professionals involved and to let them influence the development of the platform. However, the participants had a specific interest in maintaining their active lifestyle and many of them had already implemented physical exercises as part of their daily routine. They were enthusiastic about the offline modules offered by the platform, but did not use the online modules at home because of usability issues, the lack of discipline, the feeling of insecurity and the lack of a social component.

KEYWORDS

eHealth; Co-Design; Physical Activity; Healthy Aging; Elderly

1. INTRODUCTION

Physical activity is an important health behavior when it comes to preventing or slowing down disablement caused by ageing and chronic diseases (Tak et al., 2013). Physical, psychological and social changes can challenge elderly to have a physical active lifestyle. To promote healthy behavior and support elderly with staying active, many interventions have been developed. The last decennia a considerable amount of interventions is being delivered via the Internet.

Traditionally, the sequential 'waterfall' method is used to develop these web-based interventions. With this method, the planning, process and costs are strictly controlled and from the beginning there is a clear idea about what the end-product will do. However, the lack of user-involvement in this top-down, expert-driven method is often indicated as a cause for the frequently reported problems with use, adoption and attrition (Eysenbach, 2005). Today, methods are advocated and applied that include end-users from the early beginnings of the development phase (i.e. user-centered design) (Mummah et al., 2012; Bartholomew et al., 2011). The potential benefits of involving end-users from the start of a project are widely accepted and it claims to facilitate more effective interventions (Mummah et al., 2012). Yet, little is described about the operationalization of co-creating web-based products with elderly.

The LIFE project aspires to support pre-frail older adults to deploy and maintain a physical active lifestyle by providing physical activity services via a web-based platform (Van 't Klooster et al., 2017). This platform was co-created with and for the targeted population.

The goal of this descriptive paper is to i) outline how elderly and their health professionals were involved in the development and implementation of the platform, ii) how their input influenced the design, functionality and implementation of the platform. To conclude we share our lessons learned regarding the participatory process that may inspire researchers and designers who are working with web-based (activity) products and services for elderly.

2. METHOD

The LIFE project started with the idea to support the rapidly ageing population with deploying and maintaining a physical active lifestyle by means of promoting self-management. Based on the Self Determination Theory (SDT), we envisioned a web-based platform that offered a selection of activities tailored to the user's preferences and needs. According to the SDT, autonomy is an important factor to achieve goals; like the goal to keep up a physical active lifestyle (Ryan and Deci, 2000). The concept of autonomy in the platform could be operationalized by providing support without interference of professionals and giving users the opportunity to compose their own activity program out of a range of activities. These activities could include on- and offline modules. The online modules were available video clips of exercises for strength, endurance and mobility training, that were validated in previous projects (Campbell, 2005). Our idea was that users could follow these modules in their daily environment, as often and as intensive as they wish. The offline modules could contain regularly or incidental activities organized locally. At the start of the project, only the online modules (the video clips) were available. The other 'building blocks' of the platform (e.g.structure and design of the website, implementation plan) were still rough ideas.

2.1 Participants and Setting

The target group consisted of pre-frail elderly who were able to use a web-based program independently or with minimal support by a professional. Care professionals, who may play a role in the implementation and uptake of the platform (e.g by managing the local activity modules or providing support to the elderly), were also considered potential end-users. The LIFE project was introduced in a residential home for elderly with in-house (health care) services available. A group of 16 elderly (aged 74-91 years old, average 83) and professionals (physiotherapist, nurse, occupational therapist) from this home volunteered to the co-creation steps. The group composition varied per step. The project was executed in 2016 – 2017.

2.2 Development Approach

We applied a step-by-step approach (figure 1) for the development of the platform and its' implementation plan. This approach was inspired on Design Thinking, which views knowledge about users and their involvement in the design process as a central concern (Kelly and Kelly, 2013). The seven steps of the approach were not all planned in detail at the start of the project; outcomes of the first sessions, guided the goals and structure of the successive steps. Descriptive data was gathered along the iterative co-creation cycles and documented in a logbook. In this logbook the researchers documented activities, outcomes, and changes made to the intervention and implementation plan.

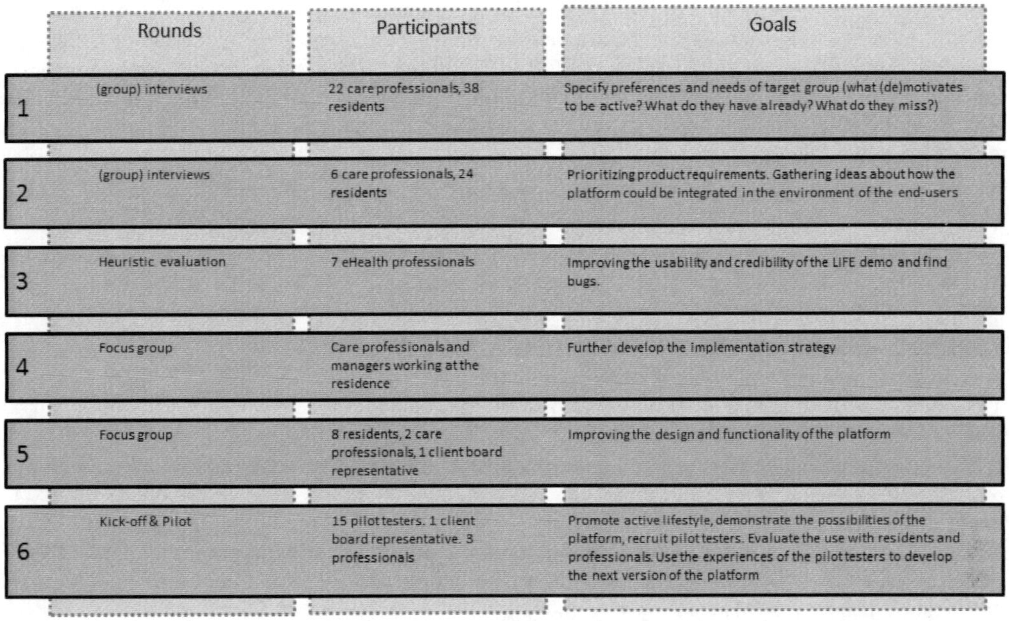

Figure 1. The Applied Step-By-Step Co-Creation Approach

The first step resulted in a list of user preferences and product requirements (Boessen, 2016). Based on these results we developed paper mockups of the platform and four user scenarios (describing the context, story and goals of an end-user representing the target group). These documents gave insight in characteristics and goals of the target group and it helped to define product requirements and the implementation plan.

In the second step, participants could reflect on the mockups and prioritize the list of product requirements and user preferences. Also, ideas were inquired about how the platform could be integrated in the daily lives of the end-users. This information was translated to care pathways (Van 't Klooster et al., 2017; Boessen et al., 2016). A care pathway can support the implementation of the platform by for example identifying relevant stakeholders, charting possible sequential activities, clarifying goals and defining the target group characteristics (Schrijvers et. Al., 2013). The requirement lists and user scenarios were further defined. With these outcomes a first web-based prototype was designed.

In the third round, eHealth experts were asked to evaluate the usability and credibility of the first web-based prototype. The evaluation was guided by a list of heuristics (i.e. recognized usability and credibility principles) (Chisnell and Lee, 2006; Fog, 2014), composed to objectively evaluate web-based interventions for elderly. The heuristics concerned consistency, user control and efficiency. With the findings of this evaluation we could solve the first bugs and adapt issues influencing the usability and credibility in a next web-based version of the platform.

The fourth round was focused on the implementation of the platform. With (health) professionals and representatives of the management team, we discussed how the platform could be integrated and used as part of their organization.

In the fifth round, the next version of the platform was presented to 11 potential end-users (elderly and professionals) aiming to evaluate the design and functionality. On a large screen, we showed the platform and demonstrated its functionalities. Attendees shared their first impressions and ideas, reflected on the visual design and functionalities. In addition also implementation issues were discussed. The platform was adapted according to the attendees' feedback and a kick-off meeting for all residents was planned.

The sixth round concerned a seven week during pilot that started with a kick-off meeting. During the kick-off, an introduction was given about active living and the platform was demonstrated. The attendees who were interested, could volunteer to pilot test the platform. Researchers supported them with registering and starting up an account on their personal computer, tablet or smartphone. Of the 26 attendees, 15 subscribed. During the pilot weeks, use of the platform elements was monitored with log files. The researchers kept in close contact with the involved professionals and pilot testers, provided support and adapted the platform based on their feedback when necessary.

3 RESULTS

3.1 The Influence on the Development of the Platform

A range of issues that were suggested by participants, guided and inspired the development of the initial product idea;

The social component; an important, recurring theme was the fact that being physically active was not a goal in itself for the elderly. Social contacts and staying independently as long as possible motivated them to be physically active. This influenced for example the way we communicated about the platform, (e.g. as part of general information about the importance of an active lifestyle and the social component of the offline modules was emphasized. Also, a functionality was developed to give users the opportunity to upload local (offline) activities such as their weekly swimming group and walking group.

Personalized advice; participants emphasized the importance of personalized advice, e.g. based on the varying activity preferences and physical limitations of users (e.g. wheelchair activities). We operationalized this by providing the users of the platform with a personal account in which activities were prioritized based on a recommender system. Yet the participants were not very enthusiastic about making a password protected personal account. At least, they wanted to learn more about the platform before they made the decision to register. For that, the homepage was adapted with more information, example modules and a short video clip introducing the platform.

Design and Structure; regarding the design of the platform, a range of usability, credibility and readability issues were developed or adjusted. For example, it was considered important to show the option to enlarge the screen clearly in the home page and the terminology that was considered too technical was adjusted. Regarding the structure of the platform, the way on- and offline modules were searched and clustered was not clear in the first version and more information was preferred about the offline activities (like available guidance, difficulty, costs). We added this information via a standardized form that needed to be completed for each activity.

Recognizability and integration; involved professionals pointed out the opportunity to use platform as an extended digital version of their activity program distributed in their monthly paper based journal and that the platform should look familiar to its' users. Therefore we customized the visual design of the platform to the corporate identity of the residential home, so users would recognize it as an in-home service.

3.2 Preliminary Findings of the Pilot

Participants were enthusiastic about the offline modules, but a range of problems arose when using the online modules. Different problems with this part of the platform were mentioned; 1) safety and insecurity issues (e.g. fear of getting injured, exercising in the wrong way), 2) usability issues (e.g. exercising while watching and operating the laptop, old software that could not run the videos) and 3) the lack of discipline to exercise alone at home.

An interesting movement was that a group of participants formed a 'LIFE exercise group'. Each Wednesday they gathered and followed together a part of the online modules that were projected on a large screen. These sessions were guided by the physical therapist. In this way, the safety and insecurity issues were solved and the social component was incorporated.

With the results of the pilot, the platform was adjusted and a second information 'kick-off' for the residents was planned.

4. LESSONS LEARNED

In this paper, we described the participatory approach applied to involve end-users in the first phases of developing a web-based activity platform. Although it was a time consuming process, we experienced that it was relatively easy to get end-users involved and to let them influence the design and functionality of the platform. However, the participating elderly all had a specific interest in maintaining their active lifestyle and many of them had already implemented physical exercises as part of their daily routine. We failed to include elderly who were more in need for support with deploying a physical active lifestyle. For the further development of the platform, we should focus specifically on reaching this group.

After the pilot, participants were enthusiastic about the offline modules, but did not use the online modules as intended. Although they had come up with a solution (the LIFE exercise group), our initial idea to promote self-management in this way, did not work out well. This result emphasizes the importance of testing (parts of) the platform in a very early stage. For example, we could have tested the online modules as separate feature, before starting with the pilot. To conclude, the influence of the end-users was valuable, but we have not reached our goals with the platform yet and further (participatory) research and development steps are needed.

REFERENCES

Bartholomew LK, et al. 2011. *Planning Health Promotion Programs: An Intervention Mapping Approach*. San Francisco, CA: Jossey-Bass.

Boessen ABCG, et al. *Co-creation of a technology supported self-management program to promote physical activity in older adults: defining user needs and requirements*. The European Journal of Public Health 26(suppl_1)

Campbell AJ, et al. 2005. *Randomised controlled trial of prevention of falls in people aged >=75 with severe visual impairment: the VIP trial.* BMJ, 331(7520), 817

Chisnell JR, Lee A, 2006. *New heuristics for understanding older adults as web users.* Technical Communication;53: 39-59

Eysenbach G, 2005. *The law of attrition.* JMIR, 7(1):e11.

Fogg BJ, accessed 2014. *A Research Summary from the Stanford Persuasive Technology Lab.* Stanford Guidelines for Web Credibility. URL: https://credibility.stanford.edu/guidelines/

Kelley T, Kelley D, 2013. *Creative Confidence: Unleashing the Creative Potential Within All of Us.* New York: Crown Business.

Mummah SA, et al. 2012. *IDEAS (Integrate, Design, Assess, and Share): A Framework and Toolkit of Strategies for the Development of More Effective Digital Interventions to Change Health Behavior*. JMIR Vol 18, No 12.

Ryan RM, Deci EL, 2000. *Self-Determination Theory and the facilitation of intrinsic motivation, social development and well being*. American Psychologist, 55(1), 68–78

Schrijvers G, van Hoorn A, Huiskes N. *The care pathway: concepts and theories: an introduction.* Int J Integr Care. 2012 Jan-Dec; 12(Special Edition Integrated Care Pathways): e192.

Tak E, et al. 2013. *Prevention of onset and progression of basic ADL disability by physical activity in community dwelling older adults: A meta-analysis*. Ageing Research Reviews Volume 12, Issue 1, Pages 329–338. Van 't Klooster JW, et al. *Introducing Personalised Self-Management to Support Physical Activity in Elderly: a Case Study.* Under review

DIGITAL NUTRITIONAL DOCUMENTATION OF PREGNANT MIGRANT WOMEN

Karin Messer-Misak
FH Joanneum Gesellschaft mbH, Eggenberger Allee 11, 8020 Graz, Austria

ABSTRACT

Pregnant women have a special need for vitamins and other nutrients. Especially for migrant women who often lack proficiency in the language of the country, it is important that they receive information on food and nutrition in an easily accessible form. The project, in co-operation with the Gebietskrankenkasse Styria, Austria (social insurance, district of Styria), examined to what extent pregnant migrant woman are already aware of dietary recommendations of the Federal Ministry of Health. Furthermore, it was examined whether pregnant migrant women already document their dietary habits and whether they would be able to document them with an app. The aim of the project is to provide information in an easily accessible form and to provide more awareness of a healthy diet during pregnancy through nutritional documentation. The results were implemented in an app that provides the desired nutritional information and a documentation of nutrition. The software informs on the basis of the entered foods units which were consumed and gives further food recommendations.

KEYWORDS

Digital Documentation, Dietary Habits, Pregnancy, App

1. INTRODUCTION AND BACKGROUND

One of the aims of the Federal Ministry of Health in Austria is to strengthen the health awareness of the Austrian population. A special focus is on the nutrition during pregnancy. Many women in Austria are not sufficiently informed about what to eat during pregnancy. That is why in 2010, an Austrian nutrition pyramid was published by the Federal Ministry of Health, and by the National Nutrition Commission. The goal was to inform the population about a balanced diet. As pregnant women have a special need for vitamins and nutrients (Bung, 2004), an expanded nutritional pyramid was published in June 2011 (BMfG, 2011) to match their needs. The question was arisen how pregnant migrant women, who are not familiar with Austrian food and the German language, can be informed about diet and special needs through a personal digital nutritional documentation.

In nutrition during pregnancy it is important to ensure that there are enough energy and nutrients for the growth and the development of the growing child as well as an adequate supply of nutrients for the pregnant woman. The right choice of food, which contains the right amount of vitamins and nutrients in addition to a sufficient liquid supply are particularly important in this phase of pregnancy. The nutrition of the mother during pregnancy does not only influence the growth of the embryo but also the future nutritional habits of the child (BMfG, 2015).

2. METHODS

Information on appropriate diet during pregnancy is easily accessible via the internet. The challenge was to present the information as comprehensible as possible, even if the users do not understand the German language. For this reason, the graphically illustrated nutritional pyramid, which was developed by the Ministry of Health together with experts from the fields of nutritional medicine, nutritional science and health promotion, was used.

The nutrition pyramid provides information on the type and quantity of food and drink that should be taken. It is structured according to a building block principle. Using the seven steps of the pyramid, you can see how often different food groups should be eaten (Öffentliches Gesundheitsportal Österreichs, 2016). The Austrian dietary pyramid shows what a healthy diet should look like at best.

In order to clarify the extent to which pregnant women are informed about the dietary recommendations by the Federal Ministry of Health in Austria and whether they document their dietary habits during pregnancy, a questionnaire was drawn up. The pretested questionnaire contained 18 questions and was published in paper and online from February 2016 to April 2016. The questionnaire was developed in cooperation with nutrition experts and psychologists who worked on the project initiated by the social insurance. The pretest was carried out within the working group, the method "thinking aloud" was selected.

The survey focused on the question whether migrant women are already aware of the dietary pyramid and the specific nutritional needs during pregnancy. Furthermore, the migrant woman were asked whether they had installed apps on their mobile phones and whether they would be interested in installing an app on diet. The main question was then whether they were currently documenting their dietary habits and whether they would also record them on their mobile phone. In the final section, it was identified which information would be needed, how often it was to be documented and what further expectations the pregnant migrant women have on an app dealing with the subject of "nutrition during pregnancy".

The questionnaires were launched paper-based in different institutions, i.e. in a pregnancy preparatory course in a midwifery center and during a workshop titled: "Baby is eating! - Nutrition workshop for pregnant women" organized by the social insurance in Styria (Austria).

3. RESULTS

3.1 Results of the Questionnaire

A total of 150 questionnaires were distributed in the workshops. 130 questionnaires were returned. The first question was "Are you pregnant?". All questionnaires answered with: "I am not pregnant" were excluded from the further evaluation. 115 questionnaires were finally qualified to be evaluated.

Of the 115 women questioned, 51.3% were between the ages of 20 and 30. 46% were between 30 and 40 years old, the remaining group was over 40 years of age. Approximately 70 percent of the women surveyed said this was there first pregnancy. The interest was highest among the women who were pregnant for the first time.

82% of pregnant women were already familiar with the dietary pyramid. But only 46% of the women knew of an extra nutritional pyramid for pregnant women, 6% were unsure and 48% did not know about it at all.

Regarding the question "Do you document your dietary habits already in any form?", it became clear that only 12% (n = 14) do in fact document their dietary habits. 57% write them down, 29% use their mobile phone and 14% use a laptop or a PC.

One of the central questions was whether they would use an app, which on the one hand informs them about nutrition recommendations and with which they can document their individual diet. 43% of the surveyed women said that they would document their dietary habits trough an app (at least once a day 50%).

Pregnant immigrants were highly interested in information about foods that should not be consumed during pregnancy (67%). 62% were interested in information about specific nutrient requirements during pregnancy. 52% were interested in recipe suggestions. Other requirements were the "ease of use of the app" (72%) and that it is available free of charge (71%). 54% expect privacy to be ensured.

The results of the questionnaire had an influence on the design and content of the app to be programmed. As it turned out, most women are familiar with the nutritional pyramid. In addition the "CINDI (countrywide integrated noncom unicable disease intervention program) dietary guide" (WHO Europe, 2000) suggests that the information should be based on foods, rather than nutrients. As people purchase and eat food, not nutrients. Therefore, it had become obvious to use the familiar graphical representation in the app. It should also be taken into account that the willingness to document the eating habits is small, so the documentation should be as simple as possible.

3.2 Results of the App

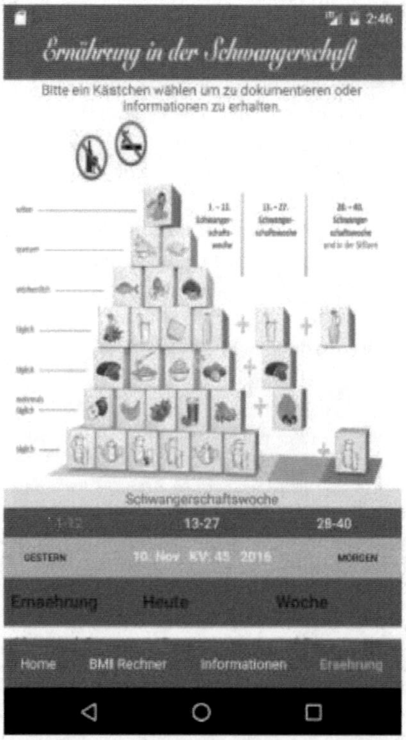

Figure 1. Screenshot – Documentation

The idea of the project was to supplement the already edited information of the graphic nutritional pyramid with a personal nutritional documentation. The app is personalized by identifying the gender, age, weight, and the pregnancy week. In this prototype the personal data and the inputs of the user are stored locally on the mobile telephone and are only accessible to the user of the mobile telephone. Basic information about the diet during pregnancy is offered. Likewise, information on foods which are not or only suitable for consumption to a limited extent. Recipe suggestions were not implemented at this stage.

The main function besides the above mentioned information was to make the daily nutritional documentation as simple as possible. By simply clicking on the respective cubes on the nutritional pyramid (see figure 1) it will be indicated how many units have already been consumed. As a result of the input, it is then automatically indicated which food, vitamins and nutrients have not yet been supplied in sufficient quantities (see figure 2). This information is displayed directly in the graphical representation in the pyramid and in an additional personalised graphic. The goal is to raise awareness about the user's balanced diet in accordance with the recommendations.

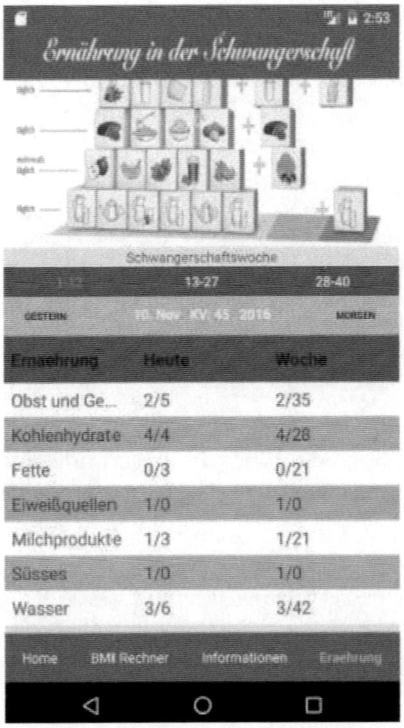

Figure 2. Screenshot – Sufficient Quantities

Technically first a mock-up was designed with the program “balsamiq" to clarify the content and structure for the application that was programmed afterwards. The main functions should be the documentation of and information about nutrition to achieve greater nutrition awareness among pregnant women. The app was programmed with “Android Studio". This tool is based on the coding language Java and supports all mobile devices with the popular operating system “Android".

4. CONCLUSION AND FUTURE WORK

The questionnaire was written exclusively in German for this pilot project. This implies that only pregnant women who are already powerful in the German language and who are interested in the topic of "nutrition during pregnancy" are included in the sample.

The result clearly showed that women are more interested in information about nutrition than in dietary documentation during pregnancy. Requirements for functions such as calendar or nutritional documentation is rather low (relevant further studies: i.e. Kennelly, et.al.; Waring, et.al.). On the subject of technology, 100% of surveyed pregnant women know how to use a smartphone and apps. This is in general a very good prerequisite for the use of this particular application.

The next step will be to test the prototype from the perspective of various experts in the area of computer science, psychologists, nutritionists and future users and to implement the evaluation results accordingly. The app can then be considered a supplement to the workshops and information events. Insurance companies do not require the documentation of dietary habits as data protection and insurance agendas have to be taken into account. The application is intended to complement the existing supply of nutritional information as a first step.

Likewise, the level of awareness of the nutritional pyramid would support the professional use of an app in addition to the existing counseling offer for pregnant migrant women. Studies on dietary habits and nutritional status are available (i.e. Elmadfa I, 2012, WHO [2], 2002), studies on the validity of special tools are also available (i.e. Ashman AM, 2016; Ashman AM, Collins CE, et.at, 2017) but concrete studies on the documentation of dietary habits on applications and their benefits are not yet available.

The present study provides a good starting point for further studies on the topic and helps to clarify to what extent are the dietary habits of the migrant women improved by the use of the app.

REFERENCES

Ashman, AM, et. al. 2016. *A Brief Tool to Assess Image-Based Dietary Records and Guide Nutrition Counselling Among Pregnant Women: An Evaluation.* JMIR Mhealth, DOI: 10.2196/mhealth.6469

Ashman, AM, Collins, CE, et. al., 2017.*Validation of a Smartphone Image-Based Dietary Assessment Method for Pregnant Women.* Nutrients, DOI: 10.3390/nu9010073.

BMfG, 02.2015. *Evaluation der Österreichischen Ernährungspyramide „Kommen die zentralen Botschaften bei der Bevölkerung an?“* Studie des Bundesministeriums für Gesundheit, URL http://www.bmgf.gv.at/cms/home/attachments/7/3/0/CH1046/CMS1290513144661/evaluation_ernaehrungspyramide.pdf

Bung, P., 2004. *Die Geburtshilfe*, Hrsg. Schneider, H., Husslein, P., Schneider, K-T., ISBN 978-3-540-30522-4, p. 224

Elmadfa I. et.at., 2012. *Österreichischer Ernährungsbericht*, 1. Auflage, Universität Wien, Institut für Ernährungswissenschaften, http://www.bmgf.gv.at/cms/home/attachments/4/5/3/CH1048/CMS1348749794860/oeb12.pdf

Öffentliches Gesundheitsportal Österreichs, 1.2.2017, https://www.gesundheit.gv.at/leben/ernaehrung/info/ernaehrungspyramide/ernaehrungspyramide

Kennelly, M.; et.al., Jan. 2016, *Pregnancy, exercise and nutrition research study with smart phone app support (Pears): Study protocol of a randomized controlled trial.* Contemporary Clinical Trials, Vol. 46, Jan. 2016, Elsevier, pp. 92-99

Waring, ME., et.al., Dec. 2014. *Pregnant women's interest in a website or mobile application for healthy gestational weight gain*, Sexual & Reproductive Healthcare, Vol. 5, Elsevier, pp. 182-184

WHO, Regional Office for Europe, Food and Nutrition Policy Unit, Denmark, ISBN 92890 11831, http://www.euro.who.int/__data/assets/pdf_file/0010/119926/E70041.pdf, p. 2

WHO [2], Regional Office for Europe, Food and health in Europe. Summary, Denmark, ISBN 92890 13648, http://www.euro.who.int/__data/assets/pdf_file/0010/98308/e78578.pdf?ua=1

DEVELOPMENT OF WORKFLOW-BASED GUIDELINES FOR THE CARE OF BURNS IN SCOTLAND

Alisa Dewanti[1], Petros Papapanagiotou[1], Charlotte Gilhooly[2], Jacques Fleuriot [1], Areti Manataki[1] and Laura Moss[2]

[1] *School of Informatics, University of Edinburgh, 10 Crichton St, Edinburgh EH8 9AB, United Kingdom*

[2] *Dept. of Anaesthesia, Pain & Critical Care, School of Medicine, Dentistry and Nursing, University of Glasgow, Glasgow G12 8QQ, United Kingdom*

ABSTRACT

Burn injuries are considered complex because they require a variety of treatments and continuous healing. Moreover, due to the relatively small number of burns patients per year in Scotland, clinicians may lack sufficient experience and familiarity with the care process, leading to errors and omissions. In this work, we captured the necessary knowledge for the first 24 hours of burns treatment for adult patients in the form of structured workflows. Our aim is to construct visual workflow guidelines that can be easily read and understood, irrespective of any workflow expertise, and can be used as a guide in every day care. Preliminary evaluation results from burns care clinicians in the Glasgow Royal Infirmary are positive and will guide our future work. We believe workflow models can be an effective methodology to document and share guidelines for patient care provided they are developed in close collaboration with clinical stakeholders.

KEYWORDS

Healthcare, Burns Care, Knowledge Acquisition, Intensive Care Unit, Knowledge Representation, Workflow Modelling

1. INTRODUCTION AND MOTIVATION

Healthcare processes are increasingly complex, as clinical staff are required to engage with long series of activities and a growing amount of information in a risky and time-pressured work environment. This is particularly the case for burns care, where patients may have different conditions and symptoms that require different treatments by a multidisciplinary team of specialist, theatre, and Intensive Care Unit (ICU) staff. The first 24 hours after a burn injury are especially critical and may reflect the degree of morbidity and mortality [Alharbi et al, 2012].

The Care Of Burns In Scotland (COBIS) network recorded an average of 340 adult burn patients per year (2010-2014), less than 7% of which were referred to the ICU. Based on this, it is difficult for ICU clinicians, who may rotate posts every few months, to develop experience in the treatment of such cases, resulting in unfamiliarity or omissions when it comes to some of the critical procedures.

Workflow models can help manage the complexity of care practices [Bastian et al, 2016]. They allow the formal representation of knowledge regarding the appropriate clinical procedures as step-by-step processes with related conditions and resources. As such, they provide a visual model of care that can facilitate decision making by forecasting what-if scenarios and reliably evaluating effects of different elements.

Such process-based analysis and improvement of medical practices is not new (see for example Marcos et al, 2002; Russo and Mecella, 2013) and there are multiple tools implemented for such purposes (such as Shahar et al, 1998; Fox et al, 2006; Papapanagiotou and Fleuriot, 2014). This not only enables the better understanding and optimisation of everyday practices based on the aforementioned parameters, but also allows the automated coordination of clinical activity in medical teams through the computer-based execution of the modelled workflows. For example, human-based processes can be integrated and coordinated through electronic checklists [Manataki et al, 2016], whereas an electronic system can send reminders and notifications to ensure the appropriate steps are performed at the right time and in the right order. However, this assumes that the appropriate knowledge is recorded in a structured way, which requires a considerable and collaborative effort.

In this particular paper, we describe our efforts to acquire and record knowledge on the treatment of adult burns patients during the first 24 hours into structured workflow-based guidelines. We aim to design workflows that:

1. are easily understandable, irrespective of any workflow expertise.
2. accurately capture the knowledge of the appropriate treatment procedures.
3. help clinicians understand and consistently deliver the treatment plan.

Our approach includes a systematic methodology, in close collaboration with a variety of medical staff involved in burns care at the Glasgow Royal Infirmary.

2. METHODOLOGY

The conceptualisation of our process-based model requires the systematic capture of medical knowledge and experience in burns treatment. For this purpose, we adjusted the Mixed-Method Research framework [Bastian et al, 2016]. Compared to other knowledge capture methodologies, it focuses on process analysis and improvement across different healthcare settings, using a broad and lean assessment and multiple stakeholder perspectives. As such it fits well to the needs of this work. In addition to the qualitative and quantitative analysis, we have extended the methodology with structured knowledge capture in the form of workflow models that have the potential for further systematic testing, simulation, and formal verification.

Our approach includes 3 phases: stakeholder analysis, process design, and model improvement. The stakeholders, which include expert burns clinicians, nurses, surgeons and ICU consultants, iteratively validate the outputs of each phase.

2.1 Phase 1: Stakeholder Analysis

This phase aims to capture the needs of stakeholders, identify the state of the current protocols for burns treatment and define the scope of the problem.

We accomplished this through unstructured interviews and multidisciplinary meetings, combining years of experience in burns care from the COBIS network with process modelling expertise from the University of Edinburgh, in a small group of 6, and for a total of 6 hours. We recorded information about typical clinical procedures, common problems and patient complications, the roles involved, and the existing IT infrastructure. We also shared medical literature, including COBIS documents and notes on standard practices. These helped establish a common understanding of the terminology and familiarity with burns treatment procedures (e.g. Hettiaratchy and Papini, 2004; Alharbi et al, 2012; COBIS, 2016).

Based on this, burns care was broken down into 4 stages:

1. Patient referral
2. The "ABC of burns care", including: Airways (A), Breathing (B), Circulation (C), Disability status (D), Exposure to external environment (E) (e.g. wounds and temperature treatment), and Fluid resuscitation (F)
3. Monitoring
4. Documentation, including the so-called Resuscitation Burns Bundle.

The outputs of the stakeholder analysis phase were (a) an activity map of burns treatment processes and (b) a table of inputs and outputs for each process.

2.2 Phase 2: Process Design

In this phase, we broke down the general processes of Phase 1, adding more detailed tasks and focusing on the information flow, interactions, and dependencies between them. The output was 10 workflow diagrams at 3 different levels of abstraction, starting with a 2-step, high-level plan down to the detailed processes of the ABC of burns care. A sample output of this phase is shown in Figure 1.

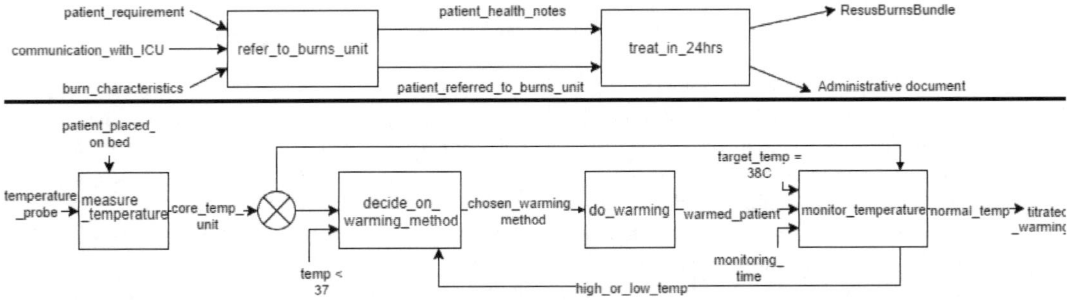

Figure 1. Sample output from Phase 2: Top level burns care (top) and temperature workflow (bottom)

The workflows reflect the considering factors at each decision point, such as the extent of burns, blood pressure, heart rate, etc. They also show the dependencies between processes so that the entire care pathway is visualized.

2.3 Phase 3: Model Improvement

This phase aims to improve the developed workflows in terms of (a) the validity and completeness of the captured knowledge with respect to actual medical practices, and (b) their understandability and usability as guidelines.

In order to improve the quality of the captured knowledge, we shared the models and collected feedback from different clinical roles in burns care, including nurses, surgeons and ICU consultants. This helped us incorporate different perspectives of the treatment plan and clarify aspects that the different roles have expertise in.

We evaluated the understandability and usability using a questionnaire, adapted from the System Usability Scale (SUS) [Brooke et al, 1996]. This included a general case scenario of the first 24 hours of care of a burns patient, a brief explanation of the workflow notation, the set of 8 developed workflows, and 2 sets of 6 questions each to assess the understandability and usability of the presented workflows. We surveyed 15 clinical participants at the Glasgow Royal Infirmary, covering all the different roles involved in burns treatment.

3. RESULTS AND LESSONS LEARNED

Preliminary survey results suggest that we acquired sufficient domain knowledge to represent the treatment of burns as a formal workflow; the majority of clinicians found the workflows clearly conveyed knowledge and complied with their experience of burns care. However, the survey identified that for the workflows to be used in clinical practice, additional knowledge about the individual patient context (e.g. medication, other medical conditions, risks) will be required.

Evidence of the understandability of our workflows was also found in every interaction with the clinical staff. During the iterative knowledge capture and model validation, the workflows were used to effectively communicate and discuss the medical practices without the involvement of the workflow experts.

We found the close collaboration between process modelling experts and clinical stakeholders to be a key challenge in the knowledge acquisition effort. Medical knowledge needs to be recorded in a way that is understandable among all involved parties. Well-organised meetings and several iterations of the model can help maximize the input provided by clinical staff given their busy schedules. Flexible activity maps and a simplified workflow notation are key elements towards communicating the results in a straightforward way to a clinical audience. The process modelling experts were required to obtain a good enough understanding of the involved practices and conditions and keep the balance between a superficial and trivial model and the years of studies and experience that the stakeholders put into practice on a daily basis. In contrast, the clinical stakeholders were required to rethink their practices and how these comply to the medical guidelines, systematically review even the parts that are well integrated and sometimes ignored as trivial, and challenge their assumptions and biases for their own line of work. These challenges were only tackled thanks to the close, devoted and open-minded collaboration between both parties, consistently through the duration of the project.

We plan to extend our work by further evaluation and refinement of models to include perspectives from different clinical roles and sites. Additionally we will investigate the representation and integration of contextual patient information in our models. Our methodology can benefit from first-hand shadowing and observation of burns treatment in practice and the use of formal methods to eliminate errors and further optimize the modelled practices [Papapanagiotou and Fleuriot, 2014]. Finally, workflow deployment, e.g. in the form of integrated checklists [Manataki et al, 2016], can help evaluate the captured knowledge towards supporting day-to-day care provision.

In summary, we believe that the Mixed-Method Research is an effective methodology for knowledge acquisition of medical procedures in a formal, structured way. Using this methodology, we can produce workflow-based guidelines with the potential of supporting clinicians to do their job effectively and consistently. Such results can only be achieved through focused and sustained collaboration between the clinical stakeholders and the process modelling experts.

ACKNOWLEDGEMENT

We would like to thank the COBIS team and the staff of the Intensive Care Unit, Glasgow Royal Infirmary for their support.

REFERENCES

Alharbi, Z. et al, 2012. Treatment of burns in the first 24 hours: simple and practical guide by answering 10 questions in a step-by-step form. *World Journal of Emergency Surgery*, Vol. 7, No. 1, pp. 1–10.

Bastian, N. D. et al, 2016. A mixed-methods research framework for healthcare process improvement. *Journal of Pediatric Nursing*, Vol. 31, No. 1, pp. e39–e51.

Brooke, J. et al, 1996. Sus-a quick and dirty usability scale. *Usability evaluation in industry*, Vol. 189, No. 194, pp. 4–7.

COBIS, 2016. Care of Burns in Scotland Managed Clinical Network - Clinical Guidelines. [online], http://www.cobis.scot.nhs.uk/clinical-guidelines/

Fox, K. et al, 2006. Decision support for health care: the PROforma evidence base. *Informatics in Primary Care*, Vol. 14, No. 1, pp. 49-54.

Hettiaratchy, S. and Papini, R., 2004. Initial management of a major burn: Ii–assessment and resuscitation. *British Medical Journal*, Vol. 329, No. 7457, pp. 101–103.

Manataki, A. et al, 2016. A workflow-driven, formal methods approach to the generation of structured checklists for intra-hospital patient transfers. *IEEE Journal of Biomedical and Health Informatics*, Ahead of print.

Marcos M. et al, 2002. From Informal Knowledge to Formal Logic: A Realistic Case Study in Medical Protocols. *Knowledge Engineering and Knowledge Management: Ontologies and the Semantic Web*. EKAW 2002. Lecture Notes in Computer Science, vol 2473, pp. 49-64. Springer

Papapanagiotou, P. and Fleuriot, J. D., 2014. Formal verification of collaboration patterns in healthcare. *Behaviour & Information Technology*, Vol. 33, No. 12, pp. 1278–1293.

Russo, A. and Mecella, M., 2013. On the evolution of process-oriented approaches for healthcare workflows. International Journal of Business Process Integration and Management (IJBPIM), Vol. 6, No. 3.

Shahar, Y. et al, 1998. The Asgaard project: A task-specific framework for the application and critiquing of time-oriented clinical guidelines. *Artificial intelligence in medicine*, Vol. 14, No. 1, pp. 29–51.

Reflection Papers

ROBOTICS AND COMPUTER SCIENCE IN MEDICAL EDUCATION

Lorenzo Brualla, Fabian Vollmer, Erdin Tokmak and Wolfgang Sauerwein
Universität Duisburg-Essen, Universitätsklinikum Essen, Strahlenklinik, Hufelandstraße 55, D-45122 Essen, Germany

ABSTRACT

This paper presents an innovative course conceived at the Medizinische Fakultät of the Universität Duisburg-Essen on robotics and computer science. Highly motivated students have participated in this course and, as a first consequence, a research has been initiated in the field of Turing machines applied to optimization of triage systems used for disasters. Additionally, a prototype of a universal Turing machine has been built using the Lego Mindstorms EV3 robotics system.

KEYWORDS

robotics, computer science, mass casualty events, triage, education, Turing machines, Braitenberg vehicles, Lego Mindstorms

1. INTRODUCTION

Given the increasing presence of robots and computerized devices in medical sciences it is desirable to offer medical students an opportunity to acquire some basic knowledge in these areas. With this objective in mind a pioneering course entitled 'Robotics and programing with Lego' has been conceived at the Medizinische Fakultät of the Universität Duisburg-Essen. This article briefly describes the course. Some of the students that participated in its first edition have initiated research projects on two subjects closely connected to it, namely the construction of a universal Turing machine and modeling casualty triage algorithms used in disasters using fuzzy Turing machines. These research projects are also briefly summarized.

2. DESCRIPTION OF THE COURSE

The elective course 'Robotics and programing with Lego' is offered in the form of a one-week seminar. It consists of 25 hours distributed in five hours a day from Monday to Friday. The number of participants is limited to four since there are only four robots. It is hands-on oriented and highly participative. The course covers an introduction to robotics and an introduction to computer science. The part related to robotics uses the Lego Mindstorms EV3 robotic system (Klassner and Anderson, 2003; Brandt and Colton, 2008). Although there already exist university courses at engineering schools based on Lego (Behrens et al., 2010), this is a pioneering course, which to the best of our knowledge, has not been offered before to undergraduate students at any medicine faculty. The syllabus of the robotics part of the course consists of: i) an introduction to the Lego Mindstorms EV3 system, ii) sensors (distance, light, temperature, sound, touch), iii) motors, iv) mathematical operations in the EV3 language, and v) Braitenberg vehicles (figure 1). The robots are programed using an easy to learn graphical language. One of the tasks is to build and program Braitenberg vehicles (Braitenberg, 1984). Although the construction and coding of these vehicles is simple, they follow complex paths that, to some extent, mimic basic social behavior (Lilienthal and Duckett, 2003; Yang et al., 2006; Buiu, 2008). Their behavior can become complex and even unpredictable (Rañó, 2012).

The main objective related to the computer science part of the course is to develop the student's abilities on abstract mathematical thinking. To this end, the Turing machine (Turing, 1936) is studied. The Turing machine is a mathematical model of computation. For any given algorithm a Turing machine that simulates the algorithm can be made. The syllabus of the computer science part is the following: i) Turing machine (exercises on language acceptors and binary addition), ii) universal Turing machine, iii) computability, iv) decidability, v) the halting problem, and vi) the busy beaver problem (Rado, 1962). The difficulties in coding Turing machines arise from the problems proposed, not from the syntax of the language, which is simple. Thus, the language is not a barrier but a tool that allows them to produce new ideas structuring their minds for solving abstract problems.

Figure 1. Braitenberg vehicle built with Lego Mindstorms EV3

This vehicle has a pair of light sensors (upper sensors with blue light) and a pair of distance sensors (lower sensors with red light). The signals from the right-hand side sensors are combined and used to control the speed of the right-hand side motor wheel. Equivalent connections are done for the left-hand side of the vehicle. In this way, the direction of movement is determined by the signals received from the sensors. Other connection maps are tested during the course.

3. CONSTRUCTION OF A UNIVERSAL TURING MACHINE

A group of students that participated in past editions of the course has started to build a universal Turing machine (UTM) using Lego Mindstorms EV3. A universal Turing machine (UTM) is a model of computation whose input is the program that solves a given problem. A UTM simulates current computers inasmuch as a given computer can solve different problems depending on the program loaded into its memory. To the best of our knowledge a pure UTM has never been constructed. Some Turing machines have been built in the past, but either are not universal, that is, they can only compute the problem for which they have been designed, or they are not pure in the sense that they use electronic components for managing the memory. The project that is being developed intends to build a UTM in the way described in the paper of Alan Turing (Turing, 1936). The 'tape' of the UTM under construction contains both, the program and the data. The 'head' can modify both, the program and the data. Thus, the program can modify itself during execution. The students participating in this project are actively involved in all its phases: proposal, design, construction, programming, testing, refinement, debugging, publication and dissemination. This approach enhances their teamwork competences and gives them a broad view on how a research project is conducted. Participating students have an opportunity to learn the skills required for conducting academic research, from idea to publication, at an early stage of their careers. A first prototype of the UTM has already been constructed (figure 2). minds for solving abstract problems.

4. FUZZY TURING MACHINES APPLIED TO TRIAGE SYSTEMS

Turing machines have been mainly used for academic problems. Although there are recent works that suggest their application to cognitive sciences and to help explain neural processes in the brain (Zylberberg et al., 2011; Hassabis et al., 2012), Turing machines have not been used for solving research problems in fields different from those related to computation and mathematics. A consequence of the course is the doctoral dissertation that one of the students is currently developing on fuzzy and non-deterministic Turing machines applied to triage systems used for mass casualty events (Iserson and Moskop, 2007; Moskop and Iserson, 2007). Although triage systems in mass casualty events are widely used, there are few studies on the adequacy of each system and these studies are inconclusive (Jenkins et al., 2008; Cross and Cicero, 2013; Timbie et al., 2013). The evaluation and optimization of the triage systems used for casualties of a disaster is an open research problem in medicine (Nocera and Garner, 1999; Garner et al., 2001; Gebhart and Pence, 2007; Lerner et al., 2008; Kahn et al., 2009; Navin et al., 2010). In 1965 L. Zadeh introduced the concept of fuzzy sets (Zadeh, 1965). In his seminal paper he already suggested the possibility of a Turing machine based on fuzzy logic. Since then a few publications have appeared developing theoretical aspects of fuzzy Turing machines and non-deterministic Turing machines (Santos, 1970; Moraga, 1999; Wiedermann, 2004; Bedregal and Figueira, 2006, 2008). However, the works published up until now on fuzzy Turing machines have only tackled academic problems. Triage systems are based on algorithms for decision-making, these decisions are taken by humans, who will always introduce subjectivity and uncertainty. This is one of the reasons that make the evaluation and optimization of triage systems difficult. The proposed approach of modeling triage systems with Turing machines exploits the resemblance between distributing colored cards among casualties and the way in which a Turing machine tape is processed. The subjectivity and the uncertainty with which decisions are taken can be modeled by means of fuzzy logic and stochastic processes, respectively. The goal of the doctoral dissertation that is being conducted in this field is to propose models of fuzzy and non-deterministic Turing machines that compute triage systems under a variety of disaster scenarios. Figure 3 shows a deterministic Turing machine simulating the Sieve triage algorithm.

Figure 2. Prototype of a universal Turing machine built with the Lego Mindstorms EV3 robotics system

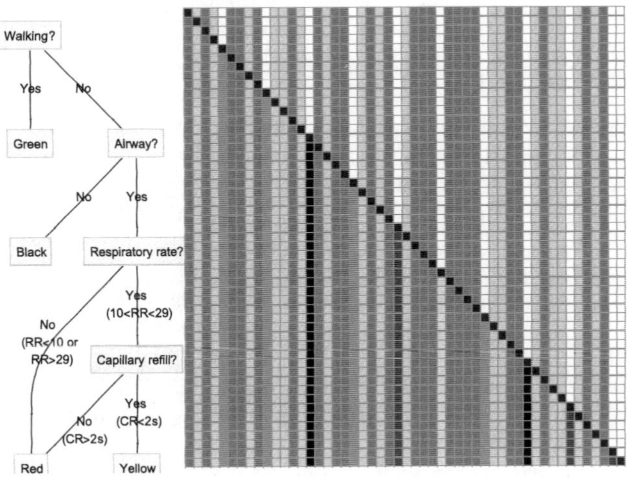

Figure 3. Sieve triage algorithm (left). Simulation of Sieve triage on a Turing machine (right)

Each casualty is represented by four binary characters and a five-state character. The binary characters indicate the answers to the questions posed by the algorithm (walking, airway, respiratory rate, capillary refill). The five-state character represents the colored card (green, yellow, red, black) assigned to each casualty. The initial state of all casualties is white, indicating that it has not been processed. The diagonal represents the evolution of the head of the Turing machine as it processes the tape.

5. CONCLUSION

The elective course on 'Robotics and programing with Lego' that we started to teach at our Faculty of Medicine has substantially evolved during one year. The course gives the opportunity to students get acquainted with the expanding field of robotics in medicine. More important, innovative solutions to the problems of modeling a universal Turing machine and evaluating triage systems for mass casualty events are arising within the course. This educational approach shows the value of interdisciplinary studies at an early stage of the medical career.

REFERENCES

Bedregal, B.C., and Figueira, S. (2008). On the computing power of fuzzy Turing machines. Fuzzy Sets Syst. *159*: 1072–1083.

Bedregal, B.R.C., and Figueira, S. (2006). Classical Computability and Fuzzy Turing Machines. In LATIN 2006: Theoretical Informatics, J.R. Correa, A. Hevia, and M. Kiwi, eds. (Berlin: Springer), pp 154–165.

Behrens, A., Atorf, L., Schwann, R., Neumann, B., Schnitzler, R., Ballè, J., et al. (2010). MATLAB meets LEGO Mindstorms - A freshman introduction course into practical engineering. IEEE Trans. Educ. *53*: 306–317.

Braitenberg, V. (1984). Vehicles. Experiments in Synthetic Psychology (Cambridge: MIT Press).

Brandt, A.M., and Colton, M.B. (2008). Toys in the classroom: LEGO MindStorms as an educational haptics platform. Symp. Haptics Interfaces Virtual Environ. Teleoperator Syst. 2008 - Proceedings, Haptics 389–395.

Buiu, C. (2008). Hybrid educational strategy for a laboratory course on cognitive robotics. IEEE Trans. Educ. *51*: 100–107.

Cross, K.P., and Cicero, M.X. (2013). Head-to-head comparison of disaster triage methods in pediatric, adult, and geriatric patients. Ann. Emerg. Med. *61*: 668–676.e7.

Garner, A., Lee, A., Harrison, K., and Schultz, C.H. (2001). Comparative analysis of multiple-casualty incident triage algorithms. Ann. Emerg. Med. *38*: 541–548.

Gebhart, M.E., and Pence, R. (2007). START Triage: Does It Work? Disaster Manag. Response *5*: 68–73.

Hassabis, D., Brooks, R., Bray, D., and Shashua, A. (2012). Turing centenary: Is the brain a good model for machine intelligence? Nature *482*: 462–463.

Iserson, K. V., and Moskop, J.C. (2007). Triage in Medicine, Part I: Concept, History, and Types. Ann. Emerg. Med. *49*: 275–281.

Jenkins, J.L., Mccarthy, M.L., Sauer, L.M., Green, G.B., Stuart, S., Thomas, T.L., et al. (2008). Mass-Casualty Triage : Time for an Evidence- Based Approach. Prehosp. Disaster Med. *23*: 3–8.

Kahn, C.A., Schultz, C.H., Miller, K.T., and Anderson, C.L. (2009). Does START Triage Work? An Outcomes Assessment After a Disaster. Ann. Emerg. Med. *54*: 424–430.e1.

Klassner, F., and Anderson, S.D. (2003). LEGO MindStorms: Not just for K-12 anymore. IEEE Robot. Autom. Mag. *10*: 12–18.

Lerner, E.B., Schwartz, R.B., Coule, P.L., Weinstein, E.S., Cone, D.C., Hunt, R.C., et al. (2008). Mass casualty triage: an evaluation of the data and development of a proposed national guideline. Disaster Med. Public Health Prep. *2 Suppl 1*: S25–S34.

Lilienthal, A., and Duckett, T. (2003). Experimental analysis of smelling Braitenberg vehicles. Environment *5*: 10.

Moraga, C. (1999). Towards a Fuzzy Computability? Mathw. Soft Comput. *6*: 163–172.

Moskop, J.C., and Iserson, K. V. (2007). Triage in Medicine, Part II: Underlying Values and Principles. Ann. Emerg. Med. *49*: 282–287.

Navin, D.M., Sacco, W.J., and McCord, T.B. (2010). Does START Triage Work? The Answer is Clear! Ann. Emerg. Med. *55*: 579–580.

Nocera, A., and Garner, A. (1999). An Australian mass casualty incident triage system for the future based upon triage mistakes of the past: The Homebush Triage Standard. Aust. N. Z. J. Surg. *69*: 603–608.

Rado, T. (1962). On Non- Computable Functions. Bell Syst. Tech. J. *41*: 877–884.

Rañó, I. (2012). A Model and Formal Analysis of Braitenberg Vehicles 2 and 3. In IEEE International Conference on Robotics and Automation, pp 910–915.

Santos, E.S. (1970). Fuzzy algorithms. Inf. Control *17*: 326–339.

Timbie, J.W., Ringel, J.S., Fox, D.S., Pillemer, F., Waxman, D.A., Moore, M., et al. (2013). Systematic review of strategies to manage and allocate scarce resources during mass casualty events. Ann. Emerg. Med. *61*: 677–689.e101.

Turing, A.M. (1936). On Computable Numbers, with an Application to the Entscheidungsproblem. Proc. London Math. Soc. *42*: 230–265.

Wiedermann, J. (2004). Characterizing the super-Turing computing power and efficiency of classical fuzzy Turing machines. Theor. Comput. Sci. *317*: 61–69.

Yang, X., Patel, R. V., and Moallem, M. (2006). A fuzzy-braitenberg navigation strategy for differential drive mobile robots. J. Intell. Robot. Syst. Theory Appl. *47*: 101–124.

Zadeh, L.A. (1965). Fuzzy sets. Inf. Control *8*: 338–353.

Zylberberg, A., Dehaene, S., Roelfsema, P.R., and Sigman, M. (2011). The human Turing machine: A neural framework for mental programs. Trends Cogn. Sci. *15*: 293–300.

THE CHARACTERISTIC FLUX OF THE E-HEALTH DEFINITION

Rune Pedersen [1], Inger Marie Holm [1] and Hege K Andreassen[1, 2]

[1] *Norwegian Centre for e-health Research - 9038 Tromsø, Norway*

[2]*Centre for Care Research, NTNU*

ABSTRACT

This reflection paper on existing e-health definitions is based on the work to define e-health for the purpose of national monitoring activities in Norway. Our aim is to encourage reflection on the challenges in defining e-health, and on the importance of definitions to succeed in monitoring and indicator work. The study was conducted by the authors from the Norwegian Centre for e-health research as part of an assignment from the Norwegian Directorate of e-health to give an account of possible concepts for a Norwegian e-health monitor. We did a web-based literature search and a hands-on search in policy papers from WHO, OECD and the EC. The results show there is growth in the interest for e-health, and that existing definitions can be grouped in three main categories: definitions based in a) target groups, b) application areas and c) generic aims. We conclude e-health definitions need to be fluid to encompass the complexity of the socio-technical context and the rapid changes in the field. Hence the choice of definition type always has to be made with regard to context, evaluation design and objectives of monitoring.

KEYWORDS

e-Health, Definition, e-Health Monitoring

1. INTRODUCTION

E-health has gradually become the dominant concept to express the practice of health, ICT and digitalization. In Norway, e-health is anchored in regional and national health care structures. The Ministry of Health has recently appointed the "Directorate of e-health" (NDE) to establish a common national direction for e-health initiatives. Furthermore, the four health regions all have their own divisions for e-health, coordinated nationally through the "National ICT" board. Several research institutions prioritize e-health. The Norwegian Centre for e-health Research (NSE) has a mediating role between policy making and research, working closely with the NDE to reach the aim of stronger national standardizations.

Since electronic communication and information systems for health started to gain ground in the 80´s, the field has been characterized by shifting nomenclatures. Telemedicine, telehealth, telecare; e-health, p-health and m-health: these are all concepts that are currently in use to point to services and solutions involving digital technology and health. The multiplicity in concepts reflect the multidisciplinarity and the presence of strong interests in the field, ranging from commercial and engineering developers; health-, social science and informatics researchers; political and policy making bodies and last but not least; the health care workers delivering day to day care as well as the receivers of care themselves. Whilst telemedicine held a strong position as lead concept in the early years, e-health now seems to have replaced telemedicine as the most used term.

Previous attempts to map definitions have concluded that the variation in content is significant. A review paper from 2007 found 104 definitions of telemedicine (Sood et al. 2007). A similar search for definitions of e-health identified 51 definitions (Oh et al. 2005). In a paper from 2012 the authors discuss the possibilities for a definition based in the International Organization of Standardizations requirements (ISO10241) (Showell and Nohr 2012). According to these a definition should include the term name itself; a denotation of the object of the definition activity; and an example.

In this paper we base our discussion on the current development, and have looked into research literature in addition to publications from international policy making organizations. Our aim is to reflect on a general definition of e-health, to be deployed in national strategy work and monitoring activities in Norway.

2. METHOD

We did an updated web-based search in the existing literature through Pubmed, the Cochrane Library, Google Scholar and Google.

We searched both with and without MeSH terms[1]. The MeSH heading when searching for ehealth is Telemedicine. Ehealth is one of the sub-categories (together with telehealth, mhealth, telemetry, telecommunication, mobile health).

We did one targeted search in WHO, OECD and EC documents and three web-searches: 'eHealth' OR 'ehealth'; 'e-Health'; 'what is eHealth' OR 'what is e-Health' AND OR 'definition of e-health'.

To analyse the papers found through search three (definitions), and the targeted search we did a qualitative content analysis; "a research method for the subjective interpretation of the content of text data through the systematic classification process of coding and identifying themes or patterns" (Hsieh and Shannon 2005 p. 1278).

3. RESULTS

Table 1. Results from Web Searches

Search term	Database	MeSH terms	Hits
ehealth OR eHealth	PUBMED	Yes	18756
ehealth OR eHealth	PUBMED	No	23445
e-health	PUBMED	Yes	4
e-health	PUBMED	No	2153
ehealth OR eHealth	Cochrane Library	No	157
e-health	Cochrane Library	No	376
'what is eHealth', OR 'what is e-Health', AND OR definition of e-health	PUBMED	No	30
'what is eHealth', OR 'what is e-Health', AND OR definition of e-health	Cochrane Library	No	43
e-health OR ehealth OR eHealth	Google Scholar	NA	59400

Results show there are fewer hits when MeSH terms are used. The interesting aspect of MeSH in this search is that the hierarchy of key words starts with telemedicine. The reason is simple; telemedicine and telecommunication were concepts that emerged earlier in time than "e-health" or "ehealth".

Two researchers separately coded the data and all authors jointly worked together to extract overall categories from this initial coding. Through this qualitative analysis of the substantial content of existing definitions we arrived at three main categories of current e-health definitions; target groups, applications and generic aims.

---

[1] MeSH terms is a comprehensive controlled vocabulary for the purpose of indexing journal articles for instance used by Pub Med. Journal articles are then all indexed with about 10–15 subject headings, subheadings and supplementary concept records. The system is built so that some of the terms are designated as major indicating the article's main topics.

4. DISCUSSION

E-health as a term for healthcare is dating back to approximately 1999 (Eysenbach, 2001, Della Mea 2001). When compared to the 2012 publication of Showell and Nøhr (op.cit.) our results show an enormous increase in interest: their searches for "ehealth" returned only 659 results from Pubmed, 18600 results for Google Scholar, and 29500,000 results for Google. We hypothesize the increased interest reflect the development in both scientific and commercial organizations.

The growth in interest and flourishing of papers calls for a reflection on the definition of e-health. As both public and private investments continue to grow the need to monitor the development, the use and not least the outcomes of e-health become ever more pressing. In order to arrive at a solid sustainable monitoring model there is, of course, a need to decide on a definition and an overall approach that can be used to single out the relevant and potential indicators.

The categories identified through our analysis, i.e, target groups, applications and generic aims, also open for a discussion approaches to e-health monitoring, as they imply different indicators to be measured.

4.1 Definitions Based in Target Groups

A good example of a definition based in target groups is that of the European commission: *"The use of modern information and communication technologies to meet needs of citizens, patients, healthcare professionals, healthcare providers, as well as policy makers".* (European Commission 2012).

For national monitoring, a strategic way to define target groups would be to identify these through a policy analysis. We have not done a through analysis of policy documents, but e.g., the most recent health-ICT policy document in Norway (MoH Norway 2012) clearly states that there are three main target groups for Norwegian e-health policy; health personnel, citizens and stakeholders who are interested in data for secondary analysis (health authorities, researchers and management/ administration of different levels).

The strength of a target group based definition of e-health would be its potential for mapping use and experienced benefits by stakeholder groups. A limitation of such a definition when it comes to its use for monitoring is that many e-health initiatives can be used by, and benefit, multiple target groups. E.g., welfare technologies to be deployed in people's homes clearly have both patient and professional users. Likewise, the use of larger systems, or "heavyweight IT" (Bygstad 2016), are anchored in day to day clinical activity, but nevertheless; the aggregation of data enabled through these systems would sometimes be of more interest for stakeholders in need for macro level control data than for individual clinicians and patients.

4.2 Definitions Based in Application Areas

Although not explicitly defining e-health per se, "The OECD guide to measuring ICTs in the Health Sector" this document has suggested one of the more influential definitions to date through its title and scope; namely that e-health is about ICTs in the health sector and that these can be divided into four application areas: provider centric electronic records, patient centric electronic records, health information exchange and telehealth (OECD 2013). The guide proposes a model survey for monitoring that has been piloted in 10 countries. In the Nordic e-health Research Network (NeRN) it has been used as point of departure for work towards identifying common indicators across the Nordic countries (Hypponen et al. 2014; 2017).

Hence, the potential of a definition based in application areas for monitoring activity has already been proved. Such definitions are specific enough to define mutually exclusive categories of indicators. A limitation could be the flexibility to include new application areas; i.e., personalized health such as self-monitoring and life style applications are one of the fastest growing fields in e-health, but was not included at the time of designing the OECD survey.

4.3 Definitions Based in Generic Aims

As an example of a definition that is based in generic aims, the WHO definition stands out: *"eHealth is the cost-effective and secure use of information and communications technologies in support of health and health-related fields, including health-care services, health surveillance, health literature, and health education, knowledge and research"* (WHO 2015).

Such definitions point to overall aims of e-health development and deployment, like economy (cost effectiveness), resource deployment, disciplines, users and results. There are theoretical models for information systems success that could correspond to such definitions, e.g., Delone and McLeans model (Delone and Mclean 2003). The use of generic standard models for defining indicator work in e-health could be useful to group the above-mentioned aims into *structural indicators* (cost effectiveness and resources), *process indicators* (disciplines and users) and *effect indicators* (results).

An evident strength of a definition based in generic aims is thus its flexibility to include new details, a highly needed feature within the fast changing field of e-health. A discussion in Norway has been on Medical technical devices, and if they are considered a part of the Electronic patient Record or m-health alternatives, or neither. e-Health also covers virtual reality, robotics, multi-media, digital imaging, computer assisted surgery, wearable and portable monitoring systems, health portals.

The main limitation however, is substantial; shall we not define as e-health all the efforts that through evaluations proves not be *"cost-effective and secure"* or to simultaneously support all *"health and health-related fields, including health-care services, health surveillance, health literature, and health education, knowledge and research"*?

5. CONCLUSION

A new definition of e-health is not what is needed. Rather, an awareness of the differences between the scope of existing concepts should be raised. When deciding on an e-health definition for the purpose of monitoring activities there are at least three distinct approaches that are of value; definitions based in target groups; application areas and generic aims. These should be considered and assessed with regard to scope and context (e.g national versus institutional or local monitoring); the evaluation design (e.g, cross sectional or longitudinal design); and objectives of monitoring (e.g., monitoring performed for governing purposes versus monitoring for clinical quality improvement).

Proposing a once and for all distinct and clear definition of the multidisciplinary field of e-health - a socio-technical practice taking place in a changing health care landscape - is challenging, and further: perhaps undesirable. We don't agree that the lack of a clear, shared definition of e-health causes problems of interest to the scientific development within the field. Rather, the characteristic flux of the e-health definition reflects the phenomenon as it plays out in contemporary health service delivery.

In our work we have focused on the change of the e-health space that looses and gain new ground based on the iterative change of the field. A good definition needs to cope with the trends to a certain degree, nevertheless; we put our faith in the application layer under the definition, what Showell and Nøhr calls "the salient components of a common and agreed ehealth space" (op.cit). It is when new technologies and socio-technical possibilities occurs and alters this application layer that real change happens.

ACKNOWLEDGEMENT

We acknowledge the contribution from the other members in our project team, Gunn Hilde Rotvold, Line Linstad and Paolo Zanaboni.

REFERENCES

Andreassen, H et al. (2016). Concepts for a Norwegian e-health monitor. NSE report series, No 10, 2016.

Author, year. Paper title. *Journal name (in italics)*, volume and issue numbers, inclusive pages.

Bygstad, B. (2016). "Generative innovation: a comparison of lightweight and heavyweight IT." *Journal of Information Technology,* Vol.32, No 2, pp 180-193.

Della Mea, V. (2001). "What is e-Health (2): The death of telemedicine?" *Journal of Medical Internet Research,* Vol. 3, No: p.e22.

Delone, W. H. and E. R. McLean (2003). "The DeLone and McLean model of information systems success: a ten-year update." *Journal of management information systems,* Vol.19, No 4, pp 9-30.

European Commission (2013), Official webpage URL: http://europa.eu.int/information_society/eeurope/ehealth/whatisehealth/index_en.htm

European Commission (2012). eHealth Action plan 2012-2020: Innovative healthcare for the 21st century. *Communication from the commission to the European Parliament, the Council, The European Economic and Social Committee of Regions*. URL: http://eur-lex.europa.eu/legal-content/EN/ALL/?uri=CELEX:52012DC0736

Eysenbach, G. (2001). "What is e-health?". *Journal of Medical Internet Research*, Vol. 3, No: p.e22.

Hsieh, H.-F. and S. E. Shannon (2005). "Three approaches to qualitative content analysis." *Qualitative health research* Vol.15, No 9, pp 1277-1288.

Hypponen, H., M. Kangas, J. Reponen, C. Nøhr, S. Villumsen, S. Koch, G. A. Hardardottir, h. Gilstad, L. Jerlvall, T. Pehrsson, A. Faxvaag, A. H, B. Brattheim, V. Vimarlund and J. Kaipio (2014). Nordic eHealth Benchmarking - Status 2014. TemaNord Report series 2015, No 539.

Hypponen, H., Koch, S., Faxvaag, A., Gilstad, H., Nohr, C., Hardardottir, G., Andreassen, H., Bertelsen, P., Kangas, M., REponen, J., Villumsen, S., Vimarlund, V. (2017). Nordic eHealth benchmarking: From piloting towards established practice. TemaNord Report series 2017, No 528.

Ministry of Health, Norway (2012). Én innbygger-èn journal. White paper (Melding til Stortinget) No 9 (2012-2013)

OECD (2013). Draft OECD guide to measuring ICTs in the health sector. OECD. COM/DELSA/DSTI(2013)3/FINAL

Oh, H., C. Rizo, M. Enkin and A. Jadad (2005). "What is eHealth (3): a systematic review of published definitions." *Journal of medical Internet research,* Vol. 7, No 1, p.e1.

Showell, C. and C. Nohr (2012). "How should we define eHealth, and does the definition matter." *Stud Health Technol Inform,* No 180, pp 881-884.

Sood, S., V. Mbarika, S. Jugoo, R. Dookhy, C. R. Doarn, N. Prakash and R. C. Merrell (2007). "What is telemedicine? A collection of 104 peer-reviewed perspectives and theoretical underpinnings." *Telemedicine and e-Health,* Vol.13, No. 5, pp 573-590.

WHO (2005). Ninth plenary meeting. Commitee A, seventh report, WHA58.28 eHealth.

Posters

THE USE OF AN ACCEPTANCE TEST FOR ACCESSING AN ELECTRONIC INFORMATION SYSTEM

Line Lundvoll Warth and Kari Dyb
Norwegian Centre for E-health Research - P.O. Box 35, N-9038 Tromsø, Norway

ABSTRACT

A national electronic information system for critical information sharing (CIS) was implemented in the period 2013-2017, and all general practitioners, doctors in emergency units, and doctors in emergency rooms were required to perform an e-learning course and pass an acceptance test in order to access the CIS. The acceptance test was seen as problematic as the users were challenged by the adjustments to the local information system, too time consuming, i.e. taking the test, picking up the PKI card, and logging on for use in critical situations. The use of CIS requires passing the test, which is determined by the national authority in Norway. The professionals feel controlled and ordered to take the test, and believe that the acceptance test is not needed in order to use the information system.

KEYWORDS

Acceptance Test, e-Learning Course, Critical Information Sharing, Implementation Work

1. INTRODUCTION

In Norway, a national electronic information system for critical information sharing (CIS) between levels of care was implemented in the period 2013–2017 (The Norwegian Directorate of eHealth, 2017). All general practitioners (doctors), doctors in emergency units in primary care, and doctors in emergency rooms (ER) in specialist services were required to perform an e-learning course and pass an acceptance test in order to access the CIS. CIS is nationally rooted and determined. Its purpose is to give fast and safe access to information about health. We have studied the preparation for the e-learning course and the acceptance test, the use of the system, and the project leaders' implementation work.

2. STUDY FOCUS

The acceptance test was devised as a door opener to the use of CIS. Passing the test gives doctors a personal identity card (PKI- Public key infrastructure) to access the system. For our research, 12 project leaders were interviewed about their preparations for acquiring the doctors' license, and 25 doctors were interviewed about their use of CIS (Charmaz K., 2014, Glaser B.G, Strauss A.L., 2009, Malterud, 1996). The research question for this part of the study was: *What were the informants' experiences with the acceptance test for accessing use?*

3. USER EXPERIENCES

Problems with Java proved to be an obstacle in taking the test. Moreover, after passing the test, the PKI card had to be picked up in person at a specified office.

Some of the project leaders' experiences with preparing the doctors accessing the test are captured here:

I met some challenges, non-updated Java, and...when arriving at the acceptance test...you had to put the identity card in the keyboard and finish the e-learning course, and you enter the URL for the acceptance test, but it all stops because of an out-of-date Java version. Several people are quite critical of the acceptance test. The hardest with it is actually to come so far seeing the content in the test. It's not the test itself. It's banal. The technical problems have been challenging. Picking up the card...It takes too much time to start to use it. #9

If I had been able to decide, I would not have required the test. To get people using the system faster ... E-learning would have been enough preparation [for CIS]. #6

Some of the doctors' experiences are captured here:

E-learning... I feel resigned to it...we need to spend time on it... It does not always feels rational. They know how hard it is for us to get time for training and courses... I feel controlled from the top: instructed to take these e-learning courses.... This course is banal. It is basic stuff about confidentiality and data security. #4

We were ordered to take the course. #8

It was Java-based... I tried to upgrade Java, but I could not make it work. It is stupid because people could not access it in the beginning. #17

I cannot look it up every time because it takes too long to log in... It's not that easy. It takes about 30 seconds. That does not sound so time consuming, but in relation to consultations it is. #23

The acceptance test was easy in itself, but the users met technological challenges and found that it was time consuming.

4. DISCUSSION AND CONCLUSION

The acceptance test was seen as problematic as the users were challenged by the technology and the adjustments to the local information system. It was also too time consuming for the practitioners from the perspective of their other work as it involved taking the test, picking up the PKI card, and logging on for use in critical situations. They experienced the medical content in the test as easy, but the tool itself was technologically complicated and time consuming. The use of CIS requires passing the test, which is determined by the national authority in Norway. The professionals feel controlled and ordered to take the test. As its content is similar to the principles they follow in daily practice without using CIS, they believe that the acceptance test should not be needed in order to use the information system.

REFERENCES

Charmaz K., 2014: Constructing grounded theory. Sage.

Glaser B.G, Strauss A.L., 2009: The discovery of grounded theory: Strategies for qualitative research. Transaction publishers.

Malterud, K. 1996: Kvalitative metoder i medisinsk forskning. En innføring, Aurskog, Tano Aschehoug.

The Norwegian Directorate of eHealth, 2017 (https://ehelse.no/english) [accessed, 03.04.2017]

IMPACT OF OBSERVIA-SANDOZ'S APPLICATION FOR CONDUCTING PHARMACEUTICAL INTERVIEWS ON THE EVALUATION OF KNOWLEDGE ACQUISITION OF ASTHMATIC PATIENTS AND PATIENTS TREATED BY ANTICOAGULANTS

Geoffroy Vergez[1] and Gersende Guédon[2]

[1] *CEO, Observia SAS, Pépinière d'entreprise Cochin, 29 rue du Faubourg Saint Jacques, 75014 Paris, France*

[2] *Doctor of Pharmacy, Observia SAS, Pépinière d'entreprise Cochin, 29 rue du Faubourg Saint Jacques, 75014 Paris, France*

ABSTRACT

Since 2009, the role of French pharmacists have evolved in the accompaniment of chronic patients due to the establishment of pharmaceutical interviews. Observia in partnership with Sandoz has developed an interactive and educational application to facilitate and manage patient learning. The objective was to evaluate the impact of the Observia-Sandoz's application on the progress of knowledge acquisition in asthmatic patients and in patients treated by anticoagulants (AVK / AOD) as measured by the change in overall score between first interview and the last one.

KEYWORDS

Application, Asthma, Anticoagulants, Pharmacy, Pharmaceutical interviews

1. INTRODUCTION

Starting in 2009, a French law (HPST: Hôpital Patient Santé Territoire) defined the new role of pharmacists in public health: the accompaniment of chronic patients and the prevention of iatrogenic risks that was formalized by a pharmaceutical interview. The pharmaceutical interview is an opportunity for the pharmacist to apply his knowledge and his advisory role in therapeutic education in order to ensure personalized and optimal patient care. Moreover, it should strengthen the pharmacist's role of counselling, education and prevention for patients. Due to their proximity and the frequent renewal of treatments, French pharmacists are well positioned to follow-up asthma patients and patients treated by anticoagulants. They are able to periodically accompany patients by verified the knowledge they acquired during the pharmaceutical interviews. Furthermore, a recent study shows that 72 % of asthmatic patients are non-adherent to their treatment and largely 60 % of chronical patients are non-adherent. The role of the pharmacist is major in improving patients' knowledge and their compliance with chronic diseases in particular through pharmaceutical interviews.

Observia, in partnership with the pharmaceutical firm Sandoz, has designed and developed a comprehensive interactive and educational application to facilitate and manage pharmaceutical interviews. With this study, we would like to evaluate the use of this application on the improvement of knowledge in asthmatic patients and patients treated by anticoagulants who have used the solution.

2. METHODS

When pharmacists use the application to conduct interviews, they evaluate their patient's knowledge on several topics (diet, everyday life, treatment, complications, adverse effects, biological monitoring, health professionals and inhalation technique for asthma). The content of the questionnaire was defined by the

"Actualités Pharmaceutiques – Elsevier Masson" and fits with the recommendation of the French Health Autorities. Pharmacist give a note on the patient's knowledge: « A » for acquired (score 1 point), « PA » for partially acquired (score 0.5 point) and « NA » for not acquired (score 0 point). At the end of the interview, the patient obtains an overall score expressed a 5-point Likert scale as a percentage for all topics (notes A (81-100 % of knowledge acquisition), B (61-80 % of knowledge acquisition), C, (41-60 % of knowledge acquisition), D (21-40 % of knowledge acquisition), E (0-20 % of knowledge acquisition). This evaluation is carried out at a given moment on the entire database for eligible asthmatic patients and patients treated by anticoagulants that have more than one interview (2105 pharmacies). Data is detailed by mean, standard deviation, median and quartiles for quantitative and actual variables and percentage for qualitative variables. The statistical analysis is carried out on the basis of the student t and Khi2 test (before and after) for 5 notes A, B, C, D, E carried over to a 5-point Likert scale from 2009 to 2017. Intragroup comparisons of the quantitative variables are carried out using repeated series t-tests, intra-group comparisons of qualitative variables by MacNemar Chi-square tests. The acquisition of knowledge is measured by the evolution of the overall score at the end of each interview. The statistical significance threshold is set to alpha = 0.05.

3. RESULTS

Fifty-four patients had at least two interviews on the Asthma's topic, and 293 had at least two interviews on the anticoagulants' topic. Furthermore, 287 patients retained the same anticoagulant between the first and last visit (including 266 AVK : Anti-Vitamins K and 21 AOD : oral anticoagulants).

Table 1. Number of visits per patients (Asthma)

		Total N=329
Number of visits	N	329
	1	275 (83.6%)
	2	42 (12.8%)
	3	11 (3.3%)
	4	1 (0.3%)

Table 2. Number of visits per patients (Anticoagulants)

		Total N=1454
Number of visits	N	1454
	1	1161 (79.8%)
	2	245 (16.9%)
	3	34 (2.3%)
	4	6 (0.4%)
	5	7 (0.5%)
	6	1 (0.1%)

In the first "Asthma" interview (N = 31), 3.2% of patients were rated "A", and 71% were rated "E". At the last Asthma interview (N = 48), 2.1% of patients obtained "A" and 56.3% had "E". Slightly more than half of the patients (51.7%, 15 patients) retained the same score, 3.4% (1 patient) had their score decreased and 44.8% (13 patients) had their score improved. The change in the overall score between the two interviews was significant (p-value = 0.006, Wilcoxon's signed rank test, N = 29). Pharmacist who used the Observia-Sandoz's application for pharmaceutical interviews have better chance of improving the knowledge of their asthmatic patients.

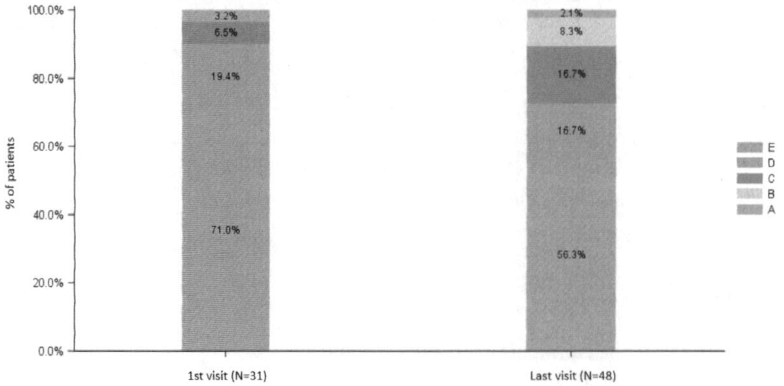

Figure 1. Asthmatic patients' score at the first and the last visit

In the first anticoagulants interview (N = 250), 17.6% of the patients obtained the grade "A", and 7.6% obtained the grade "E". In the last anticoagulants interview (N = 274), 35% of the patients obtained "A" and 6.2% the "E" score. In general, the patients' level of information appeared to be much better for the "Anticoagulants (AVK/AOD)" theme than for the "Asthma" theme. Half of the patients (50%, 120 patients) retained the same score, 12.1% (29 patients) had a decreased score and 37.9% (91 patients) had improved their score. The evolution of the overall score between the two interviews was significant (p-value <0.001, Wilcoxon's signed rank test, N = 240). Pharmacists who used the Observia-Sandoz application for pharmaceutical interviews have a better chance of improving the knowledge of their patients treated with anticoagulants (AVK/AOD).

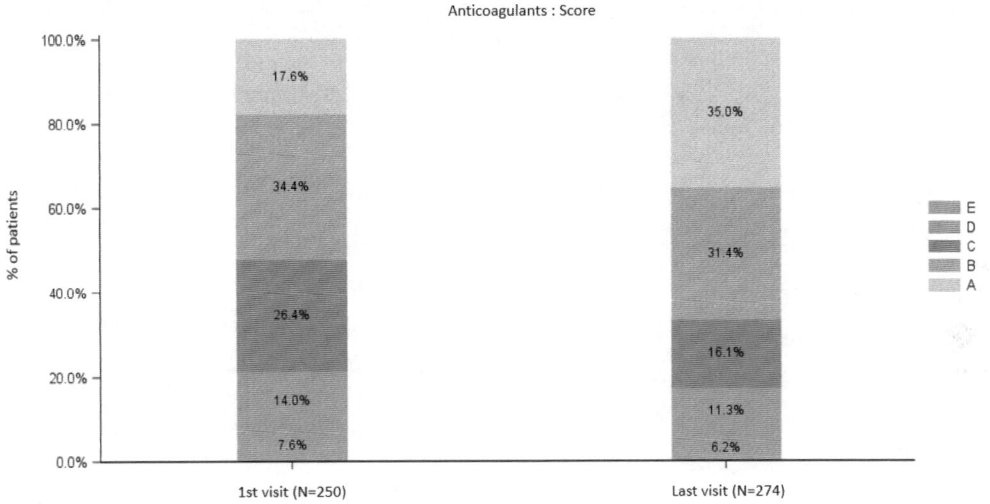

Figure 2. Patients treated with anticoagulants score at the first and the last visit

4. CONCLUSION

The objective was to evaluate the impact of the Observia-Sandoz's application on the progress of knowledge acquisition in asthmatic patients and patients treated with anticoagulants (AVK / AOD) as measured by the change in overall score between first interview and the last one. This study demonstrates that the change in the overall score between the first and last interviews on asthma was significant (p-value = 0.006, Wilcoxon's signed rank test) despite the lack of data. Furthermore, the evolution of the overall score between the first and last interviews on anticoagulants was also significant (p-value <0.001, Wilcoxon's signed rank test, N = 240). There is no obligation for pharmacists to inform the data on the application. The large proportion of missing data strongly limits the results, which must be taken with caution.

REFERENCES

Ministère de la santé et des sports, 2009. *LOI n° 2009-879 du 21 juillet 2009 portant réforme de l'hôpital et relative aux patients, à la santé et aux territoires.* JORF n°0167 du 22 juillet 2009 page 12184 texte n° 1.

QuintilesIMS, 2017. *Observance thérapeutique – Des leviers pour agir.* CRIP.

IMS Health, 12 novembre 2014. *L'observance en France : Plus de 9 milliards d'euros d'économies potentielles en 1 seule année sur 6 pathologies chroniques !* CRIP.

AUTHOR INDEX